PONZI REGULATION

Myth vs. Reality
in Fighting Financial Fraud

By Chidem Kurdas

TABLE OF CONTENTS

—

—

PREFACE

Some 14 years ago, I started to write about the aftermath of a financial fraud, expecting to wrap up the story in a short while. To my surprise, it kept going on. And on. While the scheme itself lasted a little over three years, the sequel under government auspices went on for over a decade. Eventually I realized that this case connected to arguments on regulation.

The main mission of financial regulation, as repeatedly stated through the past 80 years, is to protect investors. But what I observed gave the lie to that claim and led to the conclusion that financial regulation failed in its fundamental rationale. How did we get to this point? Why did an agency considered the triumph of the New Deal turn into an abject failure? What can be done? This book came out of a search for answers.

Had Rip von Winkle gone to sleep in America circa 1900 and woken up a century later, he would have found himself bewildered not only by new technologies, products and fashions but also a new mode of governance. A novel system had developed, consisting of numerous federal offshoots with clunky titles. Reduced to acronyms, they are collectively known as the alphabet soup of agencies.

The ideas that underpin this development were impressive in their time and are widely accepted still. Starting in the late 19th century, American thinkers in law and social sciences made a powerful case for the regulation of economic activity. Their arguments remain the touchstone of what regulators are supposed to do.

Regulatory agencies form a realm of their own, shaped by social, legal and economic notions once considered radical but now taken for granted. Embodied in this – as we will see – largely independent domain, the regulatory state is a mode of governance that lies beyond the traditional tripartite division of legislature, executive and judiciary. A many armed octopus engaged in numerous activities, it is almost impossible to perceive in its entirety. Certainly no single author can usefully grapple with it.

My target here is limited to just one segment, the regulation of securities markets and investments. And limited still by a focus on one issue, the prevention of financial fraud. The arguments and failures I document are related to this particular matter. Other areas of regulation are subject to different rationales and failures, though key issues cut across the system.

On the face of it, this limited subject is an uncomplicated corner of the regulatory state. Stamping out fraud is not a controversial goal. There is broad agreement that false information subverts markets, that deceiving investors is a bad thing and that misleading claims should be discouraged. Criminal laws against fraud are included in the night-watchman state, the limited but effective government to protect life and property envisioned by the founders of the United States. Fighting swindles is part of the government's basic mandate.

Indeed, how well the government deals with fraud has long been part of the larger issue of how well it performs its core duties. But in the 20th century a new vision arose of a comprehensive oversight system that would intervene to prevent deception, not just prosecute it after the fact. The arguments for an expansive regulatory state pointed to the shortcomings of individuals and private institutions, promising to overcome the deficiencies.

The policy goal of preventing deception is not only backed by near consensus but also has the unusual virtue of being relatively clear. It is readily comprehensible not only to government players responsible for making and implementing rules but also to a significant part of the public. Much is known about the topic and there is a wealth of experience to draw from. What Charles Ponzi did in the early 20th century is not fundamentally different from a Ponzi scheme headlined in today's news. Whether a conman uses postage stamps, an insurance company, a bank, a hedge fund or some other ruse, the basic mechanism is the same. While the specific instruments change, the mechanics of deception don't.

Regulators have the wherewithal to improve their craft by learning from the long history of similar schemes. The mission is achievable. Hence preventive actions against fraud should be reasonably effective. This is possibly the least contentious, most straightforward and best documented policy goal, well within the powers of the sprawling United States financial oversight system. It can be taken as the benchmark for the success of the regulatory state — if any such effort can succeed, this is it. Yet regulation against financial deception has been a failure by any common sense standard.

By media and official telling, fraud is a problem of markets and the government appears in the guise of cavalry coming to the rescue of besieged civilians. Between that reassuring image and reality is an immense chasm. My quest here is how and why so promising a regulatory venue failed. The broader issue of what the regulatory system as a whole achieves and whether the achievements are worth the resources spent and freedoms curtailed, is beyond the scope of the book — though the same problems arise in almost every type of economic intervention.

The reasons for the failures I document lie in large part with the original ideas upon which the regulatory state rests. The arguments that support financial laws and agencies make certain assumptions; these are wrong; therefore the resulting system could not but fail to achieve the end it was meant to serve.

The chapters below flesh out the points I've summarized here. The book is organized around three main questions: What is financial fraud-related regulation supposed to do? What does it in fact do? Why is it a failure and how can it do better?

The men who provided the rationale for and built the regulatory state answered the first question. Their arguments reshaped the American government and remain potent. Key figures and their ideas are the subject of the first part of the book.

The second part examines the role of regulators in three Ponzi schemes, from early in the process to the aftermath when the perpetrator is arrested or sidelined and the government takes over. The point is to see how performance compares to promise.

The third part explains why regulatory failure happens and offers a policy alternative for preventing financial fraud. Realistic regulation requires recognizing the error of the old assumptions that go back to the turn of the past century.

This book developed from a confluence of financial journalism and my interest in public policy. I owe a large debt to the participants in the New York University colloquium on market institutions and economic processes led by Mario Rizzo and David Harper. They kept me appraised of relevant academic research. The colloquium's format of reading a paper before discussing it with the author makes for great ongoing education.

Thanks also to Thomas and Donna McQuade, who provided helpful suggestions for an earlier manuscript on Manhattan hedge fund that became material for this book.

As always, Raymond Majewski has been a great partner, willing to act as a sympathetic sounding board for my musings even when these diverge sharply from his own view.

Innumerable members of the legal profession and financial industry provided glimpses into ways of thinking that I would otherwise not have known or understood. Though their help was often not intentional, I am grateful to them all.

PART I. Why Regulation?

Three big issues – power, conflict and irrationality – justified government incursions into the financial arena in the past hundred years. Extremes of power; conflicting interests; lack of knowledge and reasoned decision making — reformers pointed to these sources of inequity and weakness. These provided both the rationale and the guide for designing what were regarded as solutions to alleviate the social damage. Each of the following three chapters focuses on one issue and the leading thinkers who defined it.

CHAPTER ONE. Countering Power

The American regulatory state had countless sources and creators, but two remarkable men helped set it into motion. One is the activist lawyer Louis Brandeis, a leader of the movement starting in the 1890s. He led a revolution in legal thought that allowed aggressive government intervention to remedy economic problems. The other is the iconoclastic economist Thorstein Veblen, whose witty criticism of established social and economic custom impelled people to seek new arrangements.

Between them Brandeis and Veblen provided the why and the how for a radical change in governance. It is not that they created a common or monolithic body of thought — indeed, their names are rarely found in the same sentence because two more dissimilar characters would be hard to imagine. But the gist of their legal and economic ideas proved to be influential and had consequences that endured long after the men were gone.

To be sure, the ideas did not by themselves bring about a new system. Economic and political conditions were ripe for change. Even as America experienced a vast growth in production and income, disorienting breakdowns punctured prosperity.[1] There was a painful crisis in the1890s, giving rise to popular anger. Though the economy recovered strongly, there remained a sense that ordinary men and women faced outrageously unfair odds.[2]

Farmers, squeezed by low prices for their product and forced to borrow, blamed their growing indebtedness on the big banks that controlled credit. Congressmen from agricultural areas demanded action against Wall Street to loosen its suffocating grip. Stories by muckraking journalists fed the anger.[3] Against the background of rapid and volatile economic transformation and social ferment, a new political landscape evolved.

When William Jennings Bryan ran for President in 1896, his populist agenda promised not only to do away with the gold standard but more fundamentally to expand the government's economic powers. Throughout the first two decades of the 20th century Progressives pushed for measures to bring about a more just society. Some reformers went as far as to support the 1919 Prohibition on the ground that this would clean the corruption of political machines, said to operate out of saloons.

Rich and ruthless men presided over vast financial empires, against which regular people and small businesses had no chance. Brandeis came to the rescue. He attacked trusts and monopolies. He fought the banker J. P. Morgan's control over railroads and had a hand in the creation of the Federal Reserve System and the Federal Trade Commission.

In his 1914 book, *Other People's Money and How the Bankers Use It,* Brandeis argued that it was necessary to restrain the power of financial interests to protect the public.[4] He supported Woodrow Wilson, who promised to destroy the trusts. President Wilson appointed Brandeis to the Supreme Court in the face of ferocious opposition. That a militant Progressive ended up on the Supreme Court was a sign of a momentous shift. All this prepared the ground for Franklin Delano Roosevelt's economic interventionism. From Brandeis' book on banks came ideas and even words for the massive regulatory effort under the New Deal — Roosevelt used the term, "other people's money" to defend his agenda.[5] Young lawyers deeply influenced by Brandeis flocked to Washington to work for the Roosevelt administration. These acolytes of the Supreme Court justice wrote financial laws and built regulatory agencies.

Imbecile Institutions

Meanwhile, people who read Veblen – for a while he was a famous author – were left with the vivid impression that American economic and social practices were perverse. A caustic observer of human behavior, Veblen wrote about topics that ranged from dress codes to college sports. He derided mass consumerism and the powerful sway of competitive sports in American education.

Unifying his criticisms was a perspective centered around institutions, which he defined broadly as "ways of doing and thinking." These habits of thought and behavior, transmitted from one generation to the next, make up the prevalent mindset. What he studied were are not idiosyncratic personal habits but rather social routines that constitute the culture.

Institutions are distinct from organizations, though they shape organized activity at many levels. Americans' penchant to shop is an institution; your neighborhood mall is an organization. Veblen was more interested in understanding social behavior than in studying organizations. This profoundly eccentric man observed Americans with the same interest anthropologists had in distant tribes. But he followed a much older intellectual tradition.

The basic idea that the nature of a society and its economy depends on institutions went back to the Enlightenment. From that premise developed two lines of thought that diverged and had different political implications. One started with the French philosopher Jean-Jacques Rousseau, who claimed people are bad because social institutions are bad and will become nicer once institutions are reformed. The other was the brain child of 18th century Scottish philosophers David Hume and Adam Smith. They connected economic development to certain attitudes and laws that protect freedom. This explained, say, why at the time the British and Dutch advanced and increased their wealth while China seemed to be stationary — despite having long been a rich and highly sophisticated civilization.[6]

Veblen followed in the footsteps of these thinkers but his focus was on American society and his conclusions were based on what he observed. He saw habit formation in all aspects of life, from the trivial to the serious, from notions of fashion to attitudes to government. Habits of thought become entrenched as social customs, values and official laws — these various types of rules control how people behave and hence determine the character of society.[7]

In Veblen's grand scheme, social behavior results from interactions between biology and institutions. Hardwired human nature – the biological imperatives and predispositions common to our species – is the raw material that institutions channel. Among the predispositions people have, he believed, is a strong tendency to admire and defer to persons of distinction. Another is a need to dominate others. But customary norms tell us what particular qualities to admire and defer to. Laws indicate acceptable and unacceptable ways of dominating others. This is why societies vary so much over time and from each other, even as human nature remains constant.

Habituated rules are resistant to change but evolve over generations. Veblen's description of how institutions develop suggests a process that is beneficial, at least in part. Past societies channeled the instinct to dominate into certain types of violence. Aristocratic honor codes valued the slaying of challengers and rivals, not the making of ploughs. In those times the highest accolades went to men who exhibited an "extraordinary predatory efficiency in war or a quasi-predatory efficiency in statecraft."[8] People imbued with this habit of thought made their living by preying on and threatening others, not by producing goods. Societies that reward predation remained economically backward and poor.

By contrast, when the focus is on industry, wealth becomes the criterion for social standing and people work on acquiring property. "Gradually as industrial activity displaces predatory activity in the community's everyday life and in men's habits of thought, accumulated property replaces trophies of predatory exploit as the conventional exponent of prepotence and success," Veblen wrote.[9]

The shift to industrial institutions makes for a more comfortable and affluent society. In that way it is a beneficial change, except that Veblen saw accumulated property as the modern equivalent of "trophies of predatory exploit" like scalps that attest to a tribesman's ability as warrior. His unique mix of analysis and irony offers a complex picture of institutions.

Collecting property versus collecting scalps – two ways of channeling the same disposition – have different economic consequences. But modern society's conventions need not be any more rational than the magical beliefs of hunter-gatherer tribes. From studies of past and contemporary societies, Veblen concluded that inherited habits of thought often hinder wellbeing. Many modern institutions, including occupational divisions, work rules, class distinctions and consumption patterns, inhibit efficiency or use up resources without satisfying real needs.

Collective mindsets can persist even while wrecking social or economic havoc. He wrote: "history records more frequent and more spectacular instances of the triumph of imbecile institutions over life and culture than of peoples who have by force of instinctive insight saved themselves out of a desperately precarious institutional situation..."[10] Civilizations do die and typically the intransigence of their institutions is the cause. Even if an external enemy is the immediate reason for the collapse, destructive habits of mind render a society vulnerable to attacks from the outside.

When a civilization disintegrates, there is chaos. Weak or nonexistent social rules mean that behavior is uncontrolled. As ancient Rome fell, Veblen observed, the institutional fabric crumbled and "left mankind naked and unashamed and free to follow the promptings of hereditary savage human nature."[11] Then a new set of rules emerged, integrating some elements from the past—like a new biological species that contains older genes.

In America, he saw "imbecile institutions" primarily in the making and spending of money. Traditional means of establishing status by proving prowess in war, politics or sports do not disappear in a modern society, but money becomes the measure of success. Those who don't have it receive no respect even in their own eyes. People compete by engaging in conspicuous consumption — the term Veblen coined to describe purchases undertaken to establish one's identity and financial status, unnecessary except as a way of showing off.

And this is where fraud comes in. American public opinion tends to admire people who make a lot of money, encouraging attempts to acquire wealth through hook or crook, whether financial shenanigans or dubious deals. "Pecuniary occupations" – including but not confined to finance – are exclusively about making money. These are like games, Veblen opined, where strategy tends to develop into "finesse and chicane."[12]

Under a perverse value system, people are prone to chicanery to pay for their wasteful and hollow lifestyle. The race is non-ending. No matter how much you acquire, there is always someone else who has more. Since the main point of acquiring is to show that one is better than others, people are dissatisfied even if they possess ever-increasing amounts of goodies.

What is even worse, there is no joy left in work, just as there is no joy left in much of consumption. When money is the one and only object, work becomes merely a means to conspicuous consumption and property, to signal one's worth. Work ceases to be enjoyable in itself. Americans' obsession with moneymaking to the exclusion of other values militates against the instinct of workmanship, the pride and interest in useful work that Veblen thought existed in handicraft systems.

Probably this view was fueled by nostalgia for his childhood in mid-19th century Minnesota, where he grew up in an isolated rural community of immigrant Norwegian farmers. Veblen was rooted in a world where families built their cabins, made their clothes, churned their butter. One can argue that non-industrial work was nothing as satisfying as he presumed – he himself spent his life reading and writing, not tilling the land – and also question the accuracy of his depiction of American society.

For our purpose the germane point is that he believed key American institutions encourage fraud. The mindset that glorifies the making and spending of money makes for deceptive behavior. A predatory "leisure class" – another term he originated – controls the economy and the financial system. This class speculates and manipulates markets for its own advantage, disrupts industries and wastes the productive potential of technology.

Veblen's explanation of what's wrong with America brings to mind the possibility of deliberate action to change bad institutions. Laws could clamp down on the power of the leisure class, loosen its control on the economy, discourage financial speculation. People might find ways to enjoy their work rather than regard it as necessary drudgery to make money. Corrective public education could focus the younger generation's minds on things other than wealth and its accoutrements, dispelling the fiction that nothing else matters.[13]

Remarkably, Veblen himself did not advocate corrective state action. It is obvious why he did not do so. His view of the government was even darker than his view of robber barons. He regarded politicians as dangerous opportunists who, in order to get themselves elected or consolidate their power, whip up people's feelings of solidarity into mass malevolence against particular groups or societies. This resulted in discord, violence, wars.

Of course, there are different types of state and different mindsets that go with them. Veblen contrasted the British concept of the commonwealth that serves the citizen versus the German convention of the citizen as a subject who serves the higher ends of the state. He argued that the German way of thinking is especially dangerous because it directs the population to blindly follow leaders. But self-serving politicians everywhere are liable to sow resentment and goad people to harmful adventures.

More fundamentally, governments are not outside society but rather embody the prevalent way of thinking. They are likely to protect rather than challenge the worst institutions. Given this critical view, Veblen did not advocate the extension of government power in the economic sphere.

While rejecting official action, he wrote of a vague hope as to how American society might improve. Technical experts such as engineers could become endowed with different mental habits from the rest of the population. They could escape from destructive social rules and somehow reconstruct institutions so as make society both more productive and equitable. Economic activity would then be freed from the control of the leisure class, with its frittering away of resources to maintain itself in style, and be redirected to satisfy everybody's real needs.

This idea sits awkwardly with Veblen's own analysis of institutional change as a slow, cumulative process — operating through incidental developments that become entrenched as habits of mind. Even so, his vision of rational and selfless technicians who would deliberately design better institutions encouraged faith in collective action.

He was astonishingly prescient on some topics, as in his 1918 forecast that in the coming years Germany would pose a serious threat to international peace and minorities, it particular the Jewish population in Europe. But he did not provide a blueprint for improving institutions. John Commons, the second outstanding institutionalist thinker, played a greater role in the making of the regulatory state — as we will see.[14]

Reformers influenced by Veblen's vision crafted a simpler message by leaving out the troublesome bits about government. They ignored his strictures on the dangers posed by politicians. Left out was his notion that to create better institutions people have to be truly exceptional — possessed of an entirely different mindset from the rest of society, immune to money lust as well as to old custom. Veblen did not claim that scientists, engineers or any other group had evolved a new way of thinking; he hoped they might do so in the future.

Shorn of those impractical caveats that barred social redesign by government, his criticism of business institutions became part of the reform agenda. What had to be done was to build a public-minded technocracy. This new entity would not only prevent the ravages caused by robber barons and their ilk, but more fundamentally control the corrosive influence of the wealth nexus and the greed and chicanery it creates. So the Progressives and their successors went to work.

They Crossed the Rubicon

While Veblen exposed the American economy and in particular the financial system as wasteful and given to deception, lawyers looked to remake the law into a tool for reform. A most far-reaching aspect of the Progressive movement was the resulting revolution in legal thought.[15] Brandeis advocated "realist" jurisprudence, that is, shaping laws to meet the needs of a modern society, even if this violates established principle. The legal system had to be freed from the past and realigned to support cures for social ills.

The notion that judges should make law to deal with the issues of the day challenged the basic premise behind the old Classical "rule of law" — that judges discover and apply existing social norms. From the legal realist perspective, the point is to find practical solutions. Judges should craft their arguments to cover needed social or economic measures. By implication, so should regulators. They are supposed to create new rules that solve social and economic problems, not stay under musty old institutions.

Thus was laid the foundation of myriad interventions. In the words of one of Brandeis' most promising law clerks and disciples, James Landis, the realists "crossed the Rubicon of legal tradition to declare openly that judges made rather than discovered the law."[16] This philosophy had already gained many adherents in the late 1930s, when Landis surveyed the changing legal-regulatory landscape.

Now it is conventional wisdom. Thus the scholar-judge Richard Posner dismisses the notion that judges should defer to the rulings of their predecessors or privilege the past in any way. He claims we could start from scratch and design a more efficient system. Early 20th century Progressives would have agreed with that, though Posner is not necessarily an advocate of current progressive causes.

Mario Rizzo contrasts Posner's concept of top-down legal reasoning, based on a theory of what is desirable, with bottom-up reasoning based on common law and custom.[17] The latter does not rely on criteria derived from economic reasoning but on evolved rules familiar and agreeable to the public. From the late 19th century on, reform advocates fought to replace the bottom-up approach with top-down reasoning. Their success was ensconced in the legal profession by the time Landis commented on the change.

This was progress. You could do whatever necessary to promote equity or efficiency, ignoring the past. You had full scope to go in new directions. The vision may have started in the judiciary but spread and freed government action in general from the restrictions of custom. A less commented aspect of the shift was that it gave the legal-political elite greater power. By contrast, Classical jurisprudence set bounds by insisting on following established norm.

In some matters, top-down may converge with bottom-up. Richard Epstein has argued that the utilitarian economic calculus Posner and other modern legal thinkers favor can lead to rules no different from social custom — defined as "the implicit norms that grow up within a community."[18] Even so, there is the danger that legal sanctions will crowd out or weaken beneficial customs. Does society as a whole benefit from replacing its institutions with a state-created and imposed regime? That question faded as interventionism gained momentum in numerous fields.[19]

Classical economics had stood alongside classical legal principles as a bulwark against interventionism. Both were responses to an ugly history going back to medieval and earlier times. Public authorities had in fact long meddled in markets, whether to relieve social tensions, protect local guilds or cater to other interests. The price of bread was fixed; merchants were hung for charging too much for commodities at times of scarcity; and people were punished, even executed, for selling innovative products that took markets away from politically powerful guilds.

With the Enlightenment came the recognition that such measures were wasteful and an impediment to material wellbeing—not to mention oppressive. Economics and law combined to protect freedom in markets as well as in other areas. In the United States, government involvement in business was limited by a commitment to a general legal framework and the courts, with minimal intrusion otherwise.

The founders sought to encourage commerce and industry by establishing the right framework, one that would discourage fraud and theft but also deter political favoritism. Regarding bankruptcy and criminal provisions to prevent fraud, the question was whether the effect was clear and generally agreed-upon. In 1787 James Madison defended the power the proposed constitution gave to the federal government to establish uniform bankruptcy laws, as necessary to prevent fraud.

Having a system that covered all states "will prevent so many frauds where the parties or their property may lie or may be removed into different states, that the expediency of it seems not likely to be drawn into question," he wrote in the *Federalist Papers*.[20] Such was the minimalist approach fashioned by Classical economic and legal precepts—agreed-upon laws with clear goals.

To 20th century reformists, that was not enough to contain the destructive shenanigans inspired by avarice and enabled by unequal economic power. New measures were necessary to reduce the waste caused by greed and fraud; the old limits obstructed policies to promote economic justice and fairness. Established principles of limited government came to be viewed as the dead hand holding society back from a bright, egalitarian, efficient future.

This view harkened back to the 18th century radical, Rousseau. He favored discarding old institutions and making a new society based on reason, run by the "general will" of the people. American lawyer-reformers did not dwell on the similarity between their own thought and the philosopher associated with the French revolution but the aptness of the comparison emerges in retrospect.

The United States crossed the Rubicon into a previously forbidden land, to use Landis' stylistic flourish. Had someone pointed out that Julius Caesar's crossing the little stream had disastrous consequences, heralding the end of the ancient Roman Republic, Landis might have shrugged. He was a determined advocate of an all-encompassing regulatory state and knew well that building it required dispensing with old legal and economic precepts.

Being a Brandeis follower and legal realist, though in certain respects a moderate one, Landis was sanguine about the bold reforms. This was rational policymaking in action. And there was no turning back.

To Protect the Savings of the Country

Wall Street was widely blamed for stock market losses after the 1929 crash.[21] Financial manipulators and short sellers were seen as causing prices to fall. Whether or not financial industry insiders caused the slump – in fact many of them lost their wealth in the fracas – they were an easy target for shareholders and politicians.

Securities markets were regulated by state governments, which had statutes against fraudulent stock issues, called "blue sky" laws in reference to con men who promised gullible investors shares in the sky. States appear to have enforced these laws somewhat haphazardly. There was no federal regulation of securities, though fraud in general was a crime.

President Herbert Hoover was under pressure to do something but unwilling to impose federal securities oversight. In 1930 he warned the head of the New York Stock Exchange, Richard Whitney. The NYSE handled nearly 90% of stock transactions in the country (on a dollar basis). Unless you curb speculative practices that benefit insiders at the expense of the public, said the President, federal regulation is inevitable.

Hoover later recalled that Whitney made promises but did not deliver.[22] The NYSE had imposed requirements on issuers and its members in the 1920s. But the exchange did not restrict certain practices that drew shareholders' ire – in particular short selling. Prodded by Hoover, the NYSE called for daily reports on short sales and in 1931 banned short sales, but only briefly.

Meanwhile Whitney and his allies, an old guard who long controlled the exchange, faced opposition within the NYSE. There was a reform faction pushing for new rules. The old guard held on to power but other members kept trying to take control and change the way things were done at the exchange.

Franklin D. Roosevelt came into office promising to "protect the savings of the country from the dishonesty of crooks and from the lack of honor so common in high financial places." Speaking as the presidential candidate at the at the Democratic National Convention, he endorsed the party's call for the regulation of stock exchanges, broker-dealers and investment banks. However, it was not clear what exactly should be done.

Among the brain trust competing for the new president's ear were Adolf Berle, a Wall Street attorney and law school professor, and Rexford Tugwell, a Columbia University economist inspired by Veblen.[23] In 1932 Berle co-authored, with Gardiner Means, a notable book on the modern corporation. It showed that American manufacturing was no longer a world of small, owner-operated businesses. Much of the economy was under the control of big companies run by professional managers. The 200 largest corporations owned nearly 50% of American industry. This was the case in finance as well, with banking increasingly concentrated in the hands of a few giants.

Unlike the traditional family firm, modern companies had numerous shareholders, most of whom held only a small fraction of the company. These shareholders, in contrast to owners of family businesses, had neither the incentive nor the ability to supervise the operation. It was professional executives who controlled the business and made corporate decisions. They could operate in ways that ran contrary to the owners' interest.

On the basis of these findings, Berle argued that the federal government should protect shareholders by overseeing security issues and financial firms. He admitted that the NYSE itself has gone some way with its information requirements for listed companies but found this insufficient. For the rest of his career in academia, government and the law, Berle advocated financial regulation for the benefit of shareholders.

Tugwell thought the modern corporation with its power over the market had caused the Great Depression and if not controlled would create other economic calamity. But Tugwell and Berle also credited large corporations with technological and organizational improvements and high productivity — by contrast, Brandeis questioned whether productivity grew with size.

The problem as Tugwell saw it was that corporations did not pass on lower costs to consumers by reducing the prices of their products. Neither did they pass productivity gains to their workers via higher wages. They kept the gains to themselves, so that business profits ballooned in the 1920s. Huge profit margins bolstered the stock market and fed a speculative bubble.

Tugwell neatly tied together long-term trends and the "roaring" 1920s. Accumulating profits stimulated investment, which created more productive capacity. But because corporations tamped down on wages, consumer purchasing power and sales did not keep pace with production. Corporate and investor riches camouflaged growing economic malaise. The weakness in demand eventually caught up with businesses, inventories piled up, profits turned downward and companies stopped investing.

Once stock market speculators noticed this, the buying frenzy ended and everybody tried to unload shares. So the bubble burst in 1929 and the economy that had looked solid turned into quicksand. Tugwell substituted the executives of giant companies for the old leisure class but otherwise his analysis was in keeping with Veblen's view of business behavior and financial markets.

From this diagnosis one could go to a Keynesian policy prescription. If large corporations monopolized productivity gains and by so doing unwittingly brought about economic catastrophe, some would argue for the government to tax and spend the proceeds to prop up demand. But that was not the advice Tugwell gave Roosevelt — he saw government spending as a short-term nostrum that treated the symptom, not the underlying condition.

Tugwell instead looked to wide-ranging government regulation of prices and wages to cure what he identified as the root cause of the disease, the market's inability to bring a balance between productivity growth and what consumers paid for the product and workers received for making it. The "real, visible guiding hand" of the government had to take the place of the invisible hand of the market, which according to Tugwell did not really exist.[24]

Within the administration and more broadly among reformists was a major divide. The trust busters, followers of Brandeis, wanted to break up large companies. Tugwell and Berle instead proposed controlling the productive potential of big business for the public good. In effect, they wanted to regulate large industrial and financial corporations in the same way that utilities are regulated, officially accepting and even protecting monopoly power.

Tugwell and Berle's agenda underpinned the National Recovery Administration. That experiment was short lived because Brandeis joined conservative Supreme Court justices to vote it down. The aged Progressive warned President Roosevelt: "we're not going to let this government centralize everything."

Successors to the Progressives and New Dealers never resolved the conflict between the twin goals of regulating industry and promoting competition.[25] Regulation favors large scale. Big companies can spread the cost across numerous customers; whereas small, competitive businesses can't and may be destroyed or never created because of the burden of regulation. This relationship works in the other direction as well – scale facilitates regulation. It is difficult to effectively oversee numerous competitors. Soviet central planners realized that they could more easily control a few big enterprises than many small ones, so they created gigantic enterprises.

The trade-off between competition and regulation does not stop left-wing critics from wanting more of both. For example, Nobel-winner Joseph Stiglitz has advocated the break-up of big banks but also heavier regulation[26] – which as a side effect encourages bigness. Current arguments on this issue are to a large extent a rehash of past policy battles which left a residue of pro-big-business, competition-reducing regulation that co-exists with anti-big-business political rhetoric. We will encounter examples.

Securities and Dams

New Dealers believed the financial industry required specialized regulation. For one thing, complaints that corporate insiders and exchange members manipulated stock prices had to be addressed. It was not enough that a group of bankers organized as a self-regulating entity under the NRA and persevered after it ended. They lacked a sufficient number of members and anyway government control was needed.

After an early attempt to write a comprehensive financial law failed, Roosevelt turned to Harvard law professor Felix Frankfurter, another Brandeis disciple. Frankfurter put together a group of his protégés to prepare a bill. Among them was Landis. He and two other lawyers, Thomas Corcoran and Benjamin Cohen, were so identified with Frankfurter in Washington that they came to be known as the "Happy Hotdogs." The three wrote and got through Congress the 1933 and 1934 securities laws, which in the main remain in place to this day.

Corcoran was – for a while – Roosevelt's top political operative and close associate, nicknamed "Tommy the Cork" by the president. While on occasion he helped draft legislation, his main function was to push people to go along with the boss's program. Cochrane refined the art of influencing members of Congress to vote in the direction the president desired. Without forceful arm twisting by this skilled political horse trader, major 1930s laws might not have passed. A congressman from Maine publicly accused Cochrane of threatening to hold up the construction of a dam in the man's district if he did not vote as instructed on a bill.[27]

The 1933 Truth-in-Securities Act was minimally intrusive regulation, requiring companies to disclose material facts when issuing a security. This was not controversial — in fact the New York Stock Exchange already required issuers to provide such information in order to list a security. The law went through Congress easily. It was to be administered by an existing agency that Brandeis helped create decades ago, the Federal Trade Commission.[28]

Landis, who as a Harvard academic had done a study of state blue sky laws, was named a Commissioner of the FTC. He became renowned for his hard work, intelligence and zealous enforcement of the law, emerging as the prototype regulator.[29]

Berle, sitting on a committee formed by the NYSE to recommend reforms for the exchange, was not satisfied. The 1933 law was a measure against fraudulent new issues but did not limit the financial power of investment bankers. He argued that the government had to take a greater role to counterbalance this power and transform high finance from a master into a servant of society.

Among the ardent reformers who were unhappy with the mild 1933 Act was a Yale law professor influenced by Veblen and Brandeis, William O. Douglas. He thought the Act was useless because most investors would not be able to absorb the large body of information securities registration statements had to contain. It was secondary to a "thoroughgoing and comprehensive program for social control in this field." Douglas soon had opportunity to shape financial regulation.

The following year, more ambitious financial legislation expanded regulators' remit. The 1934 law established oversight of financial markets with the aim of eliminating "unwise and destructive speculation" (in Roosevelt's words). It created the U.S. Securities and Exchange Commission and gave it wide powers. Exchanges were required to register with the new agency and obey its rules. The disclosure of information was mandated for all securities, not just new issues.

Landis had carefully written into the bill provisions that empowered regulators to formulate rules as they saw fit and gave them subpoena power to compel testimony when they wanted information. He made it a penal offense to disobey an SEC subpoena. The goal was to make regulators as independent as possible from the rest of the government. Landis' view was that lawmakers should delegate power to administrators. As a result, the SEC was given huge leeway in how it applied laws and the authority to take pre-emptive action against undesirable potential developments.

The bill gave rise to ferocious opposition from Wall Street, led by Whitney of the NYSE. To weaken the opposition, Corcoran allowed certain investment bankers to help redraft parts of the bill. This could be seen as a necessary compromise with the financial industry, reconciling opposed interests. But there was criticism from inside the administration that the bankers who made the deal were getting special benefits.

Corcoran successfully defended the 1934 bill in Congress. During his speech at the key hearing, he argued that it was necessary to give the new agency broad powers. Otherwise the financial interests that were being regulated would "regulate the regulators".[30] Despite opposition, the law passed with overwhelming support.

This was thanks to the Southern Democrats allied with Roosevelt.[31] Sam Rayburn of Texas, Chairman of the Commerce Committee, shepherded the securities bills through Congress. In other matters Rayburn was a conservative free market advocate, but he had an agreement with the President and in any event his constituents believed they were abused by financial interests, so he was happy to clip Wall Street's wings. He said the 1933 law was necessary to restore confidence in American institutions and avoid the evils of socialism.

There were rewards for his cooperation. One was that Corcoran got money from the Public Works Administration for a dam in Rayburn's district.[32]

The Lawyers' Deal

Landis was initially against the creation of a new agency. He championed the established Federal Trade Commission as the proper administrator of financial rules. But once Roosevelt moved him from the FTC and made him a commissioner of the SEC, he became an ardent supporter of the nascent securities regulator. He was widely seen as the most likely candidate to be the first chairman of the SEC.

To the shock of young reformers, Roosevelt appointed Joseph Kennedy as a commissioner of the SEC and pushed to have him elected chair. The banker, speculator, liquor tycoon, moviemaker and – later – ambassador was exactly the kind of figure New Dealers blamed for the economic malaise. A magazine described the five SEC commissioners: "four grave men and true, reformers and purgers of business by natural slant and experience, are led by a jovial master of the quick money-making art, a consummate product of the era they would bury."[33]

Kennedy raised money for Roosevelt but was also a potential rival and, as is well known, an amazingly bold operator both in business and politics. When the Prohibition ended, he used his political contributions and association with the president to get himself licensed to import whisky and other British distillery products, truly a license to mint money.[34] When Roosevelt did not appoint him Secretary of the Treasury after his stint as SEC chairman, he demanded his money back from the Democratic party.[35]

Roosevelt said Kennedy's priority was to preserve his fortune. But the president apparently did not worry that this aggressive man might use the SEC to protect his own numerous interests.[36]

To be fair, Kennedy did have certain strengths as chief financial regulator. He knew where the skeletons were hidden, being personally familiar with all manner of financial maneuvers. Certainly there was no danger that he would favor patrician investment bankers — they belonged to the WASP establishment that looked down on him, an Irishman from East Boston.

In fact he was the new agency's public relations face and envoy to the financial industry. His famed charm helped bolster the repute of newly regulated Wall Street and cajole doubtful financial executives into the regulatory fold. In 1935 he resigned and Landis took over as SEC chairman. Joseph Kennedy was an anomaly at the Commission, which from the start was dominated by lawyers. His time there had no long-term repercussions except that it turned out to be a personal boon to Landis, who became a close friend of Kennedy and his family and took to mentoring the sons.

The organization owed its beginnings to Landis more than anyone else. To his mind, a separate entity like the SEC, kept independent from cabinet departments, was just the right structure for effective administration. Its independence made it more attractive to capable lawyers, who would be able to do their work with little interference. It was less subject to political influences and demands for patronage jobs.

One outstanding legal scholar Landis recruited for the SEC was William Douglas, who as a specialist in bankruptcy law prepared the way for the Bankruptcy Act and Trust Indenture Act. When this Act passed in 1939, the SEC became the top administrator in those areas, on the ground of protecting the interests of shareholders in corporate bankruptcies and reorganizations.

The New Deal was so heavily reliant on the legal profession that a historian called it the lawyer's deal.[37] The dominance of lawyers was not new; it went back to the early days of the United States. Thomas Jefferson had complained that lawyers "by their numbers in the public councils, have wrested from the public hand the direction of the pruning knife."[38] But in the 20th century the profession acquired new power.

It was not just that legal skills came to play in drafting the huge mass of legislation or that lawyers developed the detailed rules to implement the laws and then enforced those rules. There was also something intangible: the reforms embodied lawyers' way of thinking. Reformists were influenced by Brandeis and Veblen both, but not surprisingly it was the legal pioneer and Supreme Court justice who shaped the lawmaking. The institutional basis of the regulatory state was the legal mindset. Regulators naturally disregarded the satirical social scientist's strictures against government.

It followed as a matter of course that lawyers also defended businesses against the disciplinary regime their profession molded in accordance with its new mode of thought. From the outset it was clear that lawyers could quickly change sides. As regulators they oversaw businesses and subsequently as defense counsel objected to the results of the oversight of those same businesses. Almost as soon as the rules were written, regulators started to deal with their former colleagues who moved to the other side.

A dramatic instance of this happened among the first generation of agency officials. The first general counsel of the SEC, John Burns, another Harvard law professor and friend of Frankfurter, became general counsel of United Corp., a utility holding company. The SEC had the task of implementing a utility holding company law that mandated the breakup of utility systems, at least those that did not benefit from economies of scale — an anti-trust effort in the Brandeis way.

But United Corp., armed with the former SEC counsel as its legal strategist and a former assistant director of the SEC Public Utilities Division as its president, successfully fought the agency.

Not every member of the profession accepted that legal skills should rightly be fungible — easily transformed from public to private servant, and possibly back again. Frankfurter, for one, was scandalized by the spectacle of lawyer-regulators switching sides. He wanted to prevent SEC employees from using their inside knowledge for private gain and recommended that former staffers not be allowed to defend their clients against the agency for two years.

In this Frankfurter came into conflict with his one-time protégé — with whom his relations were no longer as friendly. Landis was against any such restriction; it meant losing the incentive that brought talented lawyers to the SEC. He saw no problem with what came to be known as the revolving door. Indeed, to lure legal experts he would mention this to them as a major advantage of working for the SEC — later they could go into private practice with inside knowledge of how the regulator functioned (and, presumably, make a bundle). Employee rules resembling Frankfurter's suggestion were instituted later but this matter was never resolved, as we will have occasion to notice.

Landis picked the staff for the SEC and set the method that would underlie financial regulation long after his day. A distinctive feature of this was to encourage self-regulation by the industry but under firm rules and oversight by the SEC. When Landis left the SEC to become dean of Harvard Law School, Douglas succeeded him as chairman. The agency may have been full of brainy lawyers and former academics but from the start it was not collegial. Rivalry between top officials was ferocious, apparently even when they were not competing for the same position. Thus Landis did not approve of Douglas as his successor, though he himself had brought Douglas to the SEC.

Douglas had decided to take Yale's offer to become dean of the law school if he did not become SEC chair. In a memoir written decades later, Douglas complained that Landis deliberately stayed longer than he needed at the SEC in order to block Douglas' chairmanship. By then Douglas' career at the SEC was superseded by his years on the Supreme Court and Landis was dead. It was a strangely bitter reminiscence.

—

Personal animosity notwithstanding, Douglas continued Landis' work, except that he was more aggressive. Douglas disliked the financial world for disregarding "social and human values" and aimed to make sure financiers performed their fiduciary duty in handling other people's money.[39] But like Landis he favored industry self-regulation under close supervision of the SEC.

This approach was helped by a development within the NYSE: the reform-minded opposition managed to sideline Whitney and the rest of the old guard whose representative he was. They made sure Whitney lost the NYSE presidency, excluded his allies from the governance of the exchange and instituted additional requirements for members. Those included disclosures of what they did with customer funds. The exchange's new rules showed up irregularities in the accounts of Richard Whitney & Co.

Roosevelt was astonished to hear that his Groton classmate, the famously snobby patrician Whitney, had been embezzling clients' money. As the former NYSE chief headed to Sing Sing, sentenced to five-to-ten-years for grand larceny, regulators moved to take advantage of his disgrace. Douglas said of this incident: "The stock exchange was delivered into my hands." In fact it was the reform faction in the NYSE who brought Whitney down, but Douglas pushed them to agree to additional regulation.

In 1938, legislation was enacted to regulate the over-the-counter market, that is, brokers and dealers in securities. This was a complicated problem for the SEC because brokers were numerous. Most were small businesses and there were 5,000 to 6,000 of them. Here, the desire to regulate ran directly counter to the competitive structure of the industry. The solution was to create the National Association of Securities Dealers, a trade association that acted as the industry watchdog under the aegis of the SEC.

Getting many brokers together in the association made them easier to oversee. NASD was specifically exempted from anti-trust law. In return for cooperation, organized brokers and dealers were allowed to treat differently anyone who did not belong to the association. Outside brokerages did not get the same prices for securities as NASD members; they had to pay the retail price. This was consistent with the kind of industrial arrangement advocated by Berle and Tugwell that sacrificed competition to achieve regulatory power.

NASD was given the authority to fine or suspend brokers and dealers who violated the rules. The organization built a large staff of investigators, instituted routine exams and imposed numerous sanctions on brokerages. The SEC had the power to change or reject any rule, to request disciplinary action and to review NASD cases.

Success Story

Landis, who came to be regarded as the great designer of regulatory organization as well as the brilliant legal mind that crafted impeccable financial laws, sounded confident of the success of his creation. In 1938, about a year after he returned to Harvard Law School as dean, he gave a series of talks at Yale University. Published as a book, *The Administrative Process*, the lectures attracted widespread attention and become a landmark in the history of the American regulatory state.

In effect, Landis celebrated the victory of the New Deal — in thought, in the courts and in regulatory practice. Legal realism was winning the war against the old Classical doctrine. Conservative judges had put up impediments to the regulatory state, notably through Supreme Court decisions. In 1937, a so-called "constitutional revolution" occurred. In the face of Roosevelt's scheme to pack the court with friendly justices, the Supreme Court did an about turn.

This historic legal shift had more than a few strands, as is clear from studies by Epstein (2006, 1988a) and Shughart (2004). The process was complicated. However, the end result was dramatic: legal barriers to the regulatory state rapidly fell. So Landis was justified in proclaiming success.

But traditional government, consisting of Congress, White House and the courts, did not have the ability to make and implement detailed rules for particular industries. The growth of regulation necessitated the growth of administrative agencies – as Landis described them – endowed with specialized knowledge and skills and freedom to shape policy. Independent organizations would function better than regulators inside cabinet departments. The experts at these agencies were capable of responding to changing conditions and emergencies.

Exhibit number one was the Securities and Exchange Commission. To substantiate his claims, Landis pointed to the achievements of the SEC. The agency promoted the well-being of the industry it regulated. It built confidence in financial products.

His broader vision was to tame the unruly market economy by creating a plethora of such administrative agencies to oversee other industries and functions. The greater the number of specialized agencies, the better, because that way the staff of each agency could develop detailed expertise in their particular area. Endowed with specialized knowledge, they would know how to regulate that industry. The SEC was a template for the rest of the system.

"Efficiency in the processes of government regulation is best served by the creation of more rather than less agencies," Landis asserted. "And it is efficiency that is the desperate need." For efficiency, Congress should not give detailed instructions, the expert regulators should have the discretion to do what they judged best for the public interest.

His former mentor Frankfurter had made a similar point, but more as an observation than a prescription. Frankfurter wrote that the regulation of industries, including banking, was necessary in a modern society and required decisions that legislatures or courts could not make. Therefore "These powers are lodged in vast congeries of agencies." Landis went beyond Frankfurter in presenting the observed trend as a triumph.

Those administrative "vast congeries" were becoming a "fourth branch" of government. They were to restrain economic powers and protect the little people from predatory business practices. They themselves formed a new hub of power.

Critics charged that independent regulatory agencies violated the constitutional principle of checks and balances. Landis replied that other branches of government would oversee regulators. The executive branch controlled top appointments, the legislature controlled budgets. The courts could review regulatory decisions. The problem – as Landis saw it – was not that regulators would gain arbitrary power but that they wouldn't do enough.

For the next half century, the SEC became the prime example of regulatory success. In a 1984 book Thomas McCraw described it as "the New Deal's single most successful regulatory agency."[40] The set-up created in 1938 for brokers and dealers was also seen as a fine feat of regulatory design. McCraw wrote: "NASD, closely supervised by the SEC, did an excellent job in bringing order and discipline to the over-the-counter market, a setting that once harbored some of the sleaziest characters in all of American business."[41]

Over time the SEC took on more functions and acquired more powers. It remained a model of the successful agency. As late as 2009, a history concluded that the SEC continued to advance the original goal it was given, namely to regulate finance in the interest of the public or investors.[42]

CHAPTER TWO. Wise Umpires

The desire to restrain the economic power of large business, in particular of banks and exchanges, was a powerful rationale for the growth of the regulatory state. This was a popular cause. But a more subtle and just as compelling argument came from the second great institutionalist, John Commons. He pointed out that modern society harbors numerous conflicting interests, which become destructive unless contained. The government has to act as referee and reconcile the conflicts.

That sounds like an economic version of the old Hobbesian tenet — without Leviathan, people will fight and wreck havoc. But Commons was making a less obvious point. Conflicts can be resolved in the courts, but at high cost and subject to some arbitrariness. This makes life uncertain and poorer, if not short, brutish etc. as Hobbes warned.

After analyzing myriad social and economic arrangements, Commons came up with what he believed was a better solution. It is more efficient to regulate conflicts, he concluded.

Collective Action

He started from the observation that individuals can achieve more together - whether in clans, companies or countries - than they can on their own. But to live and work together, we need ways to keep the peace. What enables people to cooperate?

Commons tackled that question at a time of acute social unrest and strife in America. Though he wrote thousands of pages, his central argument may be succinctly expressed — rules are necessary to reconcile human beings who have conflicting interests and opposed viewpoints; such rules are embodied in social customs that are obeyed automatically; but customary rules can be unfair or, even if socially beneficial, not powerful enough; therefore official rules need to be made and enforced by government. Hence the need for regulation.

Straightforward as that may sound, Commons spent a lifetime trying to develop its implications. Abstruse theorizing was part of his approach, but the purpose was practical. His theory was inspired and shaped by experience and in turn provided the basis for policymaking.[43] The reasoning never strayed far from the facts he collected.

Regulation roughly along the lines Commons advocated had been applied to railroads in the 19th century, with Massachusetts leading the way.[44] But Commons offered a systematic approach, explaining under what conditions and why regulation becomes necessary and how to go about making it.

His laboratory was the state of Wisconsin; its populist politics gave him the opportunity to put his theory into practice in the early decades of the 20th century. He knew and worked with governor Robert M. La Follette, who ran for president as the Progressive party candidate in a three-man race and lost to Calvin Coolidge in1924. Commons then became adviser to Philip La Follette.

Commons applied his insights to policies such as workers' compensation, the state civil service code, public utility rules and a minimum wage act—to pick a few examples of his handiwork. He mediated between employees and employers in labor disputes. He studied workers at print shops and steel mills and sympathized with the difficulties they faced and solutions they found.

Labor leader Samuel Gompers was a friend. But Commons also admired enterprising businessmen and great tycoons. He knew Andrew Carnegie and received assistance from him. He claimed he wanted to save capitalism by making capitalists behave responsibly.

At the University of Wisconsin where he spent much of his career, he trained students to design government programs and rules. The programs and regulations he created became models for other states and federal policy makers. Commons was an expert for the Congressional Committee that investigated the national banking industry. One of his students, Edwin Witte, led the effort to devise the Social Security system in 1935.

Citizens of an Institution

Commons' version of institutionalism focused on laws and official rules . "I had read Veblen's brilliant criticisms, beginning in 1895 ... and his suggestion that an evolutionary theory of value must be constructed out of the habits and customs of social life," he wrote. "But he had not studied the decisions of the courts which are based on these customs and I went to work with my students digging directly out of the court decisions stretching over several hundred years ..."[45]

Veblen had not asked why we obey social rules and paid little attention to the incentives that make individuals comply. This was because he focused on institutions of a certain type — informal norms embedded in the minds of members of a community. People are conditioned from an early age to observe customs; the rules are ingrained. External influence takes the form of family, peers and neighbors who may react to a violation of custom.

Commons agreed with Veblen that internalized communal rules have a powerful influence on behavior. Once established and handed over from one generation to another, social norms are taken for granted — their longevity makes them seem natural, though they are no such thing. As long as customs change slowly, he wrote, "they appear to be natural, unchallengeable, inalienable, though they are artificial, collective, transitory, forfeitable."[46]

Going beyond Veblen, Commons unpacked the notion of an institution. His work suggests a spectrum of different types of rule-based behavior. At one end are habituated near-automatic attitudes, values and habits that are rarely if ever questioned. At the other are calculated choices that depend on financial, moral or physical enforcement mechanisms — which he called collective sanctions.

Societies control behavior through different sanctions. The most potent sanction is the threat of physical coercion, ranging from having one's possessions taken away to being hauled off to jail or worse. The least coercive are moral sanctions of opinion that make us behave in ways that others in our group approve. Moral norms can be transformed into precise laws through legislation or court decisions. Thereafter what used to be an informal rule is backed by the threat of government force. This, wrote Commons, adds "organized compulsion to the unorganized working rules of custom."

His view of the relationship between custom and law is closer to classical jurisprudence than to legal realism. Certain legal doctrines are special cases of moral principles — such as the imperative that courts not violate precedent arbitrarily and treat everybody similarly under similar circumstances. Both custom and precedent reduce uncertainty by telling us what to expect. Customary rules tell us something about what a business or person is likely to do in a certain situation. Legal precedent tells us what a court is likely to decide in a certain matter.

While moral sanctions might be relatively weak in a modern society like America, economic sanctions are potent. "Customs have merely changed with changes in economic conditions, and they may today be even more mandatory than the decrees of a dictator, who perforce is compelled to conform to them," Commons wrote. "The business man who refuses or is unable to make use of the modern customs of the credit system, by refusing to accept or issue checks on solvent banks, although they are merely private arrangements and not legal tender, simply cannot continue in business ..."[47]

In purely social as well as economic situations people interact as "citizens of an institution that lived before them and will live after them," Commons declared.[48] Whether earning a living, learning new skills or hearing the gossip, we meet each other not as isolated forces of nature but "prepared more or less by habit, induced by the pressure of custom, to engage in those highly artificial transactions created by the collective human will..."

Social customs embodied in official law and backed by government coercion are highly visible and forceful institutions. Others are enforced only by more subtle moral or economic sanctions. Some are not deliberately adopted but shape behavior often from childhood and become noticeable only when violated, thereby triggering social reaction.

As the balance between sanctions evolves, the social order changes, Commons observed. Institutional economics, as he understood it, deals with the relative merits and efficiency of the three types of sanctions, drawing on the three corresponding fields — ethics, economics and jurisprudence.

Collective sanctions control individual action but also liberate and expand it. Sanctions in the form of family discipline, business conventions or government regulation forbid certain behaviors.

But sanctions also enable individuals to do things they would not be able to do on their own. Collective action liberates individuals from coercion, duress or unfair competition by others. It supports ready-made ways of doing things so that individuals know how to behave when they run a business, meet a potential date or look to purchase a house.

We all gain from collective mechanisms to reduce uncertainty and negotiate conflict. Institutions that succeed in doing this encourage transactions and hence economic activity. Without stable social structures that tell us what we need to do and how others will respond, it would be difficult and costly to achieve even a simple transaction like buying a hotdog from a vendor. Laws and customary precedents create order by reducing insecurity in transactions, making it possible for individuals to know what to expect and plan how to achieve their purpose.

A shorthand way of putting this is that collective rules reduce the cost of transacting with others. Knowing what to expect, people are able to do business more easily and efficiently. That is not the full picture, however. There are other, more deep-seated effects on ways of thinking. Thus Wesley Mitchell, a student of Veblen's and the third great institutionalist, pointed out that the spread of money created a new mentality of calculation and quantification, opening the way to new institutions that enabled economic development.

In Commons' vision, regulation is necessary because social norms are not always beneficial and even when they are beneficial, not sufficient. Private actors often make bad decisions that leave other people worse off. Businessmen do not pursue enlightened long-term self interest. Where they have market power, they abuse it and cause harm to customers and employees, creating antagonistic situations with high social costs. People deceive each other, which creates uncertainty and raises the cost of transacting.

One way the government reduces insecurity and makes transactions predictable is by preventing fraud and misrepresentation. Private institutions that control fraudulent behavior – business ethics, professional rules – are all very well but become stronger once recognized by courts and overseen by regulators. Backed by the power of law, these norms for honest behavior limit the damage that people would otherwise do to each other through deception.

More broadly, governments should fashion tools to improve social relations and economic efficiency. For Commons, regulation is the main device to harmonize conflicting interests and make all parties behave in ways that increase overall wellbeing. Properly designed interventions will improve behavior and therefore outcomes. All we need is to understand how to achieve this. Commons believed that institutional economics provides that understanding; he himself showed the way by creating workaday rules.

Do Not Get Discouraged

There was much agitation against utility companies in Wisconsin and the issue was high on the political agenda. The residents of Madison and Milwaukee were unhappy with their gas and electricity providers. The city of Madison sued the gas and electric company in 1905-1906 to make it provide higher quality service and lower the rates it charged.

Utilities were accepted as natural monopolies because the cost of the infrastructure to provide service was huge and a single provider could spread that cost over more users, reducing the cost per user. But a monopoly can exploit its customers and not pass on the lower cost. Many utility customers thought this was happening.

Commons wrote the utility law that Wisconsin passed in 1907.[49] He designed it to accommodate the interests of the utility companies and consumers without using up a lot of resources for the purpose. The statute required that the rates set by electric, gas, water and telephone service providers be approved as "reasonable" by an independent commission. Public hearings had to be held before any increase in rates.

Customers were to be protected from excessive rate hikes but at the same time the providers had a right to charge prices that earned them a "fair" return on their investment. Regulation would limit the pricing power of utility companies while making sure the price provided a profit. To Commons, a big advantage of formalized procedures for setting prices and dealing with complaints was to reduce uncertainty for both sides — they would know what to expect and how to go about making changes if they were dissatisfied. Transactions between them would be easier.

To this day, similar regulations govern public utility companies. Moreover, the line of reasoning Commons used continues to be the starting point for new regulatory schemes. Thus the 2010 Dodd-Frank law included a provision to cap the fees charged by large banks for debt cards on the ground that the credit card companies possessed market power and colluded with banks to impose the fees on retailers.[50] Card fees were to be regulated like electricity rates.

The same type of argument informed the various programs Commons devised. At the time, compensation for work-related injury and death required the injured employee or his heirs to sue the employer. This worked badly for both sides. Workplace accidents could spell disaster for families reduced to poverty while waiting for the lawsuit to be decided. Employers, for their part, did not know how much they were liable for. Some got off paying nothing while other businesses were pushed into bankruptcy when juries sympathetic to workers awarded them huge sums.

Workers also faced destitution when they lost their job. Commons drafted social programs to provide security against unemployment and work-related accidents. Employers would contribute to a common fund to compensate injured workers or their heirs. Similarly companies would pay for an unemployment insurance fund.

To get businessmen to agree, Commons made the case that these programs would reduce the litigation employers faced and lead to a more cooperative relationship with labor. The programs would promote social peace and make life more predictable and orderly for all. The transactions between employees and employers would become smoother and the travails of accidents or layoffs less damaging. Wisconsin implemented his idea. Other states as well developed disability compensation, workplace safety rules, unemployment insurance. These became enduring components of the American economy and the social landscape.

It may not be obvious but the conflict-resolution argument is very much relevant to financial fraud. Ponzi schemes typically end in a chaotic collapse. Everybody who lost money tries to recover as much as they can and fights erupt over the remaining assets. Hence it is necessary to have a referee. Regulators play the role of mediators between diverse interests — to put the matter in Commons' terms.

After a financial con game folds, the state comes in as the arbitrator. Specifically, the Securities and Exchange Commission takes control of the remnants of the fraudulent investment business. Officials then designate a receiver who has the mandate to avoid further losses and bring about a fair distribution of the assets. How this works in practice is investigated in the second part of the book.

During much of his career Commons saw grounds to be optimistic. America was slowly developing socially beneficial and reasonable rules to constrain bad behavior. These were reducing frictions between groups and hence the costs of transacting. A more efficient, equitable and fair society was in the making.

It is remarkable that he had such faith in Americans acting as a collective body, given his low opinion of humanity as a whole. His typical comment on the subject – "Man is not a rational being as the 18th century thought; he is a being of stupidity, passion and ignorance as (Thomas) Malthus thought" – suggests no ground for optimism. How does a collective of ignorant and emotional individuals design wise rules of behavior for themselves and their descendents?

To his credit, Commons did not claim that abstract blueprints drawn up by academics or policy wonks provide instant better institutions. He knew that government programs have unintended side effects. Reforms to correct perceived problems create new problems. "It is, indeed, an endless dilemma that progressive legislation in one direction brings on the need for progressive legislation in other directions," he observed. Nevertheless, he expected gradual improvement through slow, incremental trial-and-error.

During his time in Washington at the beginning of World War I he told his associates that human beings, given 12 ways to tackle a problem, will first try the eleven wrong ones before coming to the twelfth, correct, approach. This was to be expected given the limits of the human mind and could be overcome through experimentation. "Don't get discouraged," he advised.[51]

All My Devices Turned on This Assumption

One had to persist in reform efforts, Commons believed, because despite all the problems the fact remained that collective action can achieve ends that individuals can not on their own. Reformers make mistakes and create new problems. All the same, society has two key advantages over the individual. One, the collective has an extended time horizon — it exists for centuries and hence has a lot of opportunity for trial-and-error. The long span of history provides ample experience to learn from and time to derive the right lessons.

The second advantage is the diversity of talents. Societies comprise different types of individuals, some of whom are capable of learning from mistakes and using this knowledge to improve institutions. Those with such abilities can observe and correct the undesirable consequences of past interventions.

Through the learning and correction process, the collective can evolve rules that settle conflicts, restrain the harm caused by selfish individuals and reduce the unfair advantage some take of others. To achieve better learning, Commons encouraged statistical studies that would underpin policymaking. He joined Wesley Mitchell to found the National Bureau of Economic Research, which later became the leading source of information about business cycles.[52]

Unfortunately, early in his career Commons' hopes for the reforming elite shaded into self-congratulation and racism—he thought only some ethnic groups can play this role. While deprecating his own experimental "little schemes for curing economic, political and sociological disease" he nevertheless saw himself as one of the select few who would create cumulatively better institutions. He certainly made mistakes, at one time grossly misreading the fascist state in Italy as capable of reconciling conflicts in accordance with institutional theory.

But Commons recognized at least some of his errors. He was an honest observer and went on observing for a long time. In old age – though sickly and racked by all manner of family tragedy he lived into his 80s – he noticed that his confidence might not be justified, that collective action for the betterment of society could take a wrong turn and persist along a wrong path. He had assumed that the policy elite would in the main consist of individuals with strong skills and a selfless concern for the public good. Indeed, he had written a civil service code for Wisconsin aiming to create such a body.

Like Veblen, Commons did not trust politicians. For this reason he was against communism or a radical overhaul of capitalist institutions. He said of a worker-assistant who helped him investigate sweat shops: "He did not want the state, as did Karl Marx, to take over the shops and factories, for he knew the Chicago politicians...." If you knew real-life political players, you would not want them to be in charge of your shop, let alone the economy. Commons knew politicians.

But he trusted the ideal of a technocratic bureaucracy, well trained and aloof from conflicting interests. It had to be sufficiently detached to act as an impartial referee and have credibility as such. Otherwise, if people believed regulators backed certain groups against others, they would resist the rules and sanctions. The effectiveness of regulation would be impaired.

Looking back after he retired, he realized that the regulations and programs he created depended crucially on the quality of this elite: "I now see that all of my devices and recommendations for legislation in the state or nation have turned on this assumption of a non-partisan administration by specially qualified appointees."

He had envisioned capable officials negotiating with opposed groups to bring about reasonable compromises. To this end, political give-and-take and propaganda were useful components of collective action through negotiation. But officials had to act as objective and knowledgeable go-betweens who did not favor one side over another. In effect, the correct implementation of the procedures and rules required a body of impartial paragons.

The actual public bureaucracy was something else. Not only politicians but officials across the board looked to further their own standing. Commons had thought the United States was an exception to the sorry history of oppressive elites. But his observations did not support that view. "Even in democratic America I see how quickly a private citizen, when elected or appointed to public office, becomes a bureaucrat," he wrote in his memoir. He saw this as "the germ of dictatorship."

Watching the Democratic party in action shaping the Wisconsin state government apparatus for its own benefit, he wrote: "Although a good Democrat myself, I am glad I am retired."[53] As he recognized the pitfalls of the regulatory state, he wondered whether he had been wrong all along.

By then Commons' work appeared to be on its way to oblivion. Institutionalism was an alternative to mainstream neoclassical economics but by the 1940s it had been pushed to the side by anti-cyclical policies associated with John Maynard Keynes. Yet Commons is possibly the most influential little-known thinker in social science. Even Keynes may have been influenced by Commons' take on expectations in the 1930s while writing his *General Theory*.[54]

Long after Commons' death, the idea of transaction cost became a major subject of economic research. During the second half of the 20th century at least three Nobel prizewinners – Herbert Simon, Oliver Williamson and Douglas North – drew on his fundamental concepts.[55] There were efforts to reinvigorate institutional economics.[56]

Good Man Philosophy

A few judicial scholars echoed the misgivings Commons expressed in his old age. Felix Frankfurter recognized the problem early on. Laws had to be sufficiently flexible that regulators could adapt the rules to changing conditions. To be capable of doing this, regulators had to be highly trained and impartial. Everything depends on personnel, Frankfurter wrote in 1925.

New Dealers had a simple response to anyone worried about this aspect of the regulatory state: Very well, go find the right people. That was a mantra for reformers not only in the 1930s but through the century and continuing to this day.

Thomas Corcoran was characteristically bold in his expression at the hearing where he defended the 1934 Securities Exchange Act. A Congressman remarked on the potential for inequity. This was Carl Mapes of Michigan, a Republican who held his seat for some 36 years until his death in 1939 while conducting an investigative tour. An agency like the Securities and Exchange Commission might serve certain people, not others. "I hate the idea that some man can go to an administrative official and get something done that another fellow on the street cannot," Mapes said.

Corcoran was ready with the stock reply: "The answer is to pick good men on your commissions." The veteran congressman was not buying this—"Well, that sometimes is no answer at all."[57] Corcoran stood his ground. "It is the ultimate answer to any governmental problem," he told the audience, who presumably were persuaded, given that the Act passed.

Landis was a strident proponent of the right-man solution. It was the key, whatever the issue. What mattered was to cure social and economic maladies; the right men would shape the laws and rules as needed for the purpose. This went for judges and elected officials from top to bottom, as well as regulators.

Thus when the issue of Roosevelt's third term came up, Landis was persuaded to back the president despite his initial doubts. He dismissed the principle of term limits. "For my part, I distrust generalizations," he said. "I would rather pin my faith on men."[58]

Landis ran into an unexpected adversary—Roscoe Pound, the former dean of Harvard Law school, his colleague and for years ally. Pound had attacked the old jurisprudence as overly rule-bound and defended the expansion of the administrative state as a the natural result of the change from rural to industrial society.[59] But later he changed his mind.

Pound had come to realize that legal realism opened a chasm. Once traditional legal thought, with its basis of established norms, was rejected, government by law became shaky. After all, if laws are made at will, they can be remade at will. There is not much left to anchor them. The danger is that there is no law left to effectively control public agents.

In 1938 Pound attacked what he described as the "administrative absolutism" of New Deal policies. He called on lawyers to check the growth of the regulatory state and its bureaucracies. But Landis was right that the tenor of the time favored regulation and the administrative apparatus that went with it. Pound could not slow down this juggernaut, let alone stop it.

Frankfurter had certain doubts. For one thing, he was not sure presidents would pick capable regulators. He and Landis were in the same camp in arguing for agencies with wide discretion to administer the modern economy. But Frankfurter was not comfortable with the delegation of unlimited power to agencies and suspected that if it went too far it would run foul of the Constitution.

Moreover, he did not think a rule of experts unsupported by the public could work — in a similar vein, he did not favor judicial activism bereft of democratic support. It was essential for politicians to get the population behind the regulatory state. Watching regulators in practice may have been part of the reason Frankfurter became less enamored of interventionism and wrote conservative opinions as a Supreme Court justice.

While legal flexibility and a new economy run by publicly minded experts sound like modern constructs, the notion of morally and intellectually superior administrators is very old. It goes back at least 2,400 years to Socrates, who advocated rule by "those who know" — in our parlance, experts. His student Plato described an ideal state governed by philosopher-kings selected through a rigorous, lengthy process of exams and training. These scholar-rulers follow eternal laws of justice and are un-bribable and impartial. Landis appeared to be a modern incarnation of this classical ideal, what with his high scholarly standing and top position at Harvard Law School.

Socrates argued that the population should obey those who know in the same way as a patient should obey his physician. As a 20th century critic noted, later utopians of various stripes followed the same general model of paternalist government by an order of wise men — or women, as the case may be.[60]

However, Landis tried to distance the modern administrative state from past wise-ruler utopias. He acknowledged American doubts as to the " eugenic possibilities of breeding supermen to direct the inordinately complex affairs of the larger branches of private industry." He disowned any extravagant claims for regulators. One could not expect to staff Washington bureaucracies with supermen in the Platonic mold.

Nevertheless it was possible to attract smart specialists with a yen for public service, as he had done at the SEC. The solution was to hire a large number of such individuals, who might not be quite like himself with his pioneering vision, but were knowledgeable and dedicated. Brought together in numerous agencies to oversee different industries, they would impartially referee conflicts, protect vulnerable groups, keep the economy efficient and competitive.

This view of a class of experts with legal authority to permanently supervise material life was the most extreme version of statism to take root in America. It went beyond Veblen, who never trusted the government, and Commons, who favored basing formal rules on existing private institutions as much as possible. The intellectual heirs to Justice Brandeis went about boldly creating organizations and rules as needed to achieve lofty social goals.

The agenda was ambitious; it resulted in many laws, often vague, requiring elaboration by experts. At the same time, legal realism undermined the vision of a rule of law deeply rooted in immemorial social custom. Laws seen as infinitely malleable are ephemeral; the men had to be superior because they were supposed to compensate for ill-defined laws that could change before most people even understood what was required. What the rule of law lost, the rule of discretion gained.[61] It followed that the quality of the people was paramount.

In Plato's *Politicus,* a character who is the author's mouthpiece says: "The best thing is not that the laws be in power but that the man who is wise and of kingly nature be ruler."[62] It could be claimed that American government was partially remade in line with an ancient utopia, however much the reformers talked of modern industry and science and the new administrative state.

You've Got to Wear Blinders

The brash young front man of New Deal lawmaking, Corcoran, sharply exemplified the gap between the ideal and the real. He achieved results as Roosevelt's operative, nimbly using carrots and sticks to badger congressmen to pass the administration's laws. To get a Colorado senator to vote for a utility company bill, Corcoran promised that the mining office of the newly created Securities and Exchange Commission would be located in Denver as the senator wished. I've already mentioned the dams promised or withdrawn according to votes.

Neither were his services confined to policy and legislation. He solicited campaign contributions from businessmen. He solved Roosevelt's personal problems. When the president wanted to get his troublesome and unemployed brother-in-law out of Washington, Corcoran pushed the Reconstruction Finance Corp. to give a loan to the brother-in-law's Alaskan mining venture — which predictably failed.[63]

Even as the President expected him to get things done by hook or crook, his success left a trail of unsavory deals. At one time Roosevelt considered appointing him budget director. The secretary of the Treasury, Henry Morgenthau, said this was out of question. Morgenthau described Corcoran as "an intellectual crook."[64] Eventually Corcoran became too dirty and a political liability, whereupon Roosevelt discarded him.

By that time Corcoran had developed an extensive network of contacts by doing favors and getting his chums into key government jobs. At the highest levels of government were individuals who owed him a good turn. What is more, he knew intimately how Washington functions — not only Congress but also the numerous administrative agencies that Landis celebrated so enthusiastically in 1938.

As a private operator Corcoran continued to swap favors — sometimes with a long lag. He accumulated favors and called them as needed over time to serve the interests of those who paid him. Thus he went from making regulation to helping clients circumvent the rules. He helped fulfill his own warning at the 1934 Congressional hearing that the interests being regulated could instead "regulate the regulators"

Since he knew everybody, he was an obvious source of information about people. Thus William Douglas let him influence top appointments at the SEC. Corcoran found Douglas just the right apartment.[65] To an SEC chairman who was about to leave the agency, he offered valuable office space. "But I feel I owe you so much already," said the man, accepting the offer. Douglas was notably concerned about the morality of business people. But apparently he paid little attention to the morality of his wheeler-dealer friend with government connections.

We know some of Corcoran's schemes and what he said to people because the FBI tapped his phone for several years and the tapes became available after his death. The wiretap was requested by Harry Truman, who was suspicious of Corcoran and tried to prevent his influence on his own administration. J. Edgar Hoover may have agreed to the wiretap as a way of gaining the confidence of Truman.

Corcoran strongly suspected his phone was tapped but went on with his conversations and business as usual. Perhaps he reasoned that information from the wiretap could not be presented as evidence in court. His special kind of power long outlasted the Truman administration and even outlasted the decades-long reign of J. Edgar Hoover at the FBI. As a highly successful lobbyist, Corcoran was active almost till his death in 1981.

He did not invent lobbying but he offered a particularly potent version — not mere access to high officials but the possibility of achieving the clients' specific wishes, like getting around wartime rationing of raw materials. He was under no illusion that his actions served any public purpose and advised an associate that they were in the business to make money by doing whatever the client wanted.

"Once you get into this business you've got to be a draft horse and you've got to wear blinders," he said[66] It was not a matter of what you thought was good or bad, right or wrong.

Landis claimed that good men would make even bad laws – and presumably bad organizations– work. He was oblivious to the danger inherent in the get-capable-staff approach to regulation. The second career of Corcoran, Landis' confidante and a prime example of the capable lawyer he wanted to draw to the public sector, was a sign of the future. Legions followed in Corcoran's footsteps, using knowledge gained in government to serve whoever is willing and able to pay for the service.

CHAPTER THREE. Regulators Against Folly

While the Progressives started building the regulatory state primarily as a bulwark against the power of moneyed interests and 20th century reformers continued the project with the added rationale of soothing economic conflict, it was a third reason that underpinned the most invasive type of financial rulemaking.

Fraud is an exercise in persuasion. By contrast, theft depends on violence or the threat thereof. A man with a gun to the head has little choice but to turn over his valuables, whereas the target of a financial scheme is free to say no and walk away. He decides to go along with the proposition because it sounds attractive.

To persuade, the perpetrator has to be prepared. Whereas other crimes may happen in a sudden emotional flare-up, a con game takes time and is not simple to pull off. Even a three-card Monte scam on a city street corner requires preparation — to come up with the right talk, coordinate the shills, move the cards quickly.

The very word "scheme" tells you someone thought about how to do the deed. Someone figured out a ruse to convince others to give him their money, made up a reassuring story, probably created false documents. Those others mulled over the story and documents to decide whether to trust the schemer with their money. The successful swindler knows what to say and how to present the offer so that at least some of the marks find it appealing.

As a calculated act that requires thought on the part of both the perpetrators and the victims, a financial scams poses a puzzle. Both sides take the time to figure out their best advantage, often with as much care as they can, only to find themselves in a disastrous situation. They take reasoned steps to better their financial condition yet those steps lead in the opposite direction. The victims are deceived and lose money; the swindler becomes a prisoner if he is caught or a fugitive if he manages to escape. Expecting to do well, typically they end up worse off.

In retrospect it looks like they inadvertently fell into a trap, including even the perpetrator. People reason their way to an outcome they don't want. Were they really acting rationally? Perhaps they're not fit to make financial decisions. From that impression it is a short step to conclude that the public will make fools of themselves unless constrained by regulation and government overseers.

When William Douglas and others disparaged the 1933 Securities Act, they had in mind the fitness question. The 1933 law required securities issuers to provide accurate information, but Douglas doubted that people would have the time, resources or intelligence to absorb the information. They would not make the right choices despite the available information; therefore financial regulation had to go further.

This feature of financial chicanery led to distinctive policies and a specialized regulatory apparatus. Theft is not regulated by a civil government agency. It is investigated by the police and prosecuted in the criminal courts, but there is no "Theft Prevention Commission" to mirror the Securities and Exchange Commission. But fraud is subject to both criminal sanctions and financial regulation. What does the added level of intervention achieve beyond what the police and criminal courts do?

Regulators and the criminal justice system are alike in aiming to suppress undesirable behavior. Criminal punishment is expected to deter bad behavior by showing what happens to perpetrators. Regulation is supposed to do something else. If it works, it prevents deception mainly by helping potential victims not to fall for the con.

This is certainly a worthwhile goal. Prevention reduces the cost of financial transacting — the less the danger of fraud, the easier it is buy and sell securities, the lower the cost of raising capital. But there is the qualifier, "if it works."

Imperfect Calculators

History documents numerous spectacular ways people found to shoot themselves in the foot while in hot pursuit of Mammon. Charles MacKay put his 724-page chronicle of mass delusions into perspective as "a chapter only in the great and awful book of human folly."[67] That was in the early 19th century. If someone tried to extend MacKay's project through the next 200 years, they would never be able to finish because there are so many stories — I will tell a few later from the regulatory standpoint.

That human beings do foolish things was obvious to Veblen and Commons. From an institutionalist perspective, human reason is in general a weak device for the job of telling us what to think and do. That is why in many matters we follow established social custom — often absurd custom, but nevertheless a guide without which most people would be lost.

Much of 20th century mainstream economics stands in sharp contrast to this paradigm. Neoclassical economics is about the behavior of entities who are in effect perfect calculators of their own interest. Consumers maximize their satisfaction – or utility – subject to their budget constraint. Producers maximize output subject to technology and resources. These rational choices result in a balance between supply and demand. Under perfect competition and with full information, this equilibrium represents the efficient use of resources to satisfy given preferences.[68]

It is not that the theory asserts real people are always rational and fully informed, but it studies rational behavior. The more complicated neoclassical and related game theoretic models can incorporate known unknowns, to use the distinction popularized by a former U.S. Secretary of Defense. Unknown unknowns, for which there is no estimated probability, are beyond the ken of the theory.

In the second half of the 20th century, neoclassical economics replaced arguments about institutional shortcomings as the justification for regulation. If competition or information is impaired, the market fails to bring about the best use of resources. Market failures can be identified by comparing reality to models that assume fully rational and informed behavior. Government can intervene to correct these failures.

Once orthodox micro economics hardened into such models, it became obvious that the real world deviated enormously from the hypothetical ideal. One could question the usefulness of the ideal, but academic economists went the other way and described the market's deviations from models as "imperfections" — the result of a fixation on abstract models, Peter Boettke has pointed out.[69] A cottage industry developed to pinpoint departures from the assumptions of the neoclassical canon and propose interventions to bring reality better in line with theory.

A widely cited 1970 paper by George Akerlof added to interventionists' scholarly arsenal.[70] Giving used cars as the example, Akerlof suggested that when consumers can't judge quality and face dealers who have an incentive not to reveal the low quality of a car, a market may cease to function. In such cases of informational inequality markets may offer only "lemons".

In a theoretically efficient market, prices reflect all available information and all participants have the same information and draw the correct inferences. By this definition, a market in used cars where the dealer necessarily knows more about the car than the buyer is imperfect and the government should rectify the informational asymmetry. Ditto for securities and other financial products. Moreover, information can be seen as a public good — more people can benefit from it without reducing others' benefit. Market don't produce enough of such goods.

In reality used car markets continue to exist on a "buyer beware" basis, so dealers or buyers don't really behave the way Akerlof postulated. Klein (1997) and O'Driscoll & Hoskins (2006) pointed out that businesses may choose not to opportunistically make short-term profits by deceiving customers because they risk harming their reputation, the source of long-term profit. Still, Akerlof's argument left a vivid impression that without sufficient regulation markets would be inundated by bad products.

In securities markets, the government corrects for the dearth of information by requiring that more be made available, as with 1930s Acts mandating corporate disclosures. Although those laws did not prevent company executives from cooking the books on occasion, there is a strong case for having readily accessible information.

If the record is correct, it will guide investors appropriately. Conversely, if it contains falsehood, someone may notice the fake claim and make it public. The more widely information circulates, the more it will be scrutinized and the more likely a falsehood will be detected.

If everyone were fully informed and reached the right conclusion, no investor would believe in fabrications, financial fraud would no longer pay and there would be no point in attempting it. Regulation has not brought us noticeably closer to that ideal. For nearly a century there have been laws requiring sellers of securities and investment products to provide accurate data to their customers, in addition to criminal sanctions against deception. Despite that, plenty of people are vulnerable to securities shenanigans.

Typically the problem is not so much lack of information as inability to draw the correct inference. Economic actors are not perfect calculators, they make errors in processing information. A major rationale for additional financial regulation is to correct such imperfections, but neoclassical economics was of no help with that type of intervention because it provided no real insight as to cognitive errors, having assumed them away.

Fraudsters make mistakes as well. If they were perfect calculators, many of them would apply their talents in some other way. By the neoclassical model of crime and punishment pioneered by Chicago economist Gary Becker, a rational perpetrator compares the expected benefit of his scheme to its expected cost, including the chance of being detected and punished. A would-be swindler should maximize the value he receives from the crime, net of the expected cost, including the cost of going to prison.

If he is liable to be exposed quickly and punished heavily, the cost is prohibitive compared to a fleeting benefit. Hence the calculation should deter the fraud. But that supposes a correct assessment of the consequences. If a would-be con artist exaggerates the profit, ignores the risk of losses and discounts the chance of being caught, then the scheme looks promising. Taking a sanguine view, he believes that he will make money and compensate the people he hoodwinked.

It looks like he will never be charged with a crime, and even if he were, likely he will beat the rap. To a man reasoning this way, the scheme occurs as a great idea. From the skewed viewpoint, the expected costs and benefits point to a net win. Misperception is an ingredient in fraud not only on the victims' side but also on the part of the perpetrator.

In a Maze

Neoclassical economists' rationalist assumptions have been increasingly challenged.[71] Cognitive psychology and a bevy of associated disciplines such as behavioral finance documented a variety of biases in reasoning and deviations from rational behavior. Such studies in the second half of the 20th century fleshed out ancient observations of "folly."

Behavioral science precisely identifies particular human dispositions that skew reasoning. A key factor in financial mistakes is confirmation bias— the inclination to look for evidence that confirms our established view and ignore contrary facts. Having one's notions challenged causes cognitive dissonance, not a pleasant sensation. So we try to avoid it.[72]

Another source of error is vividness bias — a preference for dramatic, simple explanations. And self-serving bias, a tendency to attribute good things to ourselves but blame bad things on others. These weaknesses in rational thought become particularly damaging when we have to make choices involving the future, as every investment decision does.

A fundamental insight came from Herbert Simon, a pioneer in the use of computers to simulate human mental processes. A researcher who ranged wide, from artificial intelligence and psychology to a Nobel Prize for economics in 1988, his interest in the subject of rationality started with a chance encounter with the writings of John Commons. In his youth Simon came upon books left behind by an uncle who had been a student of the great institutionalist at the University of Wisconsin.

Commons is not easy to read, but Simon was obviously exceptional. What he learnt from the books was that there are limits to reasoned decision making. Simon sharpened and developed the idea, calling it bounded rationality. This starts from the premise that our mental resources for reasoning are scarce — there is only so much to go around. But there are conditions where the scarcity does not matter, because the decisions to be made require little thought.

These are situations where we already know what to expect, like ordering from a familiar restaurant menu. There is minimal need for analysis and it is easy to achieve the goal. The decision is routine — there is no acquiring and processing new information; the demand for inference is trivial and well within cognitive limits. Assuming the dish you order has not changed from the previous time you ate it, you are happy with your order.

The decision looks perfectly rational, but that is because the situation does not require much from reason. This is how choice appears in neoclassical economics. In the sophisticated versions, there are many menus and you don't know which one you will get, but you know the possible menus and the likelihood of getting them. You calculate your best bet factoring in the probabilities.

Simon proposed a sharply different metaphor. Life is not a known menu; it is an unknown maze. Any major choice, such as a decision whether to undertake a novel investment, is not like picking a dish from a menu or even a set of possible menus. In the maze, we don't know what the paths will lead to and don't have the wherewithal to map out the options and consequences.

We can learn the possibilities offered by the maze by exploring it, but exploration uses up time, energy and cognitive abilities. It also narrows the opportunities. When you explore in one direction, you learn about that direction and remain ignorant about the directions you did not go in. Hence the decision to explore in one direction rather than another changes your knowledge set. It creates path dependence — what someone knows depends on the path they took.

Since we can't go on exploring endlessly, there is a need to simplify the problem to make it solvable. How do we simplify problems? Simon's answer was that we construct a manageable mental model of the situation and modify the model as we go along. Usually we define a minimally satisfactory outcome and try to achieve it. If we fail, we revise downward our standard of what is satisfactory.

We may focus on a partial sample of evidence and use shortcuts. These come from our particular experience – where in the maze we happen to enter and what turns we initially take. Simplifying the problem so as to economize on reason is a reasonable response to unknowns. It makes sense to use devices like rules of thumb. But simple models are necessarily incomplete and often wrong. While we make corrections as we go along, the model we have in mind can still contain errors. Taking a bad turn can be costly and close off alternative paths.

If we repeatedly confront the same maze and are able to learn about it and map it out, we gradually transform the maze problem into a menu problem. But for that to happen, we have to repeatedly experience the same maze.

In life, we often end up in places we don't want to be through mistakes and happenstance. The result is not the one we rationally sought – given the same conditions no one would repeat the reasoning that led to an investment in a Ponzi scheme. The procedure was rational, in the sense that we used reason; but the upshot is not. The effect of reason is small in shaping the ultimate result because chance and cognitive biases are powerful influences.

There is lots of room for self-deception when confronting unknowns. Our misperceptions come to bear on what we focus on and how we choose to simplify reality. It is easy for elements of delusion to enter mental models, thereby bolstering one's inclination to believe there are wonderful riches at the end of a path. Someone who is talented at spinning fantasies can insert these into mental models. It is not that he and his acolytes do not use their reason; they do so under delusional assumptions.[73]

Nevertheless, Simon was optimistic. He thought that by and large we correct the mistakes in our mental constructs by observing the results. He was a pioneer in the use of computers. Since computers can hold much more data than human memory, the technology expands our capability to process information. This may have given Simon confidence in our ability to get rid of errors.

But he was aware of what has become evident in financial markets, namely that memory, even infinitely expandable computer memory, is insufficient by itself. For a computer to make sense of data, someone needs to create algorithms or a model to analyze the information. Otherwise, the computer has a mountain of data but not the ability to guide decisions. If the device used to make sense of the data is erroneous, the computer produces wrong results and we're just as lost as we would be with no computer.

A dramatic example of this emerged in the 2000s property boom and bust. Computerized risk models systematically underestimated the danger of mortgage investments and sophisticated quantitative finance specialists relied on mistaken risk calculations. There was no lack of data but the models were deficient. Confirmation bias may have come to play in drawing the wrong conclusions from data, given that almost everyone wanted the boom to continue and risks to be small.

Realistic Third Party

That rational decision-making ability is scarce has implications for fraud prevention. One is that people's disconnect from reality impedes the potential deterrence effect of the criminal justice system. Fraudsters can dream away the legal risk to themselves — in Simon's terms, their mental model excludes the possibility of going to prison. As a result, they're not scared.

On the other side, investors who are in the grip of wishful thinking ignore warning signs and allow themselves to be taken in. This suggests that it may be beneficial for the state to intervene in multiple ways. If criminal sanctions are not effective in deterring fraud, civil authorities might help make market players more realistic.

Regulators can impose checks and correct misperceptions. They could do things to make people less attracted to schemes, less vulnerable to being victimized. In this way they might discourage fraud beyond what the criminal justice system can achieve by arresting and punishing perpetrators.

As a knowledgeable third-party, regulators are expected to be more realistic than market players. A plausible argument can be made that they have better information and less reason to fool themselves. For one thing, experienced regulators have seen a lot of financial fraud, which presumably makes them less prone to be taken in. And they are often highly educated.

Most importantly, regulators have no personal stake in the business or investment, so there is no reason for them to emotionally delude themselves that it will succeed. For this reason alone, they should be more realistic.[74] All in all, one might take it that regulators are better informed and cool headed compared to other parties. Therefore they should be able to dispel fantasies and bring people back to earth before a con game goes far.

The belief that people need to be protected from their own mistakes justified the expansion of the regulatory state in the past and still does. Versions of the argument show up in many areas and are often taken as given. At its simplest, the reasoning is that if we can't figure out the better course for ourselves, then the agents of the state will do it for us.

This makes a strong case for all manner of intervention in the financial area, especially intertwined with the other two arguments, siding with ordinary folk against powerful players and reducing conflict. As the experienced, knowledgeable and objective third party, financial regulators appear to be qualified for the role. Who else but public agents can protect confused investors against unscrupulous operators?

Then again, consider the following history.

How Rational was the Master of the Mint?

Isaac Newton had the misfortune of making one of the worst financial mistakes known to posterity. The great physicist had interests that ranged from alchemy to the doctrine of the Trinity to stock speculation. In 1713, he invested in the South Sea Company. In April 1720, he sold at a 100% return.

So far, so good, but from April through June of that year the stock tripled. Watching other people reap profits that made his look puny, Newton was unable to resist the temptation. In July he acquired a big position at an astronomical price. That he lost a fortune when the scheme collapsed in September seems entirely predictable — though the impression of predictability comes from our hindsight.

For the rest of his life Newton did not want to hear the words "South Sea" again. Charles Kindleberger, in his classic book on financial manias and crises, suggests that this kind of avoidance is a common irrational habit after disasters. But he also notes that Newton was "presumably rational."

In fact, avoiding topics that recall one's losses could be a reasonable way of dodging further unnecessary pain. If nothing can be done to change the outcome, there is no point to bringing back the unpleasant memory. If the goal is to minimize emotional pain, avoiding the topic is rational behavior.

But why did Newton – having expressed nature's secrets mathematically – not calculate that the South Sea Company could not possibly pay the profits promised to shareholders?[75] He is said to have remarked, "I can calculate the motions of the heavenly bodies but not the madness of people." It is easy to conclude that if the genius could be fooled, anybody can be, and therefore a comprehensive regulatory regime to protect all investors is necessary.[76]

That conclusion is wrong. At the time of the debacle Newton was not just an academic; he stood at the pinnacle of the political and scientific elite and was a top regulator. From 1696 to his death in 1727 he was Britain's Master of the Royal Mint, a job that among other functions included pursuing fraudsters and counterfeiters. Also, he was president of the Royal Society. He was among the officials who would be expected to stop something like the South Sea bubble.

In fact the South Sea company was a government crony scheme backed by the Lord Treasurer Robert Harley, who whipped up publicity and encouraged share buying. As bribes, allies in the government and their associates received a kind of stock option, paid with money coming from the public.[77] It is as if the United States Treasury ran a con game, gave dibs in the proceeds to members of Congress and the brilliant scientist in charge of the money supply fell for the scam.

The event had long-term effects. When others imitated the South Sea company and similar schemes spread, government players and members of parliament connived with the company's executives to get rid of the competition in the capital market. They passed what came to be known as a bubble law, requiring joint-stock companies to be authorized by parliament or royal decree. For many years, this regulation made it difficult for legitimate businesses to raise capital, obstructing economic development.

Yet the officials involved in the fiasco appear to be highly capable. Lord Treasurer Harley was known as a very smart politician. Around him were the cream of the political class. Newton not only headed the mint with its mandate to catch cheats but was experienced in the stock market. But Harley and his associates were dishonest and Newton was fooled.

Clever officials are capable of doing things that, when done by private citizens, are thought of as indicating cognitive or moral weakness. There has to be some error in the argument that such weakness necessitates protective action by those same officials, with their own questionable judgment.

Protecting Passive Investors

Adolph Berle, in a 1967 preface to a revised edition of his book with G. Means, *The Modern Corporation,* pointed out that shares had become the dominant form of personal wealth-holding because the stock market made them liquid — that is, readily sellable. The pattern he and Means discovered in the 1930s – numerous, distant shareholders – was more pronounced by the 1960s.

The holders of this form of wealth were typically further removed from the businesses they owned. Though they had a right to vote and could sue the company for wrongdoing such as theft and fraud by the managers, they usually had no say in running the operation. Such "passive property" owners, as Berle termed them, were a large and growing segment of the population. Hence the law had properly moved to protect them by requiring regular publication of corporate information considered accurate by accounting standards.

Berle's concern in 1967 was not lack of information but how to widen stock ownership. As a solution to poverty and inequality of income, he wanted everyone to partake of shareholder wealth. Mutual funds were the main mechanism for the spread of stock ownership. Berle had his wish in the decades to come. Increasing numbers of Americans with little knowledge of the stock market and only small amounts of saving invested in mutual funds, especially through tax-protected retirement programs such as 401k accounts.

The fundamental laws concerning mutual funds and investment advisers were the Roosevelt administration's last big piece of financial regulation. These were several years in the making. The 1940 Investment Company Act, as the mutual fund legislation was called, cited information gathered under the utility company law passed in 1935. Among the findings was the fact that mutual funds channeled "a substantial part of the national savings and may have a vital effect upon the flow of such savings into the capital markets."

The 1935 investigation identified numerous problems in mutual funds, including irresponsible management and excessive borrowing. Accordingly the 1940 Act went beyond requiring the provision of information to fund investors. It imposed specific restrictions on fund portfolios. In order to make sure a fund's portfolio is diversified, the law specified the maximum percentage of ownership in any one company. And it limited borrowing and short selling.

Behind these rules was the rationale that mutual fund investors could not make the best choices for themselves. It was assumed that they could not diversify their stock holdings by buying different funds — hence a requirement that each individual fund diversify its holdings. They were not capable of understanding the risk of leveraged funds — therefore borrowing by all funds was restricted. The paternalism was much more pronounced than in previous financial laws.

Mutual funds had to be registered with the SEC and provide whatever information and documents "the Commission shall by rules and regulations prescribe as necessary or appropriate in the public interest or for the protection of investors." One exemption allowed managers of hedge funds to avoid registration as long as they ran no more than 15 funds, each fund considered one client.

The double nature of the stated goal – "in the public interest or for the protection of investors" –suggests a question. Fund investors are one group among others; what if there is a conflict between the interests of the investors versus the larger public? Which one does the regulator favor? On the basis of Landis' 1938 lecture, one could reply that the answer depends on the specific conditions and regulators should be free to figure it out.

Coupled with the mutual fund law was a 1940 Act for investment advisers. It required that they too register, periodically provide information and be available for SEC inspections. When there is a complaint of fraud, the SEC can demand information and look into the operation. Complaints can lead to in-depth investigations beyond routine exams.

The 1930s and 1940 acts were amended over the years but their basic requirements remain in place. Most of the changes expanded the scope of regulation. A 1960 amendment put all investment advisers under the anti-fraud provisions, whether or not an adviser is registered, widening the authority given to the SEC to crack down when there is any suspicion of fraud.

After waning in the Eisenhower era, the expansive regulatory trend perked up markedly in the1960s. Mainstream economists encouraged this. Robert Higgs, commenting on Lyndon Johnson's Great Society programs, describes in a nutshell the effect of neoclassical theory: "The idealized conditions required for theoretical general-equilibrium efficiency could not possibly obtain in the real world; yet the economists readily endorsed government measures aimed at coercively pounding the real world into conformity with these impossible theoretical conditions."[78]

Amid the general expansion of the regulatory state, the Securities and Exchange Commission's remit grew. One key extension arose not from any new statute but from an interpretation of the broad powers the 1934 Act gave to the SEC. When Columbia Law professor William Cary became chairman, he relied on this law to tamp down on trading on information not available to the public. Regulatory practice in this area expanded beyond corporate insiders to become an all-encompassing prohibition on almost any trading on non-public information.[79]

In 1970 Congress created another entity that would be subject to SEC supervision, establishing the Securities Investor Protection Corp. for brokerage customers. When a brokerage fails, SIPC makes sure its customers get back the stocks and bonds held in their name. If a broker steals money or securities from a customer's account, SIPC will pay up to $500,000 to the victim. To finance such payments, brokerages are required to pay assessments to the SIPC reserve fund.

The Commodity Futures Trading Commission was established in 1975 to set terms and conditions for futures contracts and exchanges. It became the main competitor to the SEC as financial regulator, but the CFTC has a narrow mandate, confined to futures exchanges and traders.

Regulators increasingly followed their own judgment rather than the commands of elected officials. In 1975 Congress passed amendments to securities laws, ordering the SEC to get rid of rules that limit competition. The goal was to reduce trading costs to investors by creating a competitive national market in exchanges and over-the-counter trading. A decade later a detailed study found that the SEC did not in fact promote competition, at least not consistently.[80]

The SEC chairman from 1977 to 1981 defended the slow progress in this area: "I am not about to be the person to come back to Congress and say I am sorry I implemented your program and it blew up," he said.[81] He and presumably SEC staff believed that it was more important to avoid disruption in existing securities trading facilities; from their vantage point, promoting competition was not a top concern. If anything, their decisions reduced competition to the NYSE, "exactly the opposite of what Congress intended by its enactment of 1975 Securities Act Amendments."[82]

Changing technology made this issue moot but it is worth noting the independence of regulators. They followed their own priority, not the directive from Congress. Leaving aside the merits of the policies, it was regulators who made the choice. Landis would have approved of this on the ground that the SEC understands securities markets better and hence makes more apt decisions than politicians.

Some historians argue that the aggressive regulatory vision lost out to the less interfering Keynesian approach.[83] Certainly Keynesian policies dominated the decades after World War II, with government spending, taxes and interest rates adjusted to keep the economy on an even keel — or so it is claimed. But the regulatory vision and the organizations created to put it into practice never went away. The agencies expanded at times and were stagnant at others, but retained their authority.

Financial regulation evolved in a piecemeal fashion, becoming a complicated patchwork of requirements and exceptions. Major spurts came in response to public anger at financial frauds and crises. Thus after the 1990s stock bubble burst and some corporations, notably Enron and WorldCom, were found to have misled shareholders, Congress passed the 2002 Sarbanes-Oxley Act mandating more paperwork and controls for public companies.

Opposition occasionally slowed down the upward trajectory, but only temporarily. Milton Friedman, a particularly effective critic, used cogent economic reasoning to explain to a wide readership the adverse impact of interventions such as price and rent controls.[84] His efforts to turn back the regulatory tide had no success with Richard Nixon, who presided over another spurt in federal agencies and rules. During the presidency of Ronald Reagan, Friedman successfully helped push deregulation in certain areas — even very limited deregulation was difficult.[85] Under following presidents, the regulatory onslaught resumed.

In the financial industry, any reduction in regulation was narrowly focused. Thus in the 1980s there was a relaxation of certain restrictions on depository organizations; a 1980 law allowed commercial banks to pay interest on checking accounts and a 1982 act removed interest rate ceilings.[86] A much-cited instance of deregulation, the reversal of part of the Glass-Steagall Act in 1999 to allow the merger of commercial banks with investment banks, was similarly narrowly focused.

By contrast broad regulatory powers remained intact or expanded, as with the passage of Sarbanes-Oxley. New regulatory capabilities were created, for instance with SIPC. Few rules were abolished, many more were added, growth was cumulative.

By the early 21st century the regulatory state was almost incomparably bigger than its antecedent of the early 20th century. The number of pages in the *Federal Register* is often cited as a rough measure of law- and rule-making activity.[87] In the first four years for which we have data, from 1936 through 1939, there were 14,271 cumulative pages in the *Federal Register*. That is tiny compared to later decades. In the 1980s, the *Register* grew by 529,223 pages; in the first decade of the 21st century, by 730,176 pages.

Wayne Crews, who tracks the growth of the *Federal Register*, suggests that the number of final rules is a better gauge than the number of pages. In the 20 years ending 2012, he counted 81,883 final rules on myriad subjects. That means federal agencies and departments on average issued almost 79 rules a week for two decades.[88]

The two most powerful financial regulators, the Federal Reserve and the SEC, between them have jurisdiction over much of the system. Commercial banks and the creation of money is under Fed oversight, while the SEC presides over brokers – through NASD – and money managers as well as securities markets. The events described in the next section were primarily under the jurisdiction of the SEC and NASD. But at times other arms of the government came to play, with SIPC taking on a dramatic role in a case I discuss in chapter eight.

In short, Landis' vision of the expanding administrative state to a significant extent became reality. The number of administrative entities grew. Politicians in Congress passed laws that left specific rules to be made and administered by agencies, each with its own regulatory turf. How the system works in practice we will see in the rest of the book. But before we get to that, it may be useful to understand Landis a bit better.

End of a Model Regulator

Occasionally a sense of regulatory stagnation, perhaps even malaise, surfaced in American political discourse. John Kennedy tackled this matter when he got to the White House. He appointed an old family friend, as Landis had by then become, as special adviser to study regulatory commissions and suggest ways to improve their performance. Thus the über regulator was given the opportunity to evaluate his life's work.

After languishing in relative obscurity, Landis once more basked in political limelight. He was seen as bringing New Deal magic to the new administration—Kennedy's choice of Berle to head a task force may have also appealed to Rooseveltian nostalgia. There was word the president might nominate Landis to the Supreme Court; Frankfurter suggested he himself could retire, giving Kennedy the opening to name Landis.

The 1960 Landis Report was a contrast to the triumphal 1938 *Administrative Process*. The regulatory commissions had become a drag on the economy, with a penchant for falling further and further behind in their work. The report blamed this on insufficient budgets, inadequate personnel and lack of coordination. In particular Landis attributed the decline to weak commissioners appointed by Truman and Eisenhower and advocated higher salaries and longer tenures for commissioners.

He wanted agency chairmen to have greater authority and direct ties to the President. In keeping with his faith that the more agencies, the better, he recommended the creation of yet another office, a sort of agency of agencies. This entity was to devise solutions for agencies' problems and act as their advocate.

As for the SEC, Landis thought it suffered mainly from too small a budget. Given enough money, it would once again become the fine agency he had created. But his proposals were not implemented. Congress, unwilling to grant yet more discretionary powers and budgets, voted down the reform bills. Even the first one, for the SEC, went nowhere.

The press called him the Regulatory Czar but Landis did not care for the title and did not wish to be appointed to head the agency of agencies he proposed. He knew his time as adviser to Kennedy was at an end; private problems ruled out future government positions. He might have survived a minor scandal—his habit of flirting with his secretaries led to a lawsuit by the husband of a new secretary. Upon being consulted, the all-knowing Corcoran said: "you can get something on anybody." The litigation against Landis was dropped, under conditions not made public.

But even Corcoran and Joseph Kennedy could not save Landis when a background check for White House clearance revealed that he had not filed tax returns for years. The president accepted his resignation.

His contemporaries as well as later historians and biographers considered Landis the prototype civil servant, the model regulator. If agencies could be staffed by the likes of him, the regulatory state would work fine—so it was believed. The problem with the agencies seemed to be that they no longer attracted "giants" such as Landis.[89]

In fact Landis is a terrible precedent for future administrators. It would be a misbegotten idea to fill agencies with characters like him, were it possible. He was as bad a guide for civil servants as his chum Corcoran was in a different way.

85

Corcoran was finely attuned to how government agencies work. He understood how to manipulate public bureaucracies — he made a fortune doing so. Landis had no such ability. He helped build the SEC under extraordinary circumstances and assumed that –given ample resources - its staff would fulfill their mission with the powers and flexibility he wrote into law. But when he had to deal with full-fledged government entities, he displayed a profound lack of understanding and an inability to function effectively.

Toward the end of World War II, Landis was sent to the Middle East as envoy for economic matters and found the State Department impossible to work with. He railed at the bureaucracy, complained to Roosevelt and went over the heads of his departmental superiors to get what he wanted. Had he not had the president's ear, the State Department would have no doubt quickly got rid of him.

Truman appointed him the chairman to the Civil Aeronautics Board, confirming his stature as the top authority on federal regulation and its administration. The board was a sluggish apparatus with years of backlogged cases. Landis intended to reform it but ran into opposition from the Commerce Department. His feud with Pan American, then the largest airline, did not help. Truman removed him from the post in less than two years. This man who literally wrote the book on public administration did not comprehend how such bodies work in practice.

Joseph Kennedy gave him a job at the family firm after he lost the Civil Aeronautics Board appointment. Later he - like so many - followed Corcoran's example and represented businesses to regulatory agencies. He acknowledged no conflict between his earlier and later careers. As a practical matter, lobbying meant ignoring conflicts of interest — "I can't be too selective," he said.

Despite making lots of money, Landis ran into severe financial difficulties. He went through a wrenching divorce to marry his secretary, became unhappy when deprived of his position as regulator and drank too much. He neglected his children and was habitually late with alimony payments. His final comeuppance was a run-in with another public body, the Internal Revenue Service.

Having trouble with a somewhat complicated tax return because he inherited stocks from his mother, Landis ignored the return and did not pay his taxes. The next year, he did not want to acknowledge that he had not filed the previous year. Again he did not file. So it went year after year. Faced with the returns he failed to file and back taxes he owed, he shelved the paperwork. This leading expert on public administration could not deal with the tax forms that are a product of one such administration, paperwork that millions of Americans are required to handle correctly.

Criminal charges against Landis could not be avoided despite an attempt within the Kennedy administration to save him. Though his lawyers argued that his failure to file and pay taxes was due to psychological problems, he was sentenced to a month in prison. Attorney General Robert Kennedy then ordered that Landis be allowed to spend this time at Columbia Presbyterian Hospital as a mental patient.

After he completed the sentence, the Kennedys wanted to make him chair of the review committee for the records of the John F. Kennedy Presidential Library. But a new chapter in his life was not to be. Landis was found floating face down in the swimming pool of his estate, dead apparently from a heart attack, though suicide was rumored. His wife scattered his ashes around the estate, which was shortly thereafter seized by the IRS in lieu of unpaid taxes.

The personal tragedy gives a glimpse of the complicated reality behind the icon of the intellectually superior and public minded regulator. Landis was the champion of the regulatory state and the bureaucratic apparatus necessary for it. He was seen as the exceptional public agent who did the right thing.

That this man was horrified whenever he came into personal contact with public organizations and had great trouble with them does not help the credibility of the case he made for the administrative state. At a minimum, his experience suggests he did not understand what that state meant. However brilliant he may have been in writing laws, he lacked a realistic sense of how government organizations function.

It is significant that he, with all his knowledge, prestige and contacts, had so much trouble. What about ordinary citizens, who have no wealthy patron or friend at the White House to help them when they tangle with a government agency? If Landis ever thought about the full impact of the administrative state on people's lives, he did not think too hard. He suggested no solution for the dysfunctions of the system he helped build and defend — except the panacea of good staffing.

NOTES

[1] In fact long-term economic growth was impressive. In the 80 years or so from 1870, American net output per person in real terms quadrupled, according to Abramovitz 1989 (drawing on Kuznets 1952). But growth was not steady; probably it was more volatile than it had been in the previous era, though there had been a financial crisis in 1857 (North 1966).

[2] The period from 1870 to the mid-20th century was subject to "striking fluctuations" beyond regular business cycles, with unemployment rising to 12% in the mid-1890s (Abramovitz p. 140, 255). Severe downturns followed long expansions—suggesting 20-year cycles, called Kuznets cycles, on top of short term cycles. The extreme volatility is an obvious economic reason for the discontent and political swing to the left even as the United States became the most affluent country in the world. Periodic losses of jobs and income must have created the feeling of social crisis at a time when, in retrospect and for the period as a whole, national output grew at a phenomenal rate.

[3] No doubt writers, politicians – Theodore Roosevelt in particular – and journalists played a dramatic role in shaping popular outrage, as one can conclude from Goodwin 2013. However, the progressive message that capitalism was not working might not have had much traction if economic volatility was not causing real hardship.

[4] For Brandeis' role in bringing about regulation, see McCraw 1984.

[5] Regulation was only one component of Roosevelt's economic program. See Folsom 2008 for a comprehensive analysis.

[6] Smith repeatedly cites China as an example for his arguments. In *The Wealth of Nations* he writes that the country "had probably long ago acquired that full complement of riches which is consistent with the nature of its laws and institutions." Hence it is stationary, but under different laws and institutions it would grow and become wealthier (Part I, ch. IX).

[7] Recent studies focus on the differences between various categories of behavioral rules such as morality and convention—for example, Bicchieri 2006. For my purpose here, is any rule that affects financial behavior is relevant.

[8] *The Portable Veblen* (ed. Max Lerner), p. 79.

[9] *The Portable Veblen*, p. 77.

[10] *The Portable Veblen*, p. 312.

[11] *The Portable Veblen*, p.489.

[12] *The Portable Veblen*, p. 44.

[13] Similar prescriptions have been offered in more recent times--see Csikszentmihalyi 1993.

[14] The other two best-known institutionalists are Richard T. Ely, who fit the Brandeis Progressive mold, and Wesley C. Mitchell, about whom more later. Mitchell was influenced by Veblen but mostly did statistical work.

[15] This is a brief review of the main points, necessary to make sense of what hasppened. See Epstein 2006 on progressive legal thought.

[16] Landis 1938; quoted in Horwitz 1992.

[17] Rizzo 1999 on Posner 1995.

[18] Epstein 1998.

[19] On the mixed economy that results from a range of interventionist policies, Ikeda 1997. For one example of the many fields shaped by government action, Butos and McQuade 2006.

[20] No. 42 of *The Federalist Papers*.

[21] Higgs 1987 explains the key role of myriad crises, including but not confined to economic ones, in ratcheting up the size and functions of the U.S. federal government.

[22] Seligman 1980 tells this history.

[23] See Shlaes 2008 and Barber 1990 on the Roosevelt administration.

[24] The quote is from Sternsher 1964, p. 13.

[25] An instance of dramatic conflict between the two goals arose in the 2008-2009 financial crisis, with too-big-to-fail banks bailed out and wrapped up in extra layers of regulation, in effect becoming the financial industry equivalent of public utilities.

[26] For instance, Stiglitz 2010 and 2013.

[27] McKean 2004, pp. 61 and 63.

[28] For a more in-depth analysis of this law, see Shughart 1988.

[29] Seligman 1980.

[30] Ernst 2009.

[31] Katznelson 2013 analyzes the reasons behind the alliance of Southerners with Roosevelt.

[32] Couch and Shughart 1998 find that Roosevelt's political concerns influenced the allotment of New Deal spending.

[33] Quoted in Seligman 1980 p. 107.

[34] Nasaw 2012 found no evidence that Kennedy was a bootlegger.

[35] Seligman 1980.

[36] For Roosevelt's comments about Kennedy, see Nasaw 2012.

[37] See Ernst 2009. The historian is Jerold Auerbach.

[38] Quoted in the introduction to Winston, Crandall and Maheshri 2011.

[39] De Bedts 1964, pp. 152-155.

[40] McCraw 1984, p. 204.

[41] McCraw, p 200.

[42] Ernst 2009.

[43] Harter 1965.

[44] McCraw 1984.

[45] Commons 1924.

[46] Commons 1934a.

[47] Commons 1931.

[48] Commons 1934b. The following quotes are also from this book.

[49] Harter 1962, pp.91-100.

[50] Epstein 2011a and 2011b makes this point.

[51] Commons 1934 p. 162.

[52] Harter 1965.

[53] Commons 1934b p.107.

[54] Kates 2010 argues this.

[55] Williamson (1985 and 1996) developed the implications of transaction costs that arise from opportunism. I discuss certain arguments from North and Simon later.

[56] Recent approaches to institutions vary. For example, Young Back Choi 1993 explains the working of markets on the basis of social learning embodied in conventions. Hodgson 1993 and 1988 follows the older institutionalist approach.

[57] Quoted in Seligman 1982, p. 101. The exchange took place at the House Commerce Committee's second hearing on National Exchange Practices, 73rd Congress.

[58] Ritchie p.100.

[59] Horwitz 1992, pp. 217-222.

[60] Ludwig von Mises, *Bureaucracy*, 1944, p. 101.

[61] The term "rule of discretion" from Rizzo 2011 indicates more clearly the nub of the matter than the old term, "rule of men".

[62] This quote is from Stone 1989 p. 96

[63] McKean, 2004, pp. 75-76.

[64] McKean, 2004, p. 72.

[65] The examples are from Lichtman 1987.

[66] Lichtman 1987.

[67] Mackay, originally published 1841.

[68] This simplified description reduces the theory to its essentials.

[69] Boettke 2010.

[70] Akerlof 1970.

[71] The quirks of human behavior came to their own as a subject of academic research in recent decades; behavioral finance made the news after Shiller 2000 used psychological factors to explain the stock bubble as that bubble collapsed. Shiller went outside neoclassical economics to use the findings of cognitive science. The fact that a cognitive psychologist, Daniel Kahneman, won the Nobel Prize in economics shows up the huge terrain left unexplored by the neoclassical theory of rational behavior.

[72] For thought-provoking discussions of our penchant to take the easy way out in perceiving the world, see Taleb 2001 and 2007.

[73] Kindleberger 1978 uses the term "borderline rationality" for situations when a decision is based on a rational model that is wrong; pp. 37-40.

[74] But objectivity is easily marred, as Chorvat and McCabe 2005 show.

[75] The question is especially relevant because Newton applied the methods he used in studying nature to his other interests such as the chronology of the ancient world (Buchwald and Feingold 2012).

[76] This tends to be argued whenever there is a major push for expanding regulation; Levenson 2009 is an example.

[77] It was not called an option but referred to as "fictitious" stock. This point is from my previous book, *Political Sticky Wicket* 2012.

[78] Higgs 2011.

[79] Manne 1966 and Boudreaux 2009 argued that this regulation reduces the information content of stock prices—in its absence prices would more fully reflect reality. I will come back to this topic in chapter 11.

[80] Seligman 1985.

[81] Quoted in Seligman 1985, p. 51.

[82] Seligman 1985, p. 53.

[83] See the articles in Fraser and Gerstle 1989.

[84] As a graduate student Friedman studied with Wesley C. Mitchell, the leading institutionalist after Veblen and Commons. He wrote that Mitchell "introduced me to the institutional approach to economic theory," Friedman 1998, p. 43. Possibly this education made Friedman more sensitive to the idiosyncrasies of institutions, though he stayed within the neoclassical framework.

[85] Tollison 1983.

[86] For a study of the effects of depository deregulation, see Barron, West and Hannan 1998.

[87] The measure is often used despite its shortcomings; for instance, Breyer 1982, Table 16.

[88] Crews 2013.

[89] Ritchie 198, p. 175.

PART II. Unmaking Ponzi Schemes

To observe what regulators do in practice and how Landis' favorite agency fared, we will examine three fraud cases. The question is whether the U.S. Securities and Exchange Commission does what it exists to do—whether it pursues the objects set forth by advocates of regulation, namely protect investors by countering powerful financial players, reduce and referee conflicts and bolster reasoned decision making.

My focus is on the SEC because this is the regulatory agency responsible for preventing securities fraud. I am not suggesting that the SEC is distinctive or different from other government agencies or departmental divisions. It may be more effective than some, less so than others. It is no doubt more transparent than many. For all I know, its personnel and mode of operation may be no different than that of other government entities.

You may object that the particular incidents I've chosen are exceptions rather than the rule and as such insufficient to establish any general conclusion. No doubt there are other ways one could approach the subject, but it is impossible to understand what regulators really do without going into the details of cases, which necessitates picking some examples.

The ones I examine span decades and suggest a persistent pattern of regulatory failure despite differences in conditions. My conclusion – the agency in the main does not pursue the professed rationale for financial regulation – follows from a history of 20-plus years, including recent scandals described in Part III. I have not seen an effective counterexample that challenges the pattern of failure.

As an alternative, one could choose many minor cases rather than a few big cases. The regulators' own preference is to go after numerous regulatory violations. This creates the impression of a lot of action and supposed achievement — which the agency publicizes in numerous press releases and interviews.

Indeed, higher-ups' preference for many, quick cases is one of the factors cited by some SEC employees to explain the failures I describe. By focusing on such actions one would get the picture deliberately constructed by the agency, a species of public relations, not a specially accurate view. My goal was to investigate surprising incidents, not to support the regulators' own choices.

The cases I draw on have the advantage of being well documented. While it is well nigh impossible to know the full story of a fraud even when there is reliable evidence, these schemes and especially their long-term consequences are described in detail in legal proceedings. This made it possible to pinpoint the regulators' role.

CHAPTER FOUR. The Art Of Persuasion

A con game requires conversation. A chat between two men in April 1999 demonstrates the dynamic. They met at a small office in Midtown Manhattan. One was a middle-aged businessman with money to invest. The other was a young hedge fund manager in need of capital. They talked for about an hour. The older man asked questions and the young man replied, using documents to illustrate his points.

The businessman was well practiced in interviewing money managers. A German citizen with interests in Latin America and the Caribbean, he traveled the world looking for promising managers to add to his extensive portfolio. To get a sense of investment opportunities, he often dined and talked with investment specialists in Zurich, London, New York and elsewhere.

Had he wished, he could have visited a large number of candidates in that very building and listened to their pitches, for this was a hedge fund nursery full of upcoming managers. Each and every one would have been delighted to tell him about their investment program and solicit a subscription. But he had a reason to be in this particular cozy, yet elegant, office.

Looking out the windows one could see similar towers all around, with hedge funds tucked away on upper floors. Within a few blocks were hundreds of these discreet little financial firms, catering to wealthy people like him but hoping to become substantial enough to raise money from pensions and insurance companies.

The nursery, a glittering glass ziggurat containing suites ready for fledgling fund managers, was run by the brokerage arm of the investment bank Bear Stearns. Hedge funds have a symbiotic relationship with banks and brokerages, on whose financial clout they rely and to whom they pay fat trading commissions and fees.

The managers did not show signs of anxiety as they passed through the gleaming marble lobby, but they were in effect taking a two-part test that only a few pass. If they raise enough capital, they can play the market. If they play it right repeatedly, they become exceedingly rich. If they get it wrong, the business won't survive for long. Most newcomers fail one or both parts of the test.

The outcome looks like a verdict on a manager's ability, but to some extent it's a matter of luck. The God of the market is capricious, at times smiling on the inept and swatting the gifted. Anyway a new manager may never get to the point of testing himself against the market with a significant amount of money. This is because he won't be able to convince people to put up enough capital, the lifeblood of such enterprise. Hundreds of funds pop up in a busy year but most never get off the ground. No money means no trades; no good trades means no profit. Either means no business.

The man who pitched his services to the businessman was only in his twenties but he was a veteran in the daunting struggle to attract investors. When he first appeared on the scene several years ago, he had been an unpromising contender. But against all odds he had succeeded in the first part of the test. His name, Michael Berger, was already known in the circles the businessman inhabited.

Where There Is A Will

Berger had a troubled youth in Austria. He got into scrapes, needed therapy and almost did not graduate from high school. His saving grace was a precocious fascination with the stock market. At high school he wrote a paper on financial developments in the United States. Later he dropped out of Johannes Kepler University and entered a teller-training program at a local savings and loan bank.

There he apparently did well, became an up-and-coming expert on the U.S. stock market, wrote research reports and started a newsletter titled *Smart Money*. He may have also picked stocks to be recommended to clients or traded on the bank's own account. Austrian publications referred to *Smart Money*, which was cited by an American magazine.

But the bank career was brief. Maybe his colleagues blocked him because they were envious or felt threatened. Berger later claimed he was held back, not given his due despite his well-regarded stock reports. For an ambitious, impatient upstart from a poor family, Austria did not seem welcoming. Old-world attitudes tamped down on a hungry would-be entrepreneur. But there may have been other factors. He had a penchant not to play by the rules and no intention of remaining a bank employee subject to the whims of a boss.

In 1993 Berger emigrated to America. For this driven 22-year-old, Manhattan was the Promised Land — an alluring citadel of gold, where securities trading is a way of life and where wealth comes to look for smart investment ideas. Determined to turn himself into a financier, he joined the moneymaking jamboree with single-minded devotion.

Until he could get ensconced in a shining monolith where he would intercept a portion of the lucre, he had to live frugally, sharing a tiny rental apartment overrun by cockroaches. A major league Wall Street job was beyond his reach and he worked for a small brokerage called Financial Asset Management, based in Columbus, Ohio. Berger came to know the owner, James Rader, and from New York generated trade ideas and cultivated clients for the broker. He and Rader started a venture to sell financial software developed by a German firm.

Only a couple of years after arriving in the U.S. with not much to his name, Berger started his own fund management company. Initially Rader objected to the Austrian's plan to launch a hedge fund business and tried to discourage the idea. The young man could continue to drum up customers for the brokerage and sell financial software — enterprises with a plausible chance of success. The hedge fund was a mere gleam in Berger's eye, utterly unrealistic, with slim to no chance.

The average Wall Street trader far outclassed him in experience, education and connections. Investors look for managers with the "pedigree" of top credentials and a history of coming up the ranks at a big bank or a well-known hedge fund. Thousands of clever young men – and a few women – prove their mettle at prestigious trading desks. Berger had not worked at an investment bank and was not at a hedge fund until he started his own. Countless stock analysts and traders hold Ivy League degrees, MBAs, doctorates. As a college dropout whose previous career was brief and obscure, Berger lacked the standard qualifications.

He was at a severe disadvantage in other respects as well. To break into hedge fund management, it helps to have wealthy relatives who will give you seed money so you can show what you can do with it. He had to raise capital from people had no obvious reason to give it to him. Investors feel more comfortable with people they know from school, previous jobs or family connections. Such contacts ease the way. Berger was a stranger in town.

Set against the crowd of accomplished rivals, the little-known immigrant's bid to create a fund business looked almost comical. Another person would not have wasted time and money in a futile effort to get access to capital. But Berger had a plan. What he lacked in conventional credentials he made up in certain other attributes.

The market was his hobby, not just his profession. He didn't have much education, experience or contacts, but he could write and speak about the market as fluently as any analyst and better than most. When it came to chatting about stocks and trade opportunities, he could keep up with Wall Street's finest in English as well as in German. Just as important, he was confident of his own ability. He believed fervidly that he was capable of figuring out the wiles of the market and had exceptional insight in picking stocks. Because he knew he was a genius, he effortlessly projected the impression of being one.

To catch the attention of investors, he had to find ways to get his name around. In Austria he had distinguished himself with his analyses and newsletter. In New York, he cultivated journalists and became a contributor to *Barron's* *magazine*. A column titled "Market Watch" contained snippets from five to ten market pundits. There, Berger regularly shared space with star investment chiefs like Barton Biggs of Morgan Stanley and Abby Joseph Cohen of Goldman Sachs. This was an excellent way to display his knack at expounding market trends. His quotes were hard-hitting and persistently critical of received opinion.

That was one way he showcased his ideas. Also he created his own weekly newsletter, titled *Wall Street Notes*, and sent it to potential clients. Every issue contained a sharp front-page commentary on the week's market-related events, topped with a little sketch — a miniature string of skyscrapers. Instantly recognizable, the stylized skyline reminded readers of Berger's firm, Manhattan Capital, and the hedge fund he managed, also called Manhattan.[90] Inside the issue he reviewed selected sectors and documented the case for the stocks he recommended.

He published *Wall Street Notes* for over four years starting in 1995, faxing the issues to more than a thousand consultants, financial advisers and wealthy individuals. The weekly display of tough, no-nonsense trader talk was his calling card — an advertisement of his skill. People became familiar with him and Manhattan Capital because they saw the newsletter or heard about it. Some mentioned it to their acquaintances.

As a trader quoted in the media and referred to in the industry, Berger was no longer an unknown. He had overcome the disadvantage of obscurity and differentiated himself from the crowd, become an established market authority who might get noticed by hedge fund investors.

To acquire a list of contacts and access to potential clients, he agreed to pay substantial fees to a Europe-based fund marketer. It was from the marketer that the German businessman heard of the talented Austrian in New York and came to investigate. This was Berger's chance to convince the seasoned investor to pick him rather than one of the many competing managers, each with his own assiduously crafted pitch. By the time the conversation took place, Berger was experienced at persuading people. At hand he had recent copies of his newsletter, which he used to expound his strategy.

Wall Street Notes was memorable – the businessman remembered it several years later, as did others who received it – but what really cinched the deal was the strategy. The businessman was willing to spend an hour of his time in that office listening to Berger because he was interested in the unusual investment program.

A Contrarian in Shangri-La

The defining feature of Manhattan Fund's strategy was to go in the opposite direction to the majority of market players. "Generally, we follow a contrarian philosophy, considering sectors attractive when the consensus is bearish and vice-versa," the prospectus announced.[91] Berger would identify the "prevailing sentiment" for sectors and companies, analyzing media coverage, market reaction to news and mutual fund holdings to determine the received wisdom of the day. Then he would go against it.

This approach underpinned all his commentaries and trade ideas. If mutual funds and the press favored a stock or industry, the price was likely too high. If everybody else was buying, he would sell, and vice versa.

In the second half of the 1990s the stock market was especially buoyant. Faithfully following the contrarian model, Berger turned pessimistic. Already in late 1995, he described "a variety of disturbing long-term factors" in *Barron's*.[92] He thought the conditions resembled the historic peaks of 1929, 1966 and 1972 — all watersheds that marked the beginning of sustained market weakness. After such turning points, prices stayed below the peak for years, sometimes decades. It looked to him like the same kind of situation was developing again.

He was certain a downturn was coming, though in late 1995 he thought the symptoms were temporarily masked by a large flow of money into equities. For the time being, this buoyed stock prices. "A prevailing slowdown in the economy, shrinking corporate profits and historical overvaluation have all been overshadowed by money pouring into the market," he wrote. "This condition will ultimately correct itself."[93]

"Ultimately" is a fuzzy word, but he mentioned a definite period. The upbeat mood had about three months to go. Maybe a little more than that; but at any rate, a few months. In the meantime, to profit from the immediate prospect he suggested buying growth-oriented technology stocks in addition to well-known large-cap names.

By the end of the first quarter of 1996, stocks appeared to be grossly overvalued. This was especially the case in the computer industry, where he expected steep declines. Dell was at $83 — his target range was $30 to $34. Oracle was almost at $42, he pegged its true value at $17 to $20. But the overvaluation was not confined to computer businesses. GE was selling at $87; he believed it was about to drop to somewhere between $50 and $54.

Many observers looked upon widespread stock investing as a wonderful thing. Adolf Berle had argued for it as a way for wealth to trickle down and help reduce inequality. By the 1990s Berle – long dead – looked prophetic as unprecedented numbers of Americans participated in the stock bonanza. About 50% of the population owned corporate equities, up from a mere 10% in 1960. Most of this ownership was through mutual funds, although a growing number of people directly bought and sold single shares.

Berger took a dim view of the trend. He claimed people were betting their financial future on what would in the long haul be viewed as the greatest Ponzi scheme in American history — the whole U.S. stock market was being shored up by new capital coming into mutual funds, just as fresh money keeps aloft a fraudulent business with no earnings. The upbeat market had such allure, the masses recklessly bet their savings and even borrowed money to acquire overpriced shares.

He had a dramatic story to tell in his writings and in meetings with would-be customers. Stock prices were artificially inflated, corporate earnings did not support those levels and the public was being conned. A gigantic game was drawing in millions of people. Investors were misled as to what stock mutual funds could deliver: "Promises of finding Shangri-La have lured an absurd percentage of individual savings into funds."[94]

Paper wealth based on inflated prices, with no corresponding growth in company profits, was an illusion. The massive inflows into mutual funds could not last and without them the extraordinary prices were not sustainable. The stream that fed the national confidence game was about to dry up. Had he still been around, Adolf Berle might have been alarmed by this prognosis, but the men and women who ran the regulatory system Berle championed took no discernable action to rein in any excess buoyancy.

In the meantime Berger presented himself as a representative of the rational, the cautious, the responsible — a judicious authority warning of imminent danger. People were acting irresponsibly, the public's stock-buying spree was irrational. The rally was fueled by a vision of ever-rising equity prices, a utopian notion that defied logic. The market bull was already grossly overweight. As he put it with a metaphoric flourish, the fat bull was "waltzing on an ice pond."[95] The ice was going to crack.

Whether by design or chance, his attacks on irrationality, recklessness and irresponsibility made it sound like he had the opposite qualities. His thesis that the whole market was operating as if it were a Ponzi scheme cast him in the heroic role of a crusader against mass Ponzi schemes. He exuded solicitude for investors' well being and concern that they were going to be hurt when the runaway prices collapsed.

It was a plausible story that met a real need. Irresistible as the giddy market was in the final years of the 20th century, veteran investors suspected that the awe-inspiring peaks were not for long and sought to protect themselves against a drop. Technology investing gurus like Alberto Vilar, the head of Amerindo Investment Advisors, argued passionately that the Internet revolution had just started. But some of the investors in funds like Vilar's worried about high-riding Internet names — were the stocks sustainable? The more prices soared, the more likely a downturn became.

People with this mindset may have been a minority among market players but they controlled substantial capital. Big investors with a lot to lose felt the need to protect themselves. In order to balance their portfolios they specifically wanted an alternative to bullish stock buyers.

In this niche the contrarian was notable. At a time when others bought frantically to gain from rising prices, he sold borrowed shares to profit from falling prices. Short sellers reverse the order of traditional long investing — they sell first and buy later. By mid-1996 Berger had fully elaborated an anti-Shangri-La investment program of short selling blue chip and technology companies across several sectors.

His doomsday scenario caught the attention of investors who wanted to hedge against a market collapse. If you wanted to diversify your portfolio, he fit the bill perfectly. He was completely immune to the investment flavor of the day, because he was a persistent contrarian — the more bullish the market, the more bearish he became.

There were very few like him. Of the 100 well-known Wall Street analysts who followed the top five companies in the Nasdaq index, not a single one had a sell recommendation at the end of 1996. Only nine analysts were neutral; the rest recommended buying and holding the top five Nasdaq names — Microsoft, Intel, Dell, Cisco and 3Com. Many were loud in their enthusiasm.

Jack Grubman of Salomon Smith Barney, an outstanding example of the celebrity-analyst cheering on the boom, had a sign behind his desk that exhorted in large letters: "BUY NOW".[96]

Berger stood out in sharp relief: he offered sell recommendations galore. At least four of the top five Nasdaq stocks were on his sell list. His contrast to the mainstream was an attraction. A time would come when buy enthusiasts, so successful now, would run into disaster. Then the contrarian was sure to turn a splendid profit. Putting some money into his anti-Shangri-La program looked like a sensible precautionary measure, especially if you invested heavily in booming Internet stocks and needed to diversify.

Word spread of the congenial young man with a distinctive point of view. People visited the Manhattan Capital office in search of an antidote to excessive bullishness. Even powerful advisers to institutions and the wealthy came to listen to the young manager's tirades against the giant Ponzi scheme of the over-extended market. Many were already familiar with his snappy bits of market wisdom from *Barron's* and may have watched him on television. "Mr. Berger appears periodically as a guest host for a German financial news network station," stated his official bio.

Face to face he was impressive. Short, slight and remarkably young looking, he nevertheless sounded mature. In interviews with journalists and investors he could become very animated as he skewered prevailing views. Afterwards, guests would recall the sturdy-sounding market philosophy that on occasion he wore on his sleeves — literally, in the form of bear-shaped cufflinks.

Then too, he was likable. With an excellent memory, a knack at sizing up people and quickly absorbing information, he could charm almost anyone. He was a sophisticate with a man who fancied European sophistication. He was a model-obsessed geek with someone who liked equations. He could be a tough-talking, down-to-earth businessman, or a dreamy intellectual speculating on the intricacies of the human psyche. It was difficult not to like him.

So Berger aced the first part of the hedge fund test. Telling a powerful story with verve, he convinced large numbers of the world's top money allocators that he was the right man. From spring 1996 on, money flowed to Manhattan Fund from around the globe. Armed with ample capital, he put into practice the program he fervently advocated. Convinced that the market house of cards was about to cave in, he borrowed and sold as many shares as he could lay hands on, expecting to buy back at low prices.

Upon the Market Deep

In late 1996 market skeptics felt validated. "Federal Reserve Chairman Alan Greenspan unexpectedly paid a visit to the bear camp and told a story about the future of the stock market,"[97] Berger gleefully reported. The chairman had spoken of the Japanese bubble of the1980s and its disastrous collapse. Greenspan pointed to the parallel with the U.S. market and used a phrase that became part of everyday language: "irrational exuberance."[98] Berger took this as support for his own view and repeated the phrase as if it were a mantra.

In fact, Greenspan had raised a question. "But how do we know when irrational exuberance has unduly escalated asset values, which then become subject to unexpected and prolonged contractions?" the Fed chairman asked.

By some yardsticks, stock values at the time were not "unduly escalated". If you had bought the companies in the Nasdaq at the time of Greenspan's speech and possessed the finances and willpower to hold them through ups and downs for the next 10 years, you would have earned a respectable return for the whole period.[99] That suggests prices overall contained little or no air in 1996 and the bubble started later. But certain shares had already gone too high.

Greenspan's remarks did not check the market for long. After some panic selling, people went back to buying and prices resumed their upward course. This Berger saw as further evidence of a sprawling yet shaky Ponzi scheme, all the more reason to short sell.

Wall Street Notes' list of sectors about to hit the skids lengthened and by the end of 1996 encompassed almost every part of the economy, with the notable exception of energy and commodities. It started with advertising, air transport, automobiles and apparel and ran through some 30 industries, ending with tobacco and toys.

His few buy recommendations were in oil, coal, natural gas and gold. Commodities were in a deep slump. Most investors avoided commodity-related businesses. Gold was at a historic low and gold producers' stocks were very cheap. To the contrarian, these looked attractive. Besides, gold is typically a darling in times of crisis and Berger foresaw a crisis around the corner. He announced to his readers: "There is a potential catastrophe looming on the horizon."[100]

In the summer of 1997, he forecast a big drop in October. This prediction was dead on. On October 27, the Dow lost 554 points, bringing back memories of a record crash in October 1987 known as Black Monday. Berger was one of the few fund managers positioned right for this event—his shorts suddenly showed triple-digit gains. This was just a start, he was sure. The tide had turned, now was his chance.

But market optimists were not discouraged. Some argued that a system put into place after the 1987 Black Monday would prevent panic selling. Regulators had instituted a rule that required a pause in the trading of U.S. stocks if the Dow Jones lost a certain number of points. If the index continued to go down, the market would be repeatedly shut off. The idea was to allow a time-out to act as a circuit breaker, stopping the plunge. Berger thought this regulation had a psychological effect in boosting the mania. "Many investors believe that the market is not allowed to drop more than a certain amount each day," he reported.[101]

He argued that circuit breakers created a false sense of security and the supposed safety device could not hold. Once investors lost confidence, restrictions on selling would fuel the panic that circuit breakers were supposed to prevent. The ultimate collapse would be all the more severe because of attempts to shore up the market.[102] As the Dow dropped precipitously in October 1997, the device went into action for the first time since its introduction 10 years earlier. As Berger predicted, the stops on trading created an artificial backlog of sell orders. Knowing that they were not going to be allowed to trade for a while made people more inclined to take their money out.

Later an economist called the circuit breakers "regulatory folly".[103] Instead of breaking the market's fall, the time-out requirement acted like a magnet, pulling prices further down as traders dumped their holdings as fast as they could so as not to get caught in the breaker. After this experience, the rule was modified to make circuit breakers apply only when there is a 10% decline in the index rather than a loss of a certain number of points.

All that notwithstanding, stocks quickly recovered in 1997. Companies reported strong performance, giving the public reason to pay high prices. Berger suggested that the rosy earnings reports were not true. "Extraordinary and exotic accounting practices are being exercised to maximize earnings and minimize any shortcomings," he wrote, years before Enron and other corporate accounting scandals broke out.

By his calculation, the earnings of the top 100 U.S. companies were overstated by more than 40%. Employee stock options, a large part of compensation for the first time in history, were not included in costs. That practice alone substantially inflated profits. Then there were myriad other ploys company officers resorted to, such as fake businesses used to conceal declines in earnings. Besides employing a variety of accounting tricks, executives artificially propped up company shares by buying them back.

Perhaps Berger missed certain distinctions. Stock buybacks may reflect executives' belief that the company's shares are significantly undervalued, in which case the buybacks indicate that the stock is a good bet. Neither was he the first person to identify corporate sleights of hand. Overall, however, his analysis was strikingly prescient. To get a clearer picture of a company's future potential, he suggested factoring in stock options and excluding one-time effects. Certainly he was way ahead of regulators, who started to look into these matters only after the damage was done and the stock bubble collapsed. Years later, debates about stock options and accounting problems came to the fore.

In particular Berger suspected foul play at WorldCom and Tyco International.[104] WorldCom was one of his top four short ideas at the end of 1997. The others were America Online, Yahoo and BMC Software. While the entire telecommunications industry was badly overpriced, he felt WorldCom was especially shaky.

Bernard Ebbers had cobbled together acquired businesses. WorldCom was on its way to becoming America's second largest long-distance carrier and biggest handler of Internet data. But it was saddled with many billions of dollars of debt from Ebbers' takeover spree and earnings were feeble.

Yet investors loved WorldCom. Bullish analyst Jack Grubman enthusiastically rooted for the company. When Ebbers offered WorldCom stock in a deal to buy long-distance service provider MCI, the shareholders of MCI preferred his offer to the ready cash offered by another suitor.

Berger remarked that the shark had swallowed the whale.[105] Here was a debt-ridden predator beguiling shareholders with false visions of telecom greatness. WorldCom didn't pay dividends and its profits were more air than substance. The stock traded at around $38 in early March 1998; Berger pegged its real value at $6 to $8. But it continued to rise and by June 1999 traded at almost $65.

Similarly he described AOL as "one of the most overvalued stocks in one of the most overvalued sectors in the entire stock market." Even on the basis of optimistic estimates, the price was 98 times earnings. Every week through 1998 an 1999 he predicted a 70% to 90% drop in AOL and WorldCom; almost every week they climbed higher.

Berger kept going full tilt at the market. Not only did he throw every dollar he raised, he invested his own savings as well. It all became grist for a short-selling mill. Using the equity in the fund as collateral, he borrowed vast quantities of stocks. Because one can't borrow securities for long, he had to replace them. Then he borrowed and sold the same names all over again. Some months his trades were ten, twenty even fifty times the fund's assets.[106]

Aftershocks of a Crisis

As stocks continued to rise, he suspected that interested parties were conspiring to keep afloat the great national Ponzi game — the media, analysts, brokerages, mutual funds and the government were all acting in concert to protect the market bull. Mutual funds were spending billions of dollars promoting the buy message. Masses of investors, blitzed by sales pitches and brainwashed by perky media stories, were buying into stocks in unprecedented numbers. Regulators looked the other way, ignoring corporate abuses.

In his view, the Federal Reserve shared the blame. Why wasn't Greenspan raising interest rates to rein in the absurdly high spirits? He thought the reason was self-protection. "The Fed knows better than anyone that any hike in rates would be the catalyst for the impending downturn in the market," he wrote in *Wall Street Notes*. "And with a downturn having the potential of turning into an economic disaster, the Fed has been carefully avoiding the role of scapegoat."

In fact there were a series of rate hikes. But in 1998, when his forecast of catastrophe appeared to come true, the Fed reacted rigorously to prop up markets. A financial crisis had started in Asia. Currencies and stocks plunged in several countries. To Berger's delight, the U.S. market went on a prolonged skid.

He could not help gloating over his wisdom. The reasons for the decline, in particular the problems in Asia, had been glaringly apparent for some time. Indeed, he had pointed them out repeatedly. "(T)he final nail seems to have been driven into the coffin of the bull market," he declared triumphantly on August 5, 1998. The qualification "seems" was appropriate in view of the painful lesson he had learned — past reports of the death of the bull had turned out to be grossly exaggerated.

He could have closed his positions during the August 1998 panic run. But he did not, because he believed the sell-off was only the beginning of a long-term decline. The crisis appeared to validate his many warnings of financial doom. There would be plenty of opportunity to cash out more profitably. "Clearly, we are in the early innings of this bear market and we do not believe that the excess built up over a 16-year period can be unwound in the matter of a few months," he opined. With that prospect, he added to his shorts.

But he did not anticipate the aftershocks. For one thing, the Federal Reserve abruptly shifted policy and aggressively eased the money spigot. The target interest rate at which banks lend to each other was reduced three successive times, including an unusual decision that took place outside the regular schedule of Fed board meetings. After the first couple of interventions, Greenspan might have waited instead of cutting the rate yet again — the emergency was already abating. In 1999 the Chairman was to reverse course and try to slow the economy down, but in 1998 he sent a strong signal that he would keep the market humming.

Berger had expected a change to tighter money; instead the Fed provided ammunition to what he saws as a destructive rampage of excessive borrowing and puffy asset prices. The central bank had stoked a red-hot stock market, incidentally dealing a blow to the few struggling bears like himself. "How many more magic bullets does the Fed have left in its chamber?" he asked plaintively.[107]

Even so, he stayed the contrarian course. The effect of the cuts would soon wear off. Even the Fed did not possess a limitless supply of magic bullets. Events had just demonstrated the market's fragility. Surely the end of the boom was in sight.

But the Fed's repeated rate cuts reassured investors. Policy makers had now confirmed traders' faith that the Fed in effect guaranteed securities prices—a notion that came to be known as the "Greenspan put." After he retired, Greenspan said it wasn't true, the Fed tried to tighten but this had only a temporary flattening impact on the stock market.[108] Perhaps that was because earlier Fed actions had already created a widespread conviction that the boom was indestructible, impeding later attempts to discourage exuberance. Had policy makers not sent that message in 1998, the bubble would almost certainly have fizzled out earlier.

A surprise blow came from Russia. Oil was cheap. With its export mainstay at record lows, Russia's foreign earnings were weak. The country's foreign currency reserves continued to shrink even after the International Monetary Fund and the U.S. worked out a bailout in July. On August 17, 1998, the Russian government decided not to honor bond payments that came due.

This event had no perceptible economic consequences in the long term—Russia resumed paying its debt and became financially solvent once the price of oil recovered. Today, the country's temporary refusal to honor its bonds is memorable mainly for having destroyed Long-Term Capital Management, a large hedge fund based in Connecticut that until then was widely regarded as the crème de la crème of investment managers.[109]

Manhattan Capital and Long-Term Capital Management were as different from each other as two hedge fund businesses can possibly be. The managers of LTCM carried dazzling credentials. Headed by John Meriwether, a well-known bond chief from Salomon Brothers, the firm brought together a who's who of Wall Street heavy hitters and academic prodigies in the vanguard of finance. Two LTCM partners, Harvard theoretician Robert Merton and options pricing pioneer Myron Scholes, won the Nobel Prize in economics.

These technically brilliant experts constructed their own versions of complex trades — which turned out to be on the wrong side when Russia defaulted.

Compared to the esoteric transactions, Berger's short selling looked like child's game; compared to the huge LTCM portfolio, his fund was tiny. Nevertheless, dissimilar as they were, the two hedge fund firms had a common feature. They shared the same prime broker — Bear Stearns. The bank's top brass tried to prevent the brokerage from being dragged down by the sinking LTCM but despite the precautions Bear Stearns' stock lost over 40% from the beginning of August through September 1998. Other bank stocks also wilted.[110] When the Federal Reserve hastily organized a group of banks to take over LTCM, Bear Stearns was the only large player that declined to participate because its long-time chief wanted no additional exposure to the hedge fund.[111]

The financial sector remained shaky after LTCM was temporarily propped up to allow an orderly liquidation. Brokerages were cautious and wanted to get rid of anything that looked dangerous. Hedge funds in particular were suspect; banks sharply reduced their credit.[112] Bear Stearns, having become risk-shy, scrutinized Berger's transactions and decided to call in early some of the securities he had borrowed and sold.

In one instance, the brokerage called right before Thanksgiving to demand that he cover his position in the Internet firm Earthlink. The timing of the margin call was especially galling. Perhaps because of the holiday, it was difficult to obtain the shares. He had to pay an exceptionally high price and suspected brokers of tipping off other traders that he would have to cover. Knowing that, traders cornered the stock to profit at his expense.

Berger complained, but to no avail. He was correct in his assessment of Earthlink's prospects and would have made money if allowed to wait. Still, Bear Stearns was perfectly within its rights to ask that the shares be replaced. Brokerages all over Wall Street were making margin calls to their customers. Calling back loans of shares or money is a self-protection measure for each player, but it does spread the damage. The systemic nature of the financial industry and the danger inherent in credit showed up again a decade later. In 2008, after the near-collapse of Bear Stearns and the bankruptcy of Lehman Brothers, headlines rapped on about systemic risk and too-big-to-fail banks.

Manhattan Fund and LTCM were alike in their vulnerability. LTCM could have waited out the storm if its portfolio had not been heavily based on credit. Berger was exposed to demands that he close his positions at an inopportune time because his short selling required extensive borrowing of stocks.

In its fundamental logic, Berger's take on equity markets resembled LTCM managers' perspective on the risk premium. In both cases, research indicated that prices were not aligned with economic fundamentals. The situation could not last — there was mispricing, it was about to be corrected. So LTCM took on riskier assets as others moved away in the summer of 1998. Its managers held to their reasoning and went deeper in the direction it indicated even as markets moved the other way. Similarly, Berger added to his short trades as stock prices flew higher.

Mass psychology did not fall in line with the models as rapidly as expected. Berger and the LTCM team made the same basic mistake — both wrongly presumed that the predicted correction would be sufficiently expeditious that they could hold their positions until it happened.

Time and again, Berger predicted a market peak only to be proven wrong. In early 1998, he expected the boom to end in July. Then he pinned his hopes on autumn. But stocks recovered swiftly from their August 1998 low and by the end of the year scaled new heights. At the end of the year, he was sure the game would turn his way in early 1999. When that did not happen, he forecast "a massive top" in mid-April and immense declines thereafter. By September, he was looking forward to December.

In 1999 he added a cautionary note to his newsletter. "Even though under/overvalued stocks tend to return to fair value over time," he explained, "the timing and the exit and entry points are, in our opinion, a key element." He might have added that his own short-selling had vividly demonstrated exactly how pivotal timing is.

But he never fully overcame a weakness that dogged his strategy. There was a persistent misalignment between his research, which looked into the hazy horizon, and his trading, which targeted the immediate future. He traded as if he had insight about the here and now, when in fact he did not. Analysis showed that prices had run ahead of economic fundamentals; eventually prices would come back in line. But a likely tendency somewhere in the future does not tell you what to expect from one month to the next.

To decide when exactly to buy or sell shares, Berger supplemented his fundamental analysis with a study of market movements, a method known as technical analysis— he sought to identify inflections in prices by studying patterns in market trade volume and momentum. This was how he decided on the market "tops" that supposedly indicated prices had gone as high as they could go and were about to drop.

Technical analysis applies past patterns to current prices, but the 1990s bubble was an exceptional event during which historical patterns did not hold—it was a black swan.[113] Mass psychology, the fulcrum on which prices rose or crashed day by day, defied models derived from the past.

What made the strategy especially dangerous was that the trades could not be held for a lengthy period until the prediction kicked in. Short selling is simply not suited for long-term bets because borrowed securities have to be replaced. By contrast, a buy-and-hold strategy can have an indefinite time frame. Correct timing is essential for a portfolio consisting of shorts because keeping up the positions is prohibitively expensive.

While neither fundamental nor technical analysis provided correct timing, these methods armed him with plenty of arguments to back his case. That he knew the eventual direction several years ahead concealed the fact that he was ignorant of what mattered for trading — when he sold a security, he had not the slightest idea what the market would do before he had to buy it back. The plethora of information he gathered obscured the disconnect between his predictions and trades, reassured him that he was in the right, that stocks would collapse next month, next quarter, no later than the turn of the year.

Lost in the market, driven by an intense desire to win, he kept trading. The bad timing was an honest mistake, but it pushed him to the next step.

Mind Games

Manhattan Fund's charter spelled out at length the dangers and uncertainties inherent in the investment program — as required by lawyers. It emphasized that a major component of the strategy was short selling, which is inherently riskier than conventional bets since it involves borrowing and imposes a time constraint. Plus, if the price goes up, there is no limit on the loss because there is no limit on how high the price can go.

By borrowing stocks, a trader can sell securities of much greater value than the capital he controls. "The company will employ a high degree of leverage," Manhattan Fund's prospectus stated. If all goes well, levering up boosts returns. But when trades go bad, "the company's assets would decline in value to a greater extent than would be the case if funds were not borrowed." Not that the experienced investors who provided Berger with capital needed to be told — the risk is well known.

But knowing in the abstract that you could make a great loss is very different from facing that loss when it materializes. Berger must have been acutely aware that his clients, though willing to take the risk, would immediately pull out if losses piled up. To persuade them to invest in the first place, he had to provide proof that he was capable of delivering satisfactory profits. When he founded the business in 1995, his fund had no track record. No track record; no way to attract customers.

He finessed his way around this huge impediment. Acknowledging that the investment pool was new, the prospectus informed would-be clients that Berger had traded similar securities at previous jobs. When people came to visit, he handed out a piece of paper containing a neat table, together with issues of *Wall Street Notes*.

The table showed the track record he achieved through his stock picking career — a run of hefty returns that began in 1991 with a profit of 17.4%. It was as impressive a record as you can find. One client was absolutely entranced by the dramatic returns, observing that this amazing manager had earned 43% in the difficult year 1994.

The 1991-1995 portion of the record was prior to the launch of Manhattan Capital. A note mentions that the numbers represent Berger's performance "in his capacity as portfolio manager." In an application to the U.S. Immigration and Naturalization Service, he claimed to have been an investment manager at the German company that developed the financial software he sold in partnership with Rader, as well as at the Austrian bank.

Berger was barely 20 when he ostensibly began earning double-digit returns. At Salzburger Sparkasse Bank he was in a teller training program — a long way from portfolio manager even if the would-be cashier proved to be a supreme master of stock trading. He was supposedly promoted to the position of investment manager in 1992, when he would have been all of 21. More likely his ideas were occasionally used by other traders.

Or maybe he liked to think some of his ideas might have been implemented and in theory could have yielded those returns. In interviews with clients this was a delicate matter. Understandably, he did not say: "You'll just have to take my word that I compiled double-digit returns year in and year out, starting at age 20." He may not have been entirely clear, preferring to focus the conversation on his prognosis of market catastrophe.

While the putative, possibly hypothetical, returns from his early career should have raised doubts, he benefitted from the cult of youth that dominates the thinking of wealthy investors almost as much as it dominates fashion or sports. There is an entrenched belief that reeling in profits, like showing clothes or playing basketball, is best done by the young. This fuels an endless search for the next boy George Soros.[114]

A dazzling whiz kid who knows just the right moves to protect and expand wealth is a powerful stereotype. Like many stereotypes, it contains an element of reality. The ability to make a lot of money by trading securities usually does not suddenly emerge in middle age. And if you do not catch investment prodigies early in their career, they might get rich and lose interest in managing your money or even taking your call.

But the stereotype also contains a heavy dose of fantasy. Many boys fancy becoming the next billionaire hedge fund manager while the real thing is extremely rare. The probability that any given aspirant will prove to be the next investment genius is miniscule. To make the choice even harder, the contenders tend to be clever and authentically passionate about trading. Neither of those attributes nor any other obvious characteristic ensures success. Perhaps one day a better selection method will be devised, but at present there is no way to know beforehand who will pass the test of the market.

Recognizing this, some investors distribute small sums to a number of candidates in the hope that a few will prove successful enough to more than make up for the inevitable failures. So if you can talk the talk, you might be able to find people willing to bet on your precocious talent.[115] But confidence in a new manager is very tentative — as soon as losses show up, investors decide that the bet failed and take the capital away.

Manhattan Fund received its first investment in April 1996. Of the two million dollars that came, Berger lost about $700,000, or almost 30%, by June. He made a profit in July and August and the fund continued to attract money as it recovered. But in September there was another loss, a big one of over $5 million — more than half the capital at the time. Then in October there was a $1-million loss. In November an additional $2 million went down the drain.[116]

Every quarter the fund's investors were entitled to financial report. The deadline for the next routine quarterly report was looming.

The fund's administrator prepared the report. Berger had hired a small Bermuda offshoot of Ernst & Young as administrator. Prime broker Bear Stearns put the trades it executed for him online every day for the administrator to download. An employee of the administrator used this data to calculate the fund's net asset value. As of September 30, 1996, the fund had about $60 net assets per share. That indicated a 40% decline from the opening net asset value of $100.

Berger could easily imagine his precious clients stampeding to the exit. His extraordinary success raising capital was about to come to nothing, his dream interrupted as it became reality. And yet, he could plausibly hope that with just a bit more time the recalcitrant market would come his way.

He asked Manhattan Capital's bookkeeper in New York – an Austrian friend – to send a fax to the administrator. The fax said that the fund would soon get $2 million from Austrian investors and the report should be put off, presumably to take account of the imminent influx of money — the message was not explicit as to the exact reason for the delay. The main point was clear enough, though. The accountant in Bermuda responsible for the task was told to "please hold off the issuance of the Net Asset Value until authorized by Michael Berger ."[117]

It could wait for a few days; but investors would get curious if it were very late, so Berger could not postpone for too long.

The upshot was that he gave the bookkeeper a monthly portfolio statement to be used to calculate the new asset value. This document purported to come from his old associate Rader's brokerage, Financial Asset Management in Ohio, and was substantially at odds with the Bear Stearns record. Rader had introduced Berger to Bear Stearns and continued to do business with Manhattan Capital.

When the bookkeeper told Berger he did not think the Financial Asset Management statement was correct, the manager brusquely dismissed the objection. The bookkeeper felt he had no choice but to send this new record to the administrator. He did not mention his doubts to the accountant on the receiving end. After that, he no longer saw any Bear Stearns data, only reports from Bermuda indicating that the fund was profitable. It was his job to enter the numbers into Manhattan Capital's books and he did so.[118]

To Berger , this probably seemed like a reasonable temporary expedient. At that stage it was possible to correct the discrepancy within a matter of weeks. After all, in the summer he had regained a good part of the spring loss. Next month he could get back to the straight-and-narrow real NAV. What harm was there in fudging asset value for just one month?

If the temporary setback were revealed, the clients would lose their nerve, redeem immediately and take the loss. But if they stayed the course, he was sure to make money for them. In effect he was protecting their interest. His confidence, that quality he possessed that helped him convince people, would have told him it was going to work out.

There was no question about the correctness of his short selling program — all analysis proved that. After he reeled in the profits, the clients would thank him. Such thoughts, though obviously self-serving, were not absurd. Traders can recover from heavy losses. Sometimes investors do better by staying put. And Berger had both an unshakeable belief in his own gift and a knack for thinking up all manner of arguments. Without those attributes, he would not have come as far as he did.

The administrator obediently prepared a revised calculation using the new information faxed from Berger's office. Thus the NAV was magically transformed from $60 per share to $114 per share, which showed a respectable enough profit to reassure investors.

This maneuver demonstrated a certain virtuoso skill. By having the bookkeeper send the new record, Berger emphasized that people other than himself were involved, inspiring confidence that all was above board. And by mentioning that the fund was about to get substantial new capital, he impressed on the administrator that he was an up-and-coming manager with whom one should continue to do business — all the more reason not to annoy him with a fuss about a routine accounting matter.

He had succeeded in raising a fund thanks to his extraordinary ability to persuade people. The same ability allowed him to deceive them. He knew exactly what to say to get what he wanted.

No regulator could have discovered this deception early on. The only possible deterrent might have been a simple message on a computer screen: "The longer you fake returns, the longer will be your prison sentence. Stop now." Even that may have no effect because someone like Berger is so sanguine, he will regard prison as a very remote possibility.

CHAPTER FIVE. Illusions of Safety

A hedge fund has a private oversight system. Brokers execute its trades, the administrator prepares financial statements and the auditor vouches for those statements. The fund manager puts together these services but investors may inquire about and talk with the providers. Brokers, administrators and auditors are a source of information about funds and a check on managers.

This safeguard has a notable weakness. Service providers are beholden to the manager who picks them, pays them and can fire them. Large operations that cater to many funds, such as the prime brokerage arm of an investment bank, don't depend on any one manager. But small brokerages, administrators and auditors compete fiercely for business. For them, a fund manager is a valuable customer who can easily take his lucrative patronage elsewhere if he is dissatisfied. Challenging him can be risky.

But there is another side to the relationship. If reputable service firms refuse to do business with an investment firm, that may destroy its credibility and ability to attract customers. A manager who changes service providers will likely face inquiries from clients as to why this happened. In short, fund managers and service providers need each other. If a fund has a diverse set of service providers, it is likely that at least one of them will act as a check on the accuracy of what the manager tells his clients.

Manhattan Fund's prime broker set up a formidable barrier to any fabrication. Bear Stearns put accurate data online daily and sent out correct monthly and yearly statements to the administrator as well as to Financial Asset Management (FAM), Rader's brokerage in Ohio. Regulation played a role in how Berger subverted this system.

Bear Stearns reports tracked the fund's losses with brutal clarity, listing each trade in detail with the date, nature of the security traded and price. By contrast, the FAM spreadsheet faxed to Bermuda was sparse, containing just enough data to calculate the fund's asset value. At the beginning, the administrator did not automatically accept the spreadsheet; the accountants' own rules mandated that they verify the numbers. To check transaction prices, they asked Berger for his trade tickets.

He ignored the request. They asked again. It was as if he never received the message no matter how many times they sent it. Had the partner responsible for this issue insisted on proof, the game would have been over. But the partner did not call Berger's bluff. Then there was another spreadsheet waiting in the administrator's fax machine in Bermuda, apparently from FAM. Having accepted the first fax, the administrator accepted the next one as well, and so on.

Even as the trades in the Bear Stearns account lost large sums, the FAM spreadsheets indicated that the fund was profitable. Not that Berger's strategy always failed — some months the stocks he sold went down and his short trades made money.[119] Had he closed the shorts during the 1997 October market dip, the profit would have been enough to cover a significant chunk of the previous loss. But he missed his exit. After that, the losses towered over the gains.

According to the 1998 financial statement based on the FAM numbers Berger faxed to the administrator, net asset value was nearly $168 per share. Naturally those redeeming their investments expected to get the full $168. From the starting value of $100 per share in 1996, that was an attractive profit. Since he claimed this profit, Berger had no choice but to pay redeemers the official share value.

Calculated from the trade data Bear Stearns provided, the NAV came to less than $3 per share. New investors paid $168 for a share that in reality corresponded to $3 of assets, providing Berger with money to pay redeemers as well as capital to borrow and sell stocks. He could not avoid robbing clients to pay other clients once his fictitious returns became accepted asset value, even though by all evidence he did not start with any notion of running a Ponzi scheme. This was the unintended consequence of his trickery.

Had he thought about it, he might have noticed an eerie similarity between his fund and the market bubble — both were shored up by the influx of new money. But raging against the mass Ponzi scheme of the market bubble, he never applied the P-word to himself.

An Easy Explanation

The Bermuda accountants were always aware of the inconsistency between the Bear Stearns record and the FAM spreadsheets. Every month two radically different versions of the supposedly same reality stared them in the face. They repeatedly asked Berger if the FAM data was correct and he reassured them that it was. So the administrator went on using the faxed spreadsheets to calculate the fund's assets.

The reconciliation of the two sets of numbers was conveniently left to an annual audit, which did not take place until the following year. To audit the fund's financial reports Berger hired another Bermuda business, a small affiliate of Switzerland-headquartered Deloitte Touche Tohmatsu.

The first audit concerned the 1996 financial statement. The auditor, like the administrator, had access to the Bear Stearns trade record and, of course, immediately spotted the divergence between the two sets of numbers. Asked to explain the difference, Manhattan Capital's chief proved himself an outstanding confidence artist. Giving extensive explanations, he contemptuously dismissed any doubts.

On occasion he used other brokerages because he borrowed a wide variety of stocks, some of which were not always available at Bear Stearns. This made no difference for the financial record since all trades went through Bear Stearns and were included in its database. But Berger said Bear Stearns did not have the full picture because its data was limited to the trades it executed, while the spreadsheets showed all the trades because FAM was the custodian of the fund's assets. He further muddied the water with other specious explanations.

Later he described these conversations: "Don't pay attention to the Bear Stearns number — there was an onshore/offshore difference. I gave lots of excuses, and said if you don't understand, it's your problem."[120]

That brash line, "if you don't understand, it's your problem," became a recurring refrain in his dealings with the Bermuda administrator and auditor. The impression he conjured was of a bright young trader, very busy, annoyed with tedious questions. These bungling accountants – hired and paid by him, he might have subtly reminded them – were wasting his time.

His impudence helped convince people. Who would dare tell such bald lies? It had to be true. It helped him that the accountants on the other end sincerely wanted to believe. They were apologetic about imposing on him and no doubt would have preferred not to have to challenge him.

But the main reason the trick worked was that Rader backed him up. The broker reassured a partner at the administrator, who told the supervisor of the audit that FAM was the custodian and its statements gave the full picture. The auditor knew the administrator—the people at Bermuda financial services firms socialized, went sailing or golfing together. Rader's word spread and assured all of them.

However, to be on the safe side Deloitte Bermuda asked for a detailed transaction report. Thereupon Berger created a fictitious document that supported the monthly FAM spreadsheets. It took him six weeks to generate this massive fake. Had the trade information been real, it would have been readily available on a computer. But concocting a list of imaginary trades for a whole year to back up the imaginary asset value was a lot of work—almost as laborious as thinking up real trades, except that with hindsight he made sure the trades yielded the returns he claimed.

Upon receiving the retroactive investment masterpiece, Deloitte Bermuda again checked with FAM, the putative source of the numbers, to get independent confirmation The auditor sent FAM headquarters a letter requesting the brokerage to confirm the transaction report. Rader did not reply to the auditor—had he done so truthfully, the scheme would have ended. Instead, Rader forwarded the request to Berger.[121]

On Berger's instruction, a FAM employee sent him a package that included a cover letter from FAM to Deloitte Bermuda and an open envelope and waybill showing FAM in Ohio as the sender.[122] This material enabled Berger to mail to the auditor his fabrication under the FAM cover letter and in the FAM envelope.

With the numbers thus seemingly confirmed by the broker, the auditor decided that the fund's financial statement was accurate. Against all odds, Berger had convinced two groups of accountants to ignore the Bear Stearns record. He could not have done this without the ruse of FAM and the complicity of his ally Rader. It was no mean feat; certainly an equal match for his other remarkable achievement, talking experienced investors into entrusting him with capital.

Over time Berger became more brazen in his machinations. For the 1997 audit he wrote a cover letter that claimed to be from FAM, with a forged signature. He changed the header on the fax machine in his Park Avenue office to make it look like the false letter and account statement were sent from Ohio. Deloitte Bermuda certified as accurate the 1997 financial statement. That gave Berger the green light to report an audited profit of almost 30% for the year—a more-than-respectable performance for any fund, but an astonishing one for a short seller betting against a strong market.

In the summer of 1998 a partner in the New York office of Ernst & Young heard that there might be a discrepancy between Manhattan Fund's reported and real returns. Several investors heard the same rumor. The New York partner at once relayed the news to the Bermuda affiliate and the Bermuda administrator asked the Columbus, Ohio office of Ernst & Young to investigate FAM and make sure it was the source of the data. An executive in Columbus visited Rader to ask about Manhattan Fund. Rader said FAM was the clearing firm, with the implication that it had full information to compute asset value.

In fact FAM lacked the requisite capital to clear the fund's trades — this is why Rader had introduced Berger to Bear Stearns. FAM had only $1 million in capital, not even close to what a broker-dealer needs to clear hundreds of millions of dollars in trades. Manhattan Fund's offering memorandum plainly stated that Bear Stearns had custody of the assets. The prime broker itself announced this in its reports. Hence Rader's assertion contradicted readily verifiable facts about FAM and the fund.

There is no mention of anyone at the time checking the fund's offering memorandum. This supposedly authoritative source of information was ignored all around. Investors found it too much of a bother to read or even to keep and the administrators had no idea what it said even though they mailed copies to would-be fund clients.

The main function of the document emerged after the fund ceased to operate. At that point a small army of lawyers parsed it word by word. One is left with the conclusion that fund prospectuses, consisting mostly of boilerplate in dense legalese, are produced by attorneys for the benefit of other attorneys. The many pages of familiar disclaimers and impenetrable prose discourage non-lawyers.

Manhattan Fund's reported assets diverged from the Bear Stearns record in ever-larger amounts, presenting the administrator and auditor with a growing dilemma. The disparity between the FAM spreadsheets and Bear Stearns data went from $10 million total in December 1996 to $42 million at the end of 1997. In 1999, the Deloitte Bermuda accountant responsible for auditing the 1998 statement recognized with some anxiety that the deviation of the FAM number from the Bear Stearns number had increased substantially and was approaching $300 million.

You might think that even Berger could not paper over so large a chasm, for all his proven ability in this specialized line of endeavor. But he had another powerful factor on his side.

By then the auditor and the administrator had committed themselves to the fund's earlier statements. They had all dug themselves into the same hole. If this year's FAM reports were false, the previous ones also were likely false. The administrator had accepted those FAM spreadsheets and its partners were in trouble if the numbers were fake. The discrepancy for which they would doubtless be sued had ballooned from a few million dollars to hundreds of millions of dollars. Similarly, the auditors would have to confront the possibility that they had been tricked into certifying forged figures. To be sure they had done so in good faith, but admitting to being conned can't be a pleasant prospect for an auditor. So they tenaciously clung to the chance that all was above board.

The partner working on the 1998 audit summed up the predicament poignantly in a message: "Let's hope there is an easy explanation for this issue," he wrote.[123]

Without audited financial reports, most – if not all – investors would have likely pulled out. Rader made the audits possible by reassuring the administrator and auditor. Time and again he covered for Berger. So he played a key role in subverting the private system that otherwise would have detected Berger's trick.

The aura of being overseen by U.S. regulators helped Rader play this role. As a licensed broker under supervision, he seemed to be reliable. Both Rader and his colleague, the firm's vice president and treasurer, held U.S. securities licenses. They and FAM were subject at all times to regulation and examinations by the industry overseer NASD, itself under the authority of the Securities and Exchange Commission.

The extensive regulatory system for broker-dealers did nothing to reveal, let alone prevent, their complicity in a fraud that went on for years.[124] The peculiar aspect of FAM that should have caught the attention of NASD examiners was how heavily Rader depended on Berger. A large and growing portion of the broker's revenue came from Manhattan Capital. This merited some questions, but apparently that was not part of the examiners' routine.

End Game

Berger and Rader had trouble not from regulators but from Bear Stearns. At a cocktail party in December 1998, Bear's head of prime brokerage sales ran into an employee of a European investment firm and heard that Manhattan Fund investors made 20% that year. The next day he found out that Bear Stearns' books showed big losses for the fund and warned the administrator, auditor and FAM.[125]

Rader again referred the matter to Berger, who explained to the administrator that he traded via eight other prime brokers and Bear had only a small part of the picture, hence the discrepancy. Again he sounded insulted by any insinuation of impropriety. He triumphed once more but was increasingly embattled. Some major investors pulled out. An erstwhile ally, the Europe-based marketer who connected him to investors, sued him in London, demanding $1.6 million in unpaid fees and unspecified damages.[126]

Rumors that the fund was going downhill spread in late summer and fall of 1999. Berger fought back aggressively. In August, he filed suit in New York against five unnamed critics of his firm, alleging that these parties were spreading vicious rumors about the fund. They claimed it was down 30% when in reality its was up by 7%. Obviously he hoped that the legal threat would shut up naysayers.

Most investors had no idea that anything was amiss and continued to supply fresh money. Substantial new capital came in every month and quickly evaporated in the short-selling melee. The critics he sued for spreading rumors of a 30% loss were in fact way off the mark. Manhattan Fund was certainly in the red, but they missed the magnitude of the loss if they put it at a mere 30%. Manhattan Fund lost nearly 500% in 2008. Worse was to come.[127]

As the stock boom neared its peak, the short seller's losses likewise ballooned. As his situation became utterly desperate, Berger traded like his life depended on it — which he may have felt it did. He borrowed some $1.7 billion worth of stocks from Bear Stearns in 1999. The brokerage found the risk too much and repeatedly forced him to pare down his positions.

Securities lent for short selling come from the portfolios of brokerage clients, many of them pensions. If a borrower fails to replace the securities, the brokerage is obliged to do so. To protect itself from the danger that a customer might be unable to replace the stocks he borrowed, thereby losing the bank's money, Bear Stearns required a 35% margin for short positions. That is, to borrow and sell $100 in stocks, Berger needed to put up $35 collateral. In late 1999 the stocks he borrowed went up nonstop; to reduce its own risk, Bear Stearns raised the margin requirement to 50%.[128]

Berger did not have enough collateral and had to replace the stocks. But he borrowed and sold again. Manhattan Fund lost 1700% in the nine months from January to September 1999. Then in October he put on nearly $900 million in short sales. By the end of that month, Manhattan Fund had lost 2500% year to date.

The ruse that he made money via other brokerages looked increasingly unlikely. When Bear Stearns executives asked him for the names of those other brokers, he said it was none of their business. Toward the end of 1999, notified by the bank that there might be a problem, the SEC took control.

This is typical of how fraud comes to light — someone goes to the authorities and complains. Without complaints public overseers are highly unlikely to detect deception.[129]

At the time the SEC came in, Manhattan Fund as usual had a big portfolio of shorts, comprising some 840,000 shares. Bear Stearns immediately bought back the securities, returned them to the owners and by January had closed all of Manhattan Fund's positions. A final accounting in early 2000 showed that the accumulated losses from trades plus brokerage fees came to over $409 million.

An aggregate of $593.3 million had flowed into the fund since 1996. Some alert or lucky people had redeemed, taking out almost $144 million. What was now left in the fund's accounts was $36.5 million.

On January 14, 2000, Berger broke the bad news to investors. And that very day, the Dow Jones industrial average peaked, closing at 11,722 — in retrospect, a historic watershed. From then on, the benchmark was to fall and fluctuate at lower levels for the better part of a decade. The "top" that Berger forecast prematurely so many times and awaited so desperately had at long last arrived.

Other major stock indexes, Standard & Poor's 500 and Nasdaq, went on rising for another couple of months. In March, they too crested. It was as if the bull stayed around long enough to ruin this man who bet so ferociously against it — long enough to prove that it could outlast even the most tenacious contrarian. Then it took leave.

Joseph Schumpeter, the Austrian economist who contributed the term creative destruction to world punditry, in a less quoted comment wrote, "history sometimes indulges in jokes of questionable taste." [130] History, or rather the market, played a particularly nasty joke on Berger and his clients. They could not profit from the downturn they anticipated for years; Manhattan Fund's portfolio of shorts no longer existed.

Free Insurance

One reason so many wealthy investors and financial professionals picked Manhattan Fund was that their friends and acquaintances did so. They simply followed the example of people they knew.

Berger achieved a major coup when a Saudi prince became one of the early subscribers. This was a great boon for raising capital: a royal seal of approval, like Queen Elizabeth patronizing a certain brand of tea. Observers saw the decision by the prince's bankers as a signal of quality that validated Berger.

That started the herding. People reason that if top investors choose a fund, it has to be good. So-and-so has invested, they must know what they're doing, so we will go by their example. Hundreds followed each other to the elegantly furnished Manhattan Capital aerie — where a fabulous spin master who told them what they wanted to hear.

Ironically, these investors were farsighted. They were right that the strategy was protective against a market collapse. Short-selling does act as cover in slumps. When market indexes went into a tailspin in 2002, short-biased hedge funds demonstrated their mettle by raking in 18%. But short selling is the toughest way to turn a buck; a miniscule number of traders succeed at it over time. Anyone can easily see this by consulting the indexes. Short biased managers were the worst performing group for the 10 years from 1994, not only because they lost money but also because their returns were extremely volatile.[131]

As the market gathered steam from 1995 through 1999, short sellers lost money most years and as the boom neared its zenith they lost even more. So you could buy insurance by investing with short sellers — but you would lose until the market turned. In effect, the loss was the cost of the insurance. Such insurance, never cheap, was particularly expensive in the late 1990s because there was a bubble expanding at a rapid pace.

If a short-seller figured out how to avoid losing too much, the reward came in due course. But most were wiped out. Only a few exceptionally skilled short-sellers knew how to control the loss, and even they performed poorly in comparison to market indexes. To get cover against the future bust, you had to sacrifice a lot of current gain. It is a rare person who is willing to lose money in the midst of a thriving market.

Big investors wanted a shelter for the end of the boom, but in the meantime they did not want to pay the full price of that shelter in the form of losses. Berger gave them the comforting impression that they were buying a safeguard plus a solid return. What he appeared to offer was free insurance — a deal you can not really get.

Berger was in the limelight. His view of the bull market was well-known; he went on publishing his opinions in *Barron's* and his newsletter. He never concealed the fact that he was trading against rising prices. In that light, the reported profits were astounding. After almost 30% in 1997, he supposedly made 12.4% in 1998 while many well-known, long-established managers suffered huge losses. In 1999, betting against a market that was going up at an unprecedented rate, he claimed a 14.4% return — an achievement probably unmatched by any short seller.

His triumphal track record was available in several databases. It diverged sharply from his peers'. Other traders shorted the same stocks and ended up with large losses. They asked him how he did it. How could it be that this one manager persistently pulled in substantial profits when no one else made money short-selling in the midst of the hottest market ever? He gave some garbled explanation.

Pleased with the great deal they thought they were getting, Manhattan Fund investors stuck to idea that Berger was a whiz kid capable of doing what no other short seller could do. He was just exceptionally gifted. It looked like they were having their cake and eating it too. "He did not look like a genius and his numbers were genius numbers," said an investor later, lamenting not having pulled out.[132]

In fact Berger did have an exceptional skill, but it was not for making money trading stocks; it was for fashioning his own version of reality and convincing everyone that this was true. In trading, his wild optimism worked badly against him. Trading is a very different kind of game from selling an idea. To succeed in trading securities, you need to grasp market reality better than other people do. Successful long-term money managers are realistic in assessing the market and pragmatic in their approach.

"He who runs away lives to fight another day" is a maxim George Soros hewed to during the several decades he managed Quantum Fund, one of the few hedge funds that succeeded over a long period.[133] Soros argues that there is no predicting the future, whether in markets or life, because what happens depends on how all the players view the situation. No matter how well informed you are, your expectation may not match others' expectations. Wrong beliefs can dominate the market. So you have to watch what's happening and nimbly change direction.

This awareness that did not always save Soros from losing money, but he turned back before a loss became large enough to threaten Quantum Fund's viability. He promptly corrected course at every turn. Obeying the dictum that "the markets provide a merciless reality check," he did not stay with any idea that failed the test.

Berger completely lacked this pivotal ability. Once he made up his mind that a crash was imminent, he never budged. Only a few months after he started trading for Manhattan Fund, it became obvious that the market was not following his script. By 1998 it was clear that bringing down the stock bubble was not on the Federal Reserve's agenda. He could have reduced the short selling and hedged his bets by buying companies with strong prospects.

But he never moderated the strategy. His consistency was a draw for investors who wanted him to remain the contrarian, because that was the role he performed in their portfolio. To protect them in a downturn, he had to be the short seller.

Fraud Stories

Even as headlines proclaimed his Ponzi scheme, Berger remained coolly confident. He confronted the legal problem with the same boldness he showed in raising money and trading stocks. The SEC started civil proceedings against him in January 2000, but at the time there were no criminal charges. Berger hired a high-powered attorney to help him negotiate a deal that would forestall a possible criminal case.

Benito Romano of Willkie, Farr & Gallagher had been U.S. Attorney for the Southern District of New York in the late 1980s. He advised Berger that he could be accused of a serious crime because a substantial amount of money was involved and the falsification of documents was easily provable. This was not what Berger wanted to hear; he was determined either to avert the criminal suit or to settle it with minimal prison time.

To that end, cooperating with the authorities became his mantra. At every opportunity he piously repeated to reporters that he was "cooperating to the fullest extent." Several meetings took place with representatives of the SEC, the U.S. Attorney's office and possibly other law enforcement agencies during the first three months of 2000. Berger laid out dirty little secrets that he thought would be of interest. One was that financial advisers and private banks received kickbacks in exchange for routing their clients' money to Manhattan Fund.

His attorney encouraged him to "take responsibility" and come clean to the government. By doing so at a time when he faced civil action but no criminal charges, Berger believed he was fulfilling his side of a deal. He was under the impression that the prosecutors would reciprocate by going easy on him, especially as he provided them with stories about others' malfeasance.

He gleefully described how exactly he cooked up fake documents and browbeat hapless accountants into accepting false numbers. Given his widely publicized short selling spree, by any logic he had to be losing money. That he convinced people to the contrary was testimony to how very smart he was—not many people could accomplish so difficult a sleight of hand. After keeping this feat to himself for years, now he showed off, in effect presenting his scheme as a "look ma, no hands" act.

His counsel apparently did not restrain this tendency to brag about how ingeniously he fooled a large number of experienced people. So Berger enthusiastically shared with regulators and prosecutors the minutiae of his own hoax as well as tidbits about others.

Possibly he thought about this tactic earlier and collected information about his fellow money managers and fund marketers. As his losses mounted and the fabricated asset values diverged from the true numbers in ever larger amounts, it must have occurred to him that he needed a way out in case he did not make the money back and the police came calling. That he had a ready trove of revelations suggests that naming names may have been his hedge. He reckoned he would get the prosecutors off his back by providing them with bigger game to pursue.

Eventually he told the tales to journalists as well. The stories I heard from him were somewhat fuzzy — he had vague hunches of bogus returns at certain firms and trading on inside information at others. However, he may have given the government more in-depth accounts. In retrospect, his most dramatic revelation concerned Bernard Madoff, then known as the head of Madoff Securities, a brokerage that acted as a market maker in stocks listed on Nasdaq and the New York Stock Exchange.

Madoff's track record of avoiding any annual loss for decades surpassed the achievements of the best hedge funds. Berger said that behind this remarkably long run of success was some very bad fraud, but like his other tales, his knowledge of Madoff's malfeasance was vague. After he told the authorities in early 2000 about the fraud, Madoff seemingly went on as before, with no interference from the government.

From this observation, I started to doubt Berger's stories — perhaps he fabricated his allegations, given his penchant for making things up. How else could one explain the fact that no action was taken against Madoff? It was years later that I realized the supposed revelation that Madoff ran a scheme was in fact long familiar to the SEC. They had heard it before, had even received detailed reports and complaints on the subject going back to 1992. Those complaints had either resulted in the imposition of minor sanctions on Madoff or more frequently simply disappeared in a bureaucratic black hole.

From the government's vantage point, there would have been no value at all in getting the same old stuff second hand from Berger, who heard from others that Madoff was engaged in some shenanigan but had no specific information. So he received no brownie points from prosecutors. His tattling had one notable consequence: it gave rise to sensational pieces in the media. He held forth to journalists at length about the nasty habits of brokers, hedge fund managers and marketers, thereby instigating articles on the subject.

The disclosures had the beneficial effect – from his view – of shrinking his own misadventure to routine operating procedure. Almost everybody in the industry was doing it, Berger was one among many, not even the worst, and happy to assist officials every way he could. Surely there was no reason for them to be nasty to such an obliging fellow. That seemed to be the underlying message as he energetically condemned assorted iniquities, sounding positively shocked!

Once it became evident that he would not get the lenient deal he wanted, he worried about his heart-to-heart chats with representatives of the U.S. Attorney's office — after all, prosecutors are not the best audience for boasting of how clever you are at deception, even if you are exposing the excessive cleverness of others as well.

"Moreover, I have presented myself on a silver platter to the authorities already and it would defy logic to be counterproductive now," he wrote to his attorney, Romano, in a letter dated February 1, 2000.[134] He demanded that the attorney support him more effectively, having forked over $300,000 for his defense.

In March Romano advised his client to accept a guilty plea to criminal charges of securities fraud that were expected to come his way—but had not yet arrived. This would entail going to prison for a significant period and Berger balked. His plying the authorities with every account of financial impropriety he knew was getting no consideration. He rejected the legal advice.

A few days later Romano resigned as counsel. The reason he gave was that a conflict of interest had recently been discovered: the law firm Wilkie Farr represented some of the banks that invested their clients' money in Manhattan Fund. Among these were banks whose certain European operations Berger accused of taking kickbacks.

His next lawyer got him to plead guilty to fraud, but Berger never really accepted that he committed a crime. He blamed the fake returns on the accountants, insisting that he had not sent false information to investors—the Bermuda administrator had.[135] This was an obvious charade, as the administrator partners and staff had no motive to misrepresent the fund's performance and Berger had already described how he fooled them. He blamed his lawyers for forcing him to plea and tried to withdraw his confession.

Having met him at the time, I thought some of his notions were delusional. He claimed that the fund's offering memorandum allowed him wide discretion in valuing the portfolio and therefore he was within his rights when he engaged in a practice he delicately described as "bridging the gap between actual and theoretical value."[136]

When securities don't trade much, current prices are not readily available, making it necessary to calculate values from models. In some cases traders and brokers can honestly disagree over the value of a position and there needs to be a procedure to resolve disputes. Sometimes a crisis has an unexpected impact on instruments that are rarely traded, raising questions about the real value of the asset. In 2007, when homeowner defaults rose, there were disputes on the value of collateralized debt obligations based on mortgage bonds.

But there was no issue of valuation in Manhattan Fund. Berger bet on frequently traded U.S. stocks listed on exchanges, daily prices were readily available and there could be no difference of opinion. He also bought options, put options in particular, but these were widely used derivatives subject to no ambiguity.

What he wanted to claim was the right to impose theoretical prices that made it look like his expectations were fulfilled. The expected price necessarily gives a rosy view of a trade — it's what the trader hoped would happen. Having carte blanche to peg prices to theoretical values you expect comes to the same thing as having permission to conceal losses. Were Berger's notion of "theoretical value" universally applied, all investments would appear profitable. It was hard to believe that he truly thought this absurd excuse could help him in court.

Yet he spent his dwindling resources on legal battles around this and other chimera. No lawyer was willing to go along with his ideas for defending himself against the criminal charges; a string of attorneys took on the case but quickly resigned or were fired when they told him that his legal tactics would not help and could make his situation worse. As he went through lawyer after lawyer, railing against them, he developed detailed legal arguments that he on occasion submitted to the courts himself.

I suggested he get a law degree. That way, he could with greater authority craft legal memos and dispute his fast-changing array of attorneys. Possibly he would do less damage as a lawyer conjuring up sharp arguments than he had done as a money manager.

The recommendation that he go to law school annoyed Berger. He huffily informed me that his future was already planned and it was absurd to think he might become anything other than what he was — a hedge fund manager. He intended to reclaim Manhattan Capital and get back into business. Indeed, he filed motion after motion in the civil court to dispute penalties levied against the firm. This was possibly his most amazing illusion.

As the owner of Manhattan Capital, he consented to the appointment of a lawyer named Helen Gredd as receiver for the business after it was seized by the SEC in January 2000. Romano advised him that this was to his best interest.[137] When he left the Manhattan Capital office for what turned out to be the last time, he did not take his furniture, art and computers with him because he thought he would be back. But Gredd forbade him to come near the premises and refused to give him his belongings — though he kept trying to retrieve the computers. Romano told him Gredd regarded him as "toxic waste."

It would have been rational for Berger to forget about the residue of his unfortunate enterprise, given that it was gone and he faced a lengthy prison sentence. His attempts to take it back made no sense. I suspected he might be losing his reason altogether. Yet he often sounded not merely sane but exceptionally smart. If he were mad, it was a highly selective madness.

To Hedge and Dodge

Somehow Berger persuaded himself that he had a good chance of proving his innocence if only he could go on trial. He tried to get rid of his guilty plea on the ground that emotional problems had clouded his judgment. These, he claimed, had made him prone to behavior that harmed him and caused him to be vulnerable to his lawyers' bullying. A judge had to decide whether he was legally sane – if he was not, the guilty plea was not valid.

His psychiatrist testified that Berger had developed coping mechanisms like denial and disassociation to deal with trauma in his childhood and had narcissistic personality disorder.[138] This was in line with earlier diagnoses by Austrian psychologists. Another psychologist brought in as expert witness diagnosed a severe personality disorder with narcissistic features and bipolar disease. As a result, Berger experienced "serious cognitive distortions that lead him to deny significant aspects of both external reality and his own affects and ideas."[139]

In particular, he denied events and experiences that placed him in a bad light. That led him to believe he was justified in his market analysis and in reporting false performance data. His ability to recognize what he was doing was compromised because he rationalized his behavior to a pathological degree.[140]

External conditions can support or suppress narcissistic tendencies. An extreme version manifests as boundless political ambition and paranoia, which in an accommodating political and cultural environment can lead to dictatorial power.[141] A malignant narcissistic dictator decorates a whole country with his likeness carved in stone, painted on canvas and immortalized in film.

In the business world, market euphoria is thought to encourage the expression of this personality trait.[142] Chief executives who engage in myriad malfeasance – fudge corporate finances, misuse inside information, steal company money, spend it on lavish personal purchases – may have a touch of narcissism. But most would keep the proclivity under control if giddy markets did not create the illusion of extreme wealth and power. Thus the 1990s stock boom and the 2000s property and credit bubbles unleashed self aggrandizing tendencies. In Berger's case, his success raising large amounts of capital probably encouraged a sense of invincibility.

A government-appointed doctor agreed with the other psychologists that mental problems affected Berger's behavior during the years he perpetrated the fraud but nevertheless found him legally competent. Understandably, the prosecutor was not interested in exploring the full implications of Berger's emotional makeup or the argument that his having fooled others was not a crime because he thoroughly fooled himself. Psychiatric reports "will explain why he did what he did," wrote the assistant U.S. Attorney responsible for the case. The personality attributes that resulted in the action did not make it any less of a crime.[143]

True, fraud had not been Berger's intention, but that was not news to prosecutors. Not many white collar convicts start off planning careers as swindlers, they slip into deception willy-nilly, each little step seemingly justified at the time. That does not make a compelling legal argument. If falling into the quagmire without wanting to do so were admitted as a defense, few could ever be convicted of financial fraud.

True to form, Berger was certain that Judge Victor Marrero would grant his request to undo his admission of guilt—as sure about the legal outcome as he had been sure the Dow Jones would drop a thousand points in the next three months.

The judge had a clear impression that this defendant, who had been appearing in the criminal court for a couple of years, was unusually intelligent. Berger had the mental capacity to develop his own economic theory and argue in court that his investment strategy would have worked had it been given more time.[144] His responses during the plea hearing, wrote the judge, showed "a total command of the circumstances that demonstrated far more than average mental agility."[145]

Marrero was eloquent in describing Berger's performance. "In his answers to questions asked by the Court, as well as in impromptu remarks, he drew upon this intellectual capital to hedge and dodge, to parse nimbly the semantic nuances of legal words and to spar with the subtleties of articulated conduct, at times endeavoring to dance delicately around what was incriminating while artfully embracing the self-serving," he opined. In an attempt to control the legal damage, "Berger engaged in sophistry that would have been atypical of a truly incompetent person."[146]

All that steering, hedging and dodging, nimble parsing and delicate dancing around the fraud made Berger appear as a highly sophisticated huckster, by his own actions giving the lie to the claim that he had acted in good faith and was a hapless victim of unscrupulous lawyers.

Indeed, he was sufficiently in control to conceal his psychological problems for several years. As long as he was taking in hundreds of millions of dollars, he made no mention of his troubled psyche. He presented himself as a perfectly sane man, if anything saner than the numerous deluded fools who were paying astronomical prices for nearly worthless dotcoms. His clients were left with the impression that their money was safe with him. Had it been known that he suffered from a personality disorder that made him especially prone to delusion, it would have been obvious that he was not the person to be entrusted with large sums to invest.

But his attempt to reach a favorable deal with prosecutors having failed, he provided psychologists with evidence of mental disorder so that they could issue reports that were used in legal arguments for his benefit. He even told his doctor that he planned to ask his lawyer to request a psychiatric summary in the hope that this might "humanize" him.[147] Far from being mentally incapable, Berger demonstrated an ability to craft clever tactics.

The judge threw out the case to withdraw the plea and scheduled the sentencing for March 1st, 2002. On that appointed day, we all gathered at the frequently-filmed court building in Foley Square to hear the sentence. Marrero was expected to mete out a stiff one, at the top end of the range specified in the plea, to be served not at an easy-going place for white collar convicts but a tough prison. Berger was really in for it.

But being a very resourceful person – as the judge noticed – he had a contingency plan. It was already set into motion. When he posted bail his Austrian passport had been taken away so that he could not leave the United States, but it turned out he had another passport, a British one. We waited in vain in the courtroom. He never showed up.

About a year later, I received a call. He was broke; if I provided him with a nice advance, he would tell me his story. Not surprisingly, he declined to say where he was. I would not buy. He peddled his biography to various news organizations, but nobody was willing to pay for it. An anecdote – probably a joke – went around that a vacationing New York judge briefly encountered him, now with a moustache, at a Viennese café. The judge wanted to say hello but Berger vanished.

Several years later he was apprehended in Austria, where he went to prison for a short spell. As an Austrian citizen he was not extradited to the U.S., where the sentence would have been much longer and the prison likely less comfortable. So he did well by escaping—a successful calculation on his part. However, to a striver maniacally bent on getting rich, it must have been galling to end up penniless.

His long-time associate Rader, the broker who helped him circumvent the administrator and auditor, was investigated. The SEC found that Rader "repeatedly took steps that contributed to the fraudulent scheme perpetrated by Berger" For instance, he sent to Berger the auditor's confirmation request and the FAM letterhead for the reply. "This circumvention of the audit confirmation process … made it possible for Berger to perpetrate his fraudulent scheme."[148] Even as the fraud was about to be exposed, Berger had Rader sign and fax to Bermuda a letter saying that FAM had custody of the fund's assets and provided monthly trading and loss/gain statements.

Rader knew that the Bear Stearns reports showed immense losses and Berger had to be cooking the books, but he benefited substantially from his connection to Manhattan fund. The SEC estimated that commissions from the fund accounted for between 10% to 33% of the broker's annual revenue during the period in question.[149]

In 1998 Rader supported Berger's application to acquire immigrant status — stating in the immigration filing that "It was through Mr. Berger's efforts that our company has been able to survive." Rader's wife told Berger she relied on him to feed her family. The mutually beneficial alliance lasted for over six years, though relations were not cordial and Berger complained that his former employer threatened and exploited him. Despite the squabbles, Rader received a robust stream of income as long as Berger stayed in business.

The SEC ordered Rader and a FAM employee to cease and desist from securities law violations in the future and return $642,000 in commissions from Manhattan fund. They settled without admitting or denying guilt. At that time they did not have the money, so the SEC agreed that they would pay only $25,000. The investors sued FAM alongside the fund's other service providers and a judge found that the facts supported "a fair inference that FAM knew of Berger's fraud," making Berger.and FAM jointly liable for $288 million in damages. But this was a formality. FAM did not have assets that could to be seized.

Rader neither returned the gains from the scheme – which he'd already spent – nor faced criminal charges. He did give evidence to the government and presumably would have been a witness had the criminal case against Berger gone to trial. That was probably the reason for the leniency shown him. However, there was no trial and he ended up with a surprisingly light penalty in view of the conclusion the SEC reached that he had "made it possible for Berger to perpetrate" the fraud.

As far as this story goes, I can find no obvious useful function for regulators in preventing the scheme, beyond the criminal justice system's – ineffective – effort to punish Berger after the fact. The main effect of SEC and NASD oversight of brokerages was to enhance Rader's credibility. But there is a sequel that illuminates the role regulators do play.

Neither I, nor apparently anyone else who reported on the subject, realized at the time that the real story starts after the con man leaves the scene. The eye-opener part of the Manhattan Capital saga started after the hedge fund stopped operating. Before we turn to that in the next chapter, it is worthwhile to highlight an implication of the 1990s mass delusion, a lesson typically ignored.

Paradox of Optimism and the State

Most new businesses fail; the failure rate may be as high as 90%. If you took that number to heart, you would not go ahead. People who start a business tend to be optimistic: they believe that they're an exception to the failure statistic. Worldwide surveys show that investors in general tend to be overly confident and entrepreneurs even more so than the rest.[150]

You need to be especially sanguine to launch a hedge fund with all the odds against you. Berger could not have convinced a lot of people to invest had he not projected his belief in the investment program, his assurance that this was the right thing to do and he was the right man to do it. Wildly successful at persuading others, he was also exceptionally effective at persuading himself.[151] He found plenty of reasons to bolster his conviction that the strategy would work; in part because his diagnosis of the bubble was in fact correct.

But he put too much faith into his forecasts of imminent market bust and ignored evidence pointing to the failure of the strategy. Worse, the same confidence led him to doctor the returns and persuade accountants to use fabricated numbers. He could ignore the danger of going to prison because he ignored the chance that he would fail and be held responsible for deceiving people. If he made enough money and made the investors whole, nobody would complain and there would be no issue of fraud.

There is evidence that individuals who are more confident trade more and end up with lower returns — they would do better if they traded less. The information on which they base the trades is in fact too weak.[152] The more Berger traded, the more money he lost, and in response the more he traded. As a pitchman who feared no barriers, he was uncannily successful in selling his services. As a trader who feared no risk and kept doubling up, he was an awful failure.

As the fissure between reality and make-believe widened, the it-will-work-out assumption became increasingly implausible. By 1998, with a cumulative concealed loss of hundreds of millions of dollars, it is impossible to imagine how he could have closed the breach. Yet he went on. He must have still had hope. Optimism is a potent force for great achievements but dangerous as well.

Everyone distorts reality to some degree. Research on the sources of happiness suggests that the right level of illusion gets us through life.[153] To what extent we gloss over reality is the critical question. We need just enough optimism to keep going. We might lose our will to act if we experience the world exactly as it is—people who are seriously depressed tend to be realistic and see through comforting notions. But if the balance tips too much to the other side, one risks becoming a hostage to delusion, going astray and leading others astray.

Certainly Berger was not alone in his ability to selectively dodge unwanted observations. His clients accepted his extraordinary returns even though at the time nobody else made money short selling the same stocks. Supposedly savvy investors looked to him for safety in a market bust, entrusting large sums to an unhinged adventurer in order to protect themselves. That decision seems at least as deluded as Berger's faith that he would win back the losses if he kept on trading.

Meanwhile in the wider market investors resolutely ignored warnings that the glittering prospects of the late 1990s were not for real. As long as the boom lifted all boats, everyone could congratulate themselves on their investment acumen and ignore evidence of weakness or malfeasance. Assorted number-juggling tricks remained outside the public's awareness despite repeated warnings from Jeremiahs such as Berger, who would tell anyone who'd listen that the bull market was a giant Ponzi game.

WorldCom almost doubled in value while he loudly protested its accounting iniquities and sold it short. Neither WorldCom shareholders nor regulators looked for signs of trouble. It's not that investors were collectively crazy — rather, their decisions were warped by the penchant to seek to confirm rather than refute beliefs.[154] Berger, his clients and the millions who bought WorldCom and other stocks were united in being blind to unpleasant information. They differed only in what specifically they ignored

The bubble fed grandiose dreams. Alberto Vilar, the technology enthusiast who managed the Amerindo Technology fund in which some of Berger's clients invested, made 249% in 1999. At its peak Vilar's firm had around $6 billion in assets and notable clients such as the World Bank and big public retirement systems. Vilar the man was every bit as impressive as Vilar the high-flying money manager, giving or pledging as much as $250 million to art, education and medical research. There was a Vilar young artists program at the Royal Opera House in London, a Vilar Center for the Arts in Colorado and a Vilar spine regeneration research program in New York.[155] His name was on the grand tier of the Metropolitan Opera.

Once the market was done ruining the bears, it turned to wallop its enthusiastic supporters. Amerindo Technology Fund lost around 90% of its value from 2000 to 2002. Vilar had trouble making good on his pledges but still went on with the philanthropy spree. In December 2004 he promised tens of millions to a medical center.[156] He could not let go of the vision of fast-rising technology companies and was confident his fortune would recover. Neither could he relinquish his addiction to philanthropy as he fell deeper into a financial hole. He was arrested for stealing a client's funds and spending most of it on donations to his alma mater and other worthy causes.

A slew of corporate and market celebrities went down with the market. At that stage in the cycle demands for retribution rose. Regulators finally caught up with WorldCom chief Ebbers. Several years after Berger warned about the cover-up of WorldCom's ramshackle finances, the SEC started an inquiry into the company's accounting. After fetching $65 in 1999, the stock dropped to six cents in July 2002, even lower than Berger predicted — but having lost a small fortune short selling the stock, he was in no condition to profit from the eventual vindication of his forecast.

Another company Berger repeatedly bet against with no success, Tyco International, also ran into legal trouble once the market came down. Its chief executive went to prison for fleecing the shareholders.

The 25-year sentence meted to Ebbers meant that he'd spend most, if not all, of the rest of his existence in government custody. He could have retired years ago to a life of luxury. Instead he embarked on an ambitious but doomed effort to put together a huge fiber optic network. Surely he fooled himself when he started to play games with WorldCom's accounting, just like Berger did with Manhattan Fund's returns. Ebbers must have believed that the fiber optic network would become sufficiently profitable and his gaming the numbers would be of no consequence once the gamble succeeded. Otherwise, why take the risk?

Berger, Ebbers and Vilar are extreme examples of the paradox of optimism. They would not have been able to build businesses had they not believed in great things to come. But that same hopefulness endowed them with faith in what must have looked like temporarily useful accounting devices. The mindset that made for success led to catastrophe when the venture did not go as expected.

This is not to defend such characters; merely to point out that criminal penalties do not deter them because when they start the deception, they do not think of it as fraud. It appears as a short-term maneuver to gain time for the plan to succeed. We often engage in behavior we would reject if we were consciously aware of it — much dishonesty happens because people unconsciously fool themselves.[157] The implications of our bad acts tend to fade away. As a result, we believe ourselves to be more ethical than we are. This is a pervasive trait that shows up in behavioral experiments, like other biases.

You will recall that one rationale for financial regulation is to protect people against their own cognitive shortcomings. In the 1990s and 2000s that reasoning turned out to be broadly false. As irrational elements played out, various arms of the federal government did nothing to moderate the wild expectations. Regulators did not act to stop the games played by corporate chieftains like Ebbers.

The SEC did not try to make public company accounting more realistic — until after the bubble collapsed. In the meantime, the myth that it watches over markets fed the public's confidence, just as Rader's regulated status helped him support Berger's game.

As for the Federal Reserve, it positively egged on the perky mood. The triple rate cut in 1998 confirmed the investing public's belief in the "Greenspan put" and further spurred the market. Though afterwards officials denied that they could have stopped the bubble, at least they should not have encouraged the public's bloated confidence.

The official defense is that the Fed was not sure there was a bubble, just as the SEC had no awareness of corporate accounting fraud. We should not take such protestations of ignorance at face value. If one somewhat crazed short seller, working by himself, could see the problems ahead of time, surely officials endowed with great authority and resources could have as well.

Others in the contrarian camp sounded warnings. As the stock market got frothier, bond analyst James Grant complained that Greenspan kept rates too low for too long. In 2005, Grant again pointed a finger at the Fed: the bubble had still not popped; Washington pumped money to get the economy over any little hump, that was keeping financial markets afloat. A really loud pop came a couple of years later. If a private analyst could see it coming, why couldn't the Fed, which employs an army of economists with PhDs?

It may be that government agents were caught up in the same misconceptions as the public — a modern version of the Master of the Mint debacle. Whether or not regulators acted the fool, the fact remains that in the 1990s the regulatory state failed signally to tamp down on a gigantic bout of deluded investing and the diverse shenanigans it spawned. Regulators did not correct investors' biases in perception; if anything some policies strengthened tendencies toward deception and illusion.

CHAPTER SIX. Honey Pots

The Manhattan Capital taken over by regulators in January 2000 consisted of a small Park Avenue office where Berger's lone assistant was technically still employed. There was no other staff. This was a tiny business. The management firm owned only about $280,000 in cash and the lease for the office. But the hedge fund still contained the $36.5 million left of clients' money.

There was $15 million at the Bank of Bermuda, mostly from newly arrived subscriptions that Berger did not get a chance to lose. The rest was in New York bank accounts, left from his trades after Bear Stearns closed them. Investors could no longer take their money out because at the instigation of the Securities and Exchange Commission a District judge froze the assets in New York. A Bermuda court did the same in that country.

Asked what was going on with Manhattan Fund, a spokesman for the SEC replied that the receiver was expected to distribute the remaining money fairly to the claimants. "Generally speaking, a receiver will take charge of the remaining assets and then draw up a plan for the equitable distribution of the assets among the shareholders," he told a news service.[158] He added that a receiver may also attempt to recover assets from investors who had redeemed their shares at inflated prices.

The lawyer Gredd clearly wanted the receiver job; she and her firm, Lankler Siffert & Wohl, negotiated with the government for the receivership and agreed to give a discount of 20% from their customary hourly fee. The SEC designated her and the Justice Department gave its approval.

Estate sinecures are more lucrative than other court-appointed posts.[159] And this estate, though nothing like the gigantic estates left after the collapse of Enron and Lehman Brothers, was still substantial. Outside observers like myself knew that even with the 20% discount, Gredd received a plum assignment. But we did not fully appreciate what a plum it was. We thought the assignment consisted mainly of divvying up the assets, as officially proclaimed.

Equitably resolving conflicts between the investors was the rationale for freezing their assets and having a receiver distribute the money. For this purpose, it seemed to make sense to have a government appointee in control. It might take a year or even a bit longer, considering the lawyers would be in no hurry, but the receiver was performing a useful function. Such was my naïve impression.

Berger said he agreed to the appointment of Gredd because his lawyer Romano told him to. The judge in the civil proceeding, Denise Cote, cited Berger's consent in ratifying the receiver and noted that his lawyer had not appeared at the court on this occasion, with the inference that there was no objection.

Gredd belonged to the same legal circle as Romano and her career tracked his. Both had degrees from New York University and Columbia law school. Like him, she worked as a prosecutor at the Southern District of New York, as Assistant U.S. Attorney from 1985 to 1993. She prosecuted securities and commodities cases. She was familiar to the staff of the SEC as well as to other lawyers, though it was not obvious that she was an expert on hedge funds. No other candidate for the job was mentioned, at least in public.

Cote instructed Gredd to find out the true financial condition of the business, identify the remaining assets and ensure that all shareholders were treated fairly in the distribution. Nothing unusual in that mandate. Manhattan Capital and its fund were to pay reasonable fees and expenses incurred by the receiver in the performance of this work.

The judge also freed Gredd and persons employed by her from any liabilities and damages – unless they acted in bad faith – and forbade creditors from interfering with the receiver's disposal of the estate.[160] The investors were now officially creditors of the defunct business and what happened to their assets depended on the receiver. They could not interfere unless a judge allowed them to.

Venue Shopping

The estate did not remain under Judge Cote for long. In an action that was to have major consequences, the receiver filed for protection under Chapter 11 of the Bankruptcy Code, thereby moving out of District Court. This is the legal route typically taken by insolvent companies that continue to operate and need time to reorganize. To understand what happened to the estate, it is useful to recall the controversies on the subject.

Meant to help a business streamline and emerge from bankruptcy as a viable entity, Chapter 11 has been criticized for allowing companies to restructure at the expense of other parties—creditors and workers. Big decisions during bankruptcy include whether a company is salvageable and what businesses to sell off. Sensitive issues include not only who makes the decisions and what they're paid but also how long they take. In response to complaints, Chapter 11 law was changed to impose an 18-month time limit on company executives' right to control restructuring—a year and a half was considered enough time to pull a firm out of the morass, unless the business is exceptionally complicated.[161]

An example of the extreme case, Enron's bankruptcy took over four years, during which around $13 billion in energy-related assets were sold and the proceeds distributed to creditors. The turnaround specialist who led this massive liquidation billed $25 million as a "success fee" but cut the sum in half when the Department of Justice charged that there were billing irregularities.[162]

The 2008 Lehman Bothers collapse demonstrates how cumbersome, slow and expensive Chapter 11 tends to be. Taking Lehman through Ch. 11 bankruptcy imposed painful burdens on businesses and individuals who had relied on the bank and sent shock waves through the financial system. This led to the notion that some banks are too big to fail and therefore have to be propped by the government and subjected to extraordinary regulation, embodied in the 2010 Dodd-Frank Act.

Given the immense cost of the process, better solutions to insolvency are clearly needed. Thus John Taylor, Kenneth Scott and others (2012) proposed an simpler and expedited alternative bankruptcy route for large banks, tentatively christened Chapter 14. But that is still a proposal, not the law. For a small business, an practical alternative to Ch. 11 is Ch. 7, on which more later.

Manhattan Capital was unlike other companies that go through bankruptcy. It was unlike most small businesses, let alone a Lehman Brothers with many functioning parts. The hedge fund was a financial Humpty Dumpty broken beyond repair. It could not be put back together again under any circumstance — there was no functioning business. A hedge fund is based on the skills of one or a few individuals and is typically shuttered if the skills are not there. Berger did not have real investment ability, judging from his long run of losses. He claimed the business still had a future, having conceived the dream of operating the fund again, but that was pure fantasy.

Certainly the receiver did not obtain Chapter 11 protection to provide Berger with another shot at fund management — she did all she could to keep him away and even presented evidence of the fraud to make sure he would go to prison. There was no question of reorganizing Manhattan Capital, which had never achieved its proper goal, namely making money for investors. This was obvious before the bankruptcy filing.

Neither did Gredd need the additional legal status of bankruptcy to deal with the estate. Judge Cote's order gave her practically complete power, with the creditors not allowed to interfere. In effect, the estate was already set up for the purpose of winding down and returning the assets. For that purpose Chapter 11 protection did not appear to be necessary.

This is what some of the investors argued. They worried that while they were forbidden to touch their own money, it was likely to be spent on legal maneuvers in the course of a complicated bankruptcy process. So they sought a different legal status and possibly a different court.

The Bermuda account containing $15 million was subject to that jurisdiction. The Supreme Court of Bermuda named two specialists from the accounting firm KPMG to distribute the money. Malcolm Butterfield of KPMG Bermuda and Anthony McMahon of KPMG England were given a mandate for the Caribbean assets similar to the one Gredd received for the remaining property in the U.S., with the Bermuda court pointing out that international cooperation was necessary.

Legal opinion varies as to what law to use in winding down international hedge funds, but Chapter 11 is not the usual recommendation.[163] Butterfield and McMahon called a meeting and suggested to the creditors that Chapter 7, a simpler and cheaper process, provided a better way to deal with the assets left in America. Ch. 11 imposed enormous costs for the appointment of a creditors' committee with its own separate counsel.

Ch. 7 did not require the expense of a committee while providing all the necessary tools and powers to liquidate the assets and distribute the money. The Bermuda appointees suggested investors go to court in the U.S. and convert the case to a Ch. 7 bankruptcy.

Meanwhile in New York an alliance gathered around Gredd. In addition to her own firm, she hired as outside counsel two lawyers, Stuart and Marc Hirshfield, relatives who at the time worked at the firm Dewey Ballantine. They agreed to bill at a 10% discount from their usual hourly rate. With all the discounts, the receiver and her retinue started to sound like a great bargain.

The Chapter 11 filing brought Manhattan Capital and its fund – and related lawsuits – to the court of Burton Lifland, a long-time bankruptcy judge who knew Gredd's lawyer Stuart Hirshfield from way back. Any change had to be made through this court.

A large shareholder, the Bank of Austria, opposed Gredd's motion to become Ch. 11 trustee and tried to convert the case to Ch. 7. The bank said in a filing that the case did not belong in Ch.11 because "There is nothing to 'reorganize' and no ongoing business to wind down."[164] There was concern that Gredd would duplicate the work done by Butterfield and McMahon and the overlap of receivers would further run up costs. The investor questioned Gredd's "unfettered" status and compensation and whether the services of her law firm were really needed, pointing out that the Bermuda receivers had decades of experience in this kind of liquidation.

The lawyers in New York immediately mounted an aggressive counterattack against the Bermuda liquidators and the objecting investor. They suggested that the Bank of Austria did not represent the interests of other investors and the liquidators were in the game to line their own wallets.

Manhattan Fund's two outside directors were former employees of the bank and, according to the New York attorneys, when Berger called the directors to tell them about the SEC injunction against the fund, the bank had tried to a get a leg up on other creditors by putting a claim against the assets.[165]

Gredd complained to Judge Lifland that the Bermuda appointees showed no real interest in working with U.S. authorities, had not consulted her about the investors' meeting they arranged, did not allow her to take an active role in that meeting and had not replied to a lengthy protocol she drew up for their cooperation. She said she heard they were trying to get $2 million in fees; they were the ones wasting money, not her.

She maintained Ch. 11 was the right statute to go by and in any case the Bermuda liquidators did not have the legal standing to challenge her decision. She did not say why the less expensive Chapter 7 was unacceptable but pointed out that she gave up the receivership on becoming bankruptcy trustee and her hourly fee as trustee was no higher than it had been as receiver.

Bank of Austria made a second attempt to raise the Ch. 7 issue but Judge Lifland clearly favored Gredd and took a dim view of objectors. So the estate remained in Ch. 11, Gredd set up a creditors' committee and hired yet another legal team to represent it. This meant there were three sets of lawyers: Gredd and her firm, her outside attorneys (the two Hirshfields at Dewey Ballantine) and the firm she hired to represent the Chapter 11 creditors' committee.

This last was LeBoeuf, Lamb, Greene & MacRae, which in time merged with Dewey Ballantine. The two law firms that represented – in theory – two different interests in the estate combined to become Dewey & LeBoeuf. But the Hirshfields left Dewey Ballantine before the merger.

Lifland presided over the crowd of lawyers with aplomb. It was some years later that I came across the judge's name in the legal literature and learnt that he was famous in a certain field of study. Nobody pointed this out at the time the Manhattan estate was moved to his court, though at a deposition Stuart Hirshfield mentioned that Lifland was a distinguished judge and other lawyers as well must have known about his past.

In a sense one could say the judge was infamous. He made an appearance in a line of research about venue shopping in bankruptcy cases. In the 1980s, major corporate litigants with weak links to New York chose to file for bankruptcy in the city, in the court of Burton Lifland — him in particular, not other judges in the district. The remarkable pattern called for an explanation.

The leading researcher in this area, Lynn LoPucki, argued that competition for big cases corrupted bankruptcy courts.[166] The courts that transferred wealth from creditors to corporate managers and bankruptcy professionals were naturally preferred by managers and bankruptcy professionals. So it became common practice for them to shop for the right venue (from their point of view). In time Delaware displaced New York as the venue of choice for major bankruptcies. In both court districts, it looked like certain judges helped those who filed for bankruptcy and as a result the filers sought those judges.

Lifland favored debtors and reorganizers, among whom lawyers are the prominent group. The judge's decisions were seen as opposed to the interests of creditors. That made his court a surprising place – to say the least – for protecting fraud victims, that is, the investors in Manhattan Fund. Turned into creditors in the bankruptcy procedure, they were forbidden to interfere with the disposition of their property and the judge to whom they brought their claims was renowned for not being friendly to creditors.

The Bank of Austria episode was an early indicator of the judge's strong support for the group of lawyers around the trustee. In retrospect it is clear that any action by investors against the trustee was preordained to failure in that court — and as long as the bankruptcy continued, there was no way to go to any other court except by appealing Lifland's decisions in related cases. For the time being there were no appealable decisions and the investors were stuck.

Redeemers Pay

Gredd quickly shut down the Manhattan Capital office and got rid of the single employee. The landlord immediately offered to buy back the lease, but the lawyers decided to auction it off instead. They took about a year to organize the auction and hired an advisor for the purpose.

The same landlord bought the lease back in the auction, since the only other bid was for less money. It looked like the result that could have been achieved a year earlier without the waste of time and resources. But of course the process generated additional legal fees.

By February 2001, with the lease finally disposed of, there was no physical trace left of Manhattan Capital. It was defunct except for the bank accounts. Some of the money sitting in these accounts could have been returned to the investors, but that was the one option the three sets of lawyers had absolutely no interest in. They had other plans, as we learnt in due course.

The trustee pointed out that she worked with the SEC and the prosecutor's office. But helping the government make its case was not a long-term – or even valid – reason for billing the estate. The lawyers cast about for some other legal action to undertake.

"There are very, very few clear shots in this case …," the trustee's attorney told the judge, describing impediments such as ambiguities in jurisdiction between New York and Bermuda. But Stuart Hirshfield saw one bright spot for litigation, and with the financial analysis almost concluded, data were available by September 2000 to pursue that promising legal course.[167]

At issue were Berger's phantom profits that had become real money for the shareholders who redeemed from the fund. They had received much more than the true value of their investment, as happens in any Ponzi scheme. Although Manhattan Fund was a legitimate investment program to begin with, judges are willing to stretch the definition of a Ponzi and however one described the fiasco, it was clear that some investors benefitted at the expense of others.

Gredd's lawyers sued the redeemers. This was a highly successful legal venture, especially since the redeemers desired to avoid litigation and publicity. When Hirshfield demanded the return of the phantom gains and threatened to go to court, he quickly got results. For instance, an entity called Tower Long/Short Equities had put $20 million into Manhattan Fund in January 1999 and redeemed several months later with a supposed profit of $1.5 million. After a short negotiation, the $1.5 million was returned to the estate.[168]

Investors who did not want to be in the legal limelight had no recourse but to turn over the profits — any attempt to resist would have meant being dragged into a court proceeding. Many people or organizations across the world had invested and redeemed through financial intermediaries. They had no intention of being taken to a U.S. court. Their agents paid up once the trustee's lawyer demanded the money.

Hirshfield received the redeemers' gains without having to resort to much litigation.[169] It was a legal milestone. A precedent was clearly set, requiring beneficiaries of fraudulent schemes to pay back any fake profits they withdrew, whether or not they had knowledge of what was going on. This would affect all redeeming Ponzi scheme investors in the future.

By early 2004 Hirshfield reported to Lifland that these deals were just about complete and the additional money was part of the estate. Some time that year the assets were ready to be divided among the creditors. A long line presented themselves to be paid from the estate. The 52-page list of claims included a coffee service, publishers, a courier, a phone company and the Internal Revenue Service, in addition to hundreds of investors or their representatives.

Gredd had hired experts to investigate the market value of the investments and other assets left from the dead business, including the furniture and fixtures in the office. But that did not result in new information or any increase in the value of the estate. "Total assets cannot be determined with certainty due to the lack of complete and reliable records," stated a report several years after the investigations were complete.

So it looked like the trustee's mandate was done, the estate at long last ready to be wound down. I certainly thought so.

Who Sues Whom

If getting money back from redeemers had been the only action undertaken by the trustee coalition, the estate and the bankruptcy would indeed have ended in 2004, about five years after the hedge fund shut down. That was a long time for such a little business to be wound down—comparable to shutting down Enron, a gigantic company. However, it could possibly be justified as necessary to notify the redeemers, contact them and collect their payments.

But from the start the trustee group wanted to pursue bigger fish. They wanted to sue the fund's service providers. Toward this end, Gredd obtained open-ended authorization from Judge Lifland to compel the auditor to produce any document that might be relevant. The auditor was willing to give material to the Bermuda liquidators but not to the New York trustee, and the reason for this was obvious. As Gredd's lawyers put it in their petition to be allowed to force the issue, she was seeking information so as to craft "a strategy concerning litigation related to the collapse of the fund."

In fact, getting information was a minor issue compared to the real barrier that blocked any such litigation by the trustee. The investors emphatically did not want the estate lawyers to sue the service providers— those lawyers, chosen by regulators, were beyond their control and as likely to go against their interest as not. Neither did the investors want their cases to go the bankruptcy court and be subjected to Judge Lifland. To sue the fund's administrator and auditor, they hired independent attorneys on their own terms. Those attorneys had already started lawsuits in other courts.

As soon as the fraud surfaced, investors' representatives gathered in Geneva to make decisions. There were several countries where the victims could seek redress, including Austria, Britain, France and Switzerland. European banks and their clients loomed large among the shareholders; the American connection was by comparison weak. But U.S. law is friendlier to litigation, as American class action lawyers were at pains to point out to Berger's aggrieved clients. It did not take long for the latter to decide that they stood a better chance of getting reparation if they sued in America.

The exception was a group of 15 or so investors that had wired money to the Bank of Bermuda right before the fund was shut down and who sued in that jurisdiction to get their money back. A Bermuda court allowed them to proceed with the claim and froze the account. This caused consternation in the Gredd camp. The Bermuda liquidators, not able to use the money in Bermuda to pay their own expenses, might try to bill against the assets in America. "They were making eyes at our funds," the trustee's lawyer described the danger to the bankruptcy judge in New York.[170]

Gredd and her allies went to work and hammered out a settlement to pay investors about $8 million from the Bermuda account. That freed the rest of the Bermuda assets. From the New York lawyers' vantage, the settlement had several advantages — it allowed them dibs on what remained in the Bermuda account and reduced the portion of the estate under the control of their Bermuda rivals, while removing the reason for the latter to make claims against the assets in the U.S.[171]

The Bermuda receivers, willing to liquidate the remnants of the business, agreed to return assets to claimants in that locality. Meanwhile, other shareholders received nothing because their money remained tied up in the U.S. bankruptcy court. Like the Bermuda receivers the trustee was supposed to distribute assets to the investors as soon as possible, but that appeared to be the lowest priority.

Apart from the Bermuda angle, the consequences of Berger's numbers game were sorted out in New York courts. Given the large sums likely to change hands, numerous lawyers were more than happy to assist; law firms sought to get the job and made competing proposals to the fraud victims.[172] The latter picked from the pool the attorneys to sue the fund's administrator, auditor and brokers in U.S. District Court. At least 25 lawyers from 11 different firms worked on what became a significant class action case representing investors.

The Bermuda auditor and administrator were small firms that could simply close down, leaving little behind. So the game was to sue their corporate parents and affiliates. Thus the class action targeted three Deloitte businesses – the small Bermuda concern that audited Manhattan Fund; the much larger American firm Deloitte & Touche that was not involved in the audits; and the global umbrella corporation, Deloitte Touche Tohmatsu, with operations spanning some 130 countries.

The investors' desire to sue in the U.S. was predictably matched by the resistance of those being sued, in particular the Swiss parent of the Bermuda auditor. Defense attorneys repeatedly challenged the U.S. court's jurisdiction, arguing that the investors were foreign persons or organizations. There were American addresses in the investor list but these could belong to agents rather than to the real owners of the shares – for instance, a Chilean pension had invested via an American asset manager's New York office.

However, whether or not there were American clients turned out to be irrelevant. Regulators, prosecutors and judges found reasons to assume authority regardless of who or where the investors might be.

The Bermuda auditor was highly vulnerable to charges of breach of fiduciary duty and negligence, though the additional charge of aiding and abetting fraud was a stretch. Its reports on Manhattan Fund uniformly concluded, "In our opinion, such financial statements represent fairly, in all material respects, the financial position of the fund, in conformity with accounting principles generally accepted in the United States of America."[173] In fact the audits did not meet accepted standards and the accountants had failed to obtain reasonable assurance that the statements were accurate, especially given the Bear Stearns data showing otherwise.

But no litigation could get much from the Bermuda auditor since there wasn't much there. The parent company was a tempting target, though there was no indication that executives at the Swiss corporate headquarters of Deloitte Touche Tohmatsu were even aware of audit reports issued by a little Bermuda offshoot. The first time they heard of Manhattan Fund was probably when they were informed of impending lawsuits. The same can be said of Ernst &Young International, sued because of its relationship to the Bermuda administrator.

Various complaints were consolidated in a class action over which Judge Cote presided. She decided that the parent corporations were not involved; the use of the name was not sufficient to establish culpability. So she threw out the complaints against Ernst &Young and Deloitte Touche Tohmatsu. But the class action lawyers worked furiously to get the deep-pocketed targets back into the case and succeeded.

Most of the fund shareholders sought to make good their losses without revealing themselves — the private banks and financial businesses that had held shares for their customers continued to represent the investors without divulging their identities.

But a couple of plaintiffs stepped forward to testify against the service providers. Their replies to questioning by the defense revealed that the fund's investors had been at least as careless as the administrator and auditor they were suing.

Nevertheless, after a couple of years of legal maneuvers, the administrator settled the case. It came down to how much insurance money the investors could get from the defendants' insurer. A pact signed in December 2001 provided almost $41 million in total payment. Wrangling over the exact terms of the agreement and the compensation to be paid to lawyers went on for another several months. Some 62 investors objected to the legal fees on the ground that there was no documentation of services rendered and subpoenas were issued to get lawyers' time records and proof of expenses.[174] By the end of 2002 those matters were worked out and the administrator part of the class action put to rest.

The auditor continued to fight. Maybe Deloitte top brass did not want to set a precedent that would encourage all the hoodwinked investors in the world to haul it to American courts. But eventually the auditor – or its insurer – settled for the same total amount as the administrator.

The estate trustee and her legal entourage tried to involve themselves as much as possible in this class action, but their role was perfunctory. The attorneys who represented the investors had no wish to share the job and were mainly concerned that the trustee group not get in the way of the class action settlements. Even so, Hirshfield duly described the developments to the bankruptcy judge by way of explaining hefty charges against the estate in particular by Gredd's firm.

After several years, this rationale for holding on to the estate was wearing thin. The class action settlements were achieved by other lawyers and took effect; there was nothing more to be done. The settlements ruled out any further litigation against the auditor and administrator.

Legal Opportunity

Among the 12 defendants named in the class action in U.S. district court were Rader, his firm and Berger, but this was a mere legal formality since they lacked assets. Aside from the administrator and auditor, the main rich target was Bear Stearns. But the prime broker did not appear to be vulnerable.

After all, it had sent correct data to all concerned, repeatedly disputed Berger's fake numbers and warned the administrator and auditor. By any commonsense criterion it had functioned as a an impediment to the fraud. Indeed the class action plaintiffs themselves argued that the key to Berger's deception was his ability to convince others to ignore the reports from Bear Stearns. That suggested that the brokerage made the scheme more difficult — Berger had to work harder to hoodwink accountants.

On top of that, according to a widely accepted legal interpretation of U.S. securities law a brokerage is not responsible for deception committed by a customer. If brokers were held liable for everything their clients did, they could not stay in business and a large part of the financial sector would disappear. Hence on several grounds the bank had a strong defense, which was articulated by attorneys from the firm Schulte Roth & Zabel.

Considering the amount of money that can potentially be squeezed from an investment bank, the class action lawyers came up with ingenious arguments. Since the brokerage could not be accused of complicity in fraud for merely clearing Manhattan Fund's trades, the claims against it were based on two other issues. One was that Bear Stearns extended credit to Berger (by lending him securities to sell) that at times violated the brokerage's own margin requirements. The second matter was whether Bear executives told some people about the true state of the fund, giving them an advantage over other investors.

The class action complaint alleged that Bear Stearns allowed Berger credit in order to keep the operation going, thereby enabling favored clients to redeem their shares at artificially high values. This harmed the unsuspecting victims who remained in the fund. In fact the bankruptcy estate lawyers forced the redeemers to return those gains, but the class action made the charge against Bear Stearns anyway and demanded $1 billion in punitive damages.

Those arguments made no headway in district court. The fact remained that the brokerage owed no duty to the fund's investors, who were not its clients but its client's clients. As a practical matter Bear Stearns did even not know who the 1,000 ultimate shareholders were or how to contact them.[175] (Neither did the courts, even after years of litigation during which lawyers armed with subpoenas cast a wide global net to catch anyone who in any way had been involved with Manhattan Fund.) Bear executives happened to have business or social contacts with some investors and they alerted those as well as the administrator and auditor. This hindered Berger's deception.

As for the issue of the brokerage giving Berger extra credit, Judge Cote concluded that investors could not sue for violation of margin requirements.[176] Those rules are meant to protect the brokerage itself from taking on excessive risk by over-extending credit, not to protect its clients, let alone its clients' clients. On these considerations, the judge dismissed all charges against Bear Stearns in the class action.[177]

This was a notable decision. It looked like the bank and its attorneys had reason to celebrate. Their success was a legal landmark in affirming that brokerages do not owe fiduciary responsibility to their clients' investors and can't be held liable to the latter for temporarily violating their own margin rules. Reading Cote's decision, I had no doubt that Bear Stearns was clear of legal charges related to Manhattan Fund.

What happened next was a surprise, though in hindsight one does see a pattern. The auditor and administrator had settled, with the terms of their settlement precluding further litigation. Since the charges against Bear Stearns were dismissed in district court, it could not be sued again in that venue and on those grounds. But there was no settlement, so there was no provision preventing another lawsuit elsewhere. And the estate lawyers were all for litigation.

Only a week after Judge Cote dismissed the charges, Trustee Gredd initiated a separate lawsuit in Judge Lifland's bankruptcy court. In the name of the estate, she demanded several billion dollars from the bank. Bear Stearns' beating the class action charges turned out to be grand new opportunity for the Gredd faction.

Since the main facts and charges had already been hashed out and unambiguously rejected by Judge Cote, the new litigation had to be based on some other argument. Gredd offered a novel take on broker liability, though the basic issues remained the same. She argued that during the last 10 months of the fund's operation Bear either knew or should have known that a fraud was in process and that therefore all the transfers to the brokerage during that time were fraudulent and had to be paid back to the estate.

By this unusual reckoning, the fraudulent transfers included the securities Berger borrowed and sold, depositing the proceeds at Bear Stearns, plus the same securities bought and returned to the brokerage. Berger's 1999 stock sales added up to $1.7 billion, but shares worth $1.9 billion were returned to Bear Stearns to close the trades. In addition to those amounts, the trustee set her sight on the collateral that Berger had deposited at Bear Stearns in order to borrow securities over the 10-month period. This collateral came to $141.4 million. And she wanted Bear Stearns to be further punished by being the last creditor to be paid should it make any claim against the estate.

The trustee group contended that each transaction furthered Berger's scheme, that all transfers "were made with actual intent to hinder, delay and defraud the fund's creditors," and that "Bear Stearns cannot meet its burden of establishing that it acted in good faith in accepting the transfers..."[178] On that basis, they demanded the brokerage make a payment to the estate of no less than $1.9 billion but possibly as high as the aggregate $3.6 billion that it supposedly should not have received — because by this reasoning each and every transaction was part of Berger's scheme.

The case in bankruptcy court upped the ante but the multi-billion-dollar claim rested on the same facts as the previous suit in district court. Outside lawyers gave this attempt low odds of success. News reports predicted that lawyers for Bear Stearns would have little trouble beating the new suit as they had the previous charges.[179] That forecast eventually turned out to be correct, but eventually can mean much more time in the legal world than in a market.

Imaginative and Novel

While the case was based on the same events, there were key differences between the class action in district court and the subsequent suit by the trustee in bankruptcy court. Noteworthy was the difference in the judges' attitudes. Lifland was exceptionally amenable to the trustee and her lawyers. When she sued Bear Stearns, from the get go the bankruptcy judge sounded sympathetic to the case. Apparently well aware of this, the bank's lawyers sought repeatedly to change the venue. With these attempts they won another victory.

U.S. District Judge Naomi Buchwald granted their motion to withdraw the proceeding from bankruptcy court on the ground that the case required substantial consideration of federal securities law. Once the suit moved to district court, the bank's attorneys asked Buchwald to dismiss the main charges. Once again, they succeeded—but not completely.

Judge Buchwald made legal history by spelling out the argument as to why a trustee could not be allowed to reverse short selling transfers. The trustee's $3.6 billion claim was based on murky reasoning, Judge Buchwald's opinion showed. The $1.7 billion and $1.9 billion proceeds did not belong to the fund; the sums corresponded to securities that were loans from the brokerage and by law had to be returned. The only obligation these monies could satisfy was to cover the short sales.

These amounts were not revenue for Bear Stearns. All in all, the brokerage received $2.4 million revenue from Manhattan Fund's trades over three and a half years, mostly in the form of interest earned on balances that it held in custody. But Gredd was not trying to squeeze a modest $2.4 million; after a few years the estate lawyers' fees and expenses far exceeded that sum. It would have been hard to justify spending so much of the estate to get back a measly couple of million dollars.

As for Gredd's rebuttal that the transfers to Bear had made other creditors worse off, Buchwald saw that argument as an end-run around the earlier decision by Cote. The judge reaffirmed that the brokerage owed no fiduciary duty to its client's investors and declined "to entertain this oblique assault on (the prior) decision." [180]

On a related matter, too, Buchwald echoed the earlier opinion by Cote. She pointed out that margin requirements are there to protect brokerages, not other parties. Therefore a brokerage that continues to execute trades despite margin violations is not abetting fraud. It might be taking excessive risk itself, but that was not the issue. Gredd argued that Bear protected itself very effectively while the investors lost money and therefore should compensate them by paying the estate. This argument was rejected by the two district court judges.

Buchwald described Gredd's brief as "imaginative and novel."[181] That expression does not suggest that the trustee's argument made sense. One could, less kindly, depict Gredd's brief as implausible. It defied logic to argue that a brokerage should pay to the government-appointed overseer of its client's defunct business the value of securities it had once lent to that client, plus the value of the same securities when they were returned.

But certainly the move was bold, and it was effective in one particular respect: it allowed the trustee group to retain control over the remnants of Manhattan Fund. Were she deprived of the Bear Stearns litigation, the trustee's last reason for hanging on to the estate would have evaporated. Thus it was fortunate for her and her associates that while Judge Buchwald struck down the billion-dollar claims against Bear, one claim was left standing.

The estate was allowed to continue to sue for the $141 million collateral Berger had deposited at the brokerage in 1999 and the shrunken case was referred back to the venue the estate lawyers clearly preferred—the bankruptcy court. The trustee team became noticeably more confident upon returning to that familiar haunt, a confidence well justified by the decisions Judge Lifland handed to them.

Key Remaining Asset

Forced back to the bankruptcy court, Bear Stearns' lawyer Harry Davis sought to make a distinction between two aspects of Manhattan Fund. He pointed out that the investment program was a bona fide business with an approach fully explained to investors. Indeed, Berger had all but shouted his investment strategy from the rooftops and the short selling was perfectly legal. His deception consisted of hiding the losses from his clients.

The securities subject to fraud were Manhattan Fund's own shares, not the stocks Berger traded. Davis argued that Bear Stearns was not involved in the deception, only in the legitimate trading. Moreover, the margin transfers the trustee challenged had been disclosed to investors and were clearly above-board. Gredd claimed that all transfers are fraudulent if there is a Ponzi scheme; Davis replied that there had to be a link between the fraud and the specific transfer.[182] Berger did not commit a crime in trading or borrowing on margin and that was the business Bear did with him.

This argument is clear when applied to other types of companies: Enron's accounting fraud did not mean that its payment, say, to a supplier of pipes was also fraudulent. It would have struck most people as unreasonable to force the pipe supplier to return the money Enron paid for pipes because Enron executives concealed the company's true financial state from shareholders. A brokerage, similarly, is paid for legitimate services. Davis contended that Gredd merely repackaged in another guise arguments already rejected in district court.

In the trustee's interpretation, the trades were connected to the phony returns because the capital was obtained via fraud.[183] But in fact Berger did not need to trade at all to perpetrate deception—he could have claimed sham returns without doing a single trade. That's what Bernard Madoff did for years. Berger's trades were expressions of a genuine investment strategy, however foolhardy.

At the hearing where these exchanges took place the bankruptcy judge was as icy to Bear's attorney as he was friendly to the trustee's lawyers. Lifland cut off Davis as he explained a point. "What you are saying and what Ms. Gredd is saying, there is an issue here as to the breadth of a Ponzi presumption. I will deal with that," the judge said, curtly dismissing the defense.

As soon as the Bear Stearns contingent left and the estate attorney Hirschfield took the floor to talk about other matters, the judge became genial and even joked about the bank.[184] In view of his diametrically opposed attitudes to the two parties, it came as no revelation when he rejected Davis' argument.[185]

Thereupon the bank tried again to wriggle out of the bankruptcy court, asking Buchwald for permission to appeal the decision. But this time the district judge would not intervene. "(W)e are not persuaded that this is the type of rare situation which demands our immediate review," wrote Buchwald, opining that there was no major issue of law at that stage. Bear could later appeal the final judgment of the bankruptcy court.[186]

It seemed certain that Lifland would decide against the bank and just as certain that the bank would appeal. Bear Stearns had a reputation for fighting lawsuits to the end rather than settling.[187] Bankruptcy court decisions are frequently overturned, so the chance of an appeal is better than it would be if the verdict came from district court.

But no appeal was possible until the final judgment. After some years, it seemed that the judgment would never come. The trustee proceeded to conduct lengthy new investigations, questioning everybody involved about events that happened in December 1998, when an investment adviser who worked for financier Arpad Busson ran into a Bear Stearns managing director at a cocktail party and mentioned that they were told Berger's fund made 20% that year.

These events were well known, having been described in the district court suit and failed to persuade Judge Cote of Bear Stearns' liability. Nevertheless, the trustee insisted on questioning everybody all over again. The investigations took years and substantial resources.

Busson resided in London, where his lawyers went to the Royal Courts to oppose the order from the New York bankruptcy court. A High Court justice decided Busson was not a party to the New York litigation. British law did not allow fishing expeditions on non-party witnesses prior to a trial. So Busson could not be forced to answer questions for discovery, where the idea is to dig for any evidence. He could only be deposed for trial at a later stage, when the information sought from him had been narrowed down.

American lawyers often did not understand that difference, said the British judge. And when they don't, quipped Busson's attorney, "they run the risk of wasting a great deal of time and money, as is happening now." Thereupon the London court awarded Busson £70,000 in legal costs.

Gredd forked over the sum and agreed not to bring claims against Busson or his firm; in return he made himself available for questioning after the discovery came to an end.[188] The money came from the estate, of course, like all other expenses.[189]

It is not clear that questioning Busson elicited useful new evidence. The case did not really turn on a particular incident — the defense's key argument rested on basic tenets of securities law and if accepted made the 1998 conversation irrelevant.

Davis pointed out that the collateral did not belong to Bear Stearns, so the brokerage was not responsible for paying it back. Bear was a mere conduit to the transfers in question, the money never belonged to it and could be used legally only to meet the obligations of Manhattan Fund.[190] Since Bear could not use the collateral for its own purposes, it did not have control. Once this is granted, Davis said, it renders moot the rest of the voluminous record and evidence, for nothing else will matter.[191]

What did belong to the brokerage was the $2.4 million it made from Berger's trades. But Gredd did not sue for that paltry – considering the estate's expenses – sum.

Judge Lifland sounded irate when Davis offered to walk him through the material. "I have gone through, God knows, how many pages on this issue from you," said the judge. "And unless you don't think that you are clear in your briefs, I see no need to expand on that."[192] He obviously did not agree with the lawyer's view that this was the key issue that made everything else superfluous.

While the size of the fraudulent transfer claim had come down dramatically from the original $3.6 billion to the $141 million collateral, even a smaller settlement from the bank would be an obvious boon to the estate. Already in January 2004, Hirschfield reported to Lifland that "the Bear Stearns litigation is the key remaining asset in this estate."[193] Lifland favored the trustee's case. On the other hand, there were the previous opinions by two district court judges.

Bear Stearns, true to its reputation for fighting lawsuits, showed no evidence of being willing settle. And the trustee showed no interest in a quick resolution. Six years after she started the suit, a jury had not even been assembled. Then it turned out there would be no jury after all. Gredd moved for a "summary judgment" by the judge as a matter of law, on the ground that there was no issue of fact.

Bear Stearns contended that it was entitled to a jury trial. Lifland's final decision in the case, like all his decisions, was a boon to the trustee. He granted her request for summary judgment without a jury trial, so that the ruling was up to him alone. Unsurprisingly, he ruled in the estate lawyers' favor.

This, too, made legal history. Lifland's opinion was seen as imposing a novel standard on prime brokers, turning them into de facto regulators of hedge funds.[194] In particular, Lifland opined that the broker could not be allowed to claim good faith because its efforts to expose the fraud had been insufficient. He argued that Bear Stearns should have investigated more aggressively and earlier.[195]

The only issue on which the judge sided with Bear Stearns concerned a glaring mistake made by the trustee's law firm. It was so obvious that it should have been corrected years ago. Berger had not lost all of the $141.4 million transferred to Bear as collateral—$16.3 million was left at the brokerage. Back in early 2000, Gredd demanded that this money be turned over to her and Bear complied. Despite having already received this portion of the money, Gredd asked that Lifland order the brokerage to pay the full $141.4 million plus interest.

Davis pointed out the double counting, there being no question that the money had been in the trustee's control for almost seven years. Gredd's colleague replied that Bear had not claimed this before—but in fact it had in several court filings.

Perhaps the Gredd camp was so sure of the judge's sympathetic ear, they did not pay attention to details like having already received $16 million. They could be sloppy and still win. Lifland deducted that amount and made Bear Stearns liable for the remaining $125 million that had seven-plus years ago been collateral for Berger's trades, plus interest.

At that point the judge suggested he was expediting the matter for judicial economy and the preservation of the estate, but as he observed, "This case has been pending for seven years."[196] At the end of the hearing in 2007 he asked the defense counsel if he was going to appeal and suggested that he sounded like a mediator.

Lifland no doubt preferred that there be no appeal. Having ruled against Bear Stearns, he would not want his decision overturned by another court, an event that does not enhance a judge's reputation. If Davis negotiated a smaller sum and his client paid up, that outcome would justify the bankruptcy judge's opinion. It might also justify the estate lawyers' billings.

Very Substantial Amount

The trustee, her outside lawyers, her accountants and the attorneys she hired for the creditors' committee appeared in front of Lifland every four or six months to justify their compensation. Over the years the exact sums varied and the reasons for the billings evolved, but the central point did not change: there were legal opportunities or complications and myriad matters to attend to, which of course necessitated many billable hours.

As a veteran bankruptcy judge, Lifland was familiar with the problem. "Put another way, there are two honey pots, " he said in 2000, referring to the U.S. and Bermuda assets; "and I am fearful that before this whole thing gets off the ground in litigation form, those honey pots may be exhausted."[197] But in practice he stayed true to his reputation for favoring bankruptcy professionals. Occasional admonitions and expressions of doubt notwithstanding, he always approved the payments the lawyers made to themselves from the estate.

In the early years Hirshfield often prefaced his presentation to the judge with a reminder that the trustee's firm had agreed to a 20% discount from its customary hourly fee and he himself was billing at a 10% discount. That did little to keep down total payments. "The numbers are rather large," Lifland said in December 2000.[198] For the four-month period from the beginning of July through the end of October of that year, the various professionals had billed more than $1.4 million in total for fees and expenses.[199]

Most of these costs, Lifland noticed, had been incurred "in connection with forensic activity as a prelude to litigation and administration of the wind down of the business." But the business was already wound down "and the numbers here are quite high." That was just the beginning. The 2000 billings Lifland expressed concern over were in fact merely the harbinger of numerous rounds to follow.

In 2000 and 2001, a major source of billable hours was the Gredd team's desire to examine the records of the fund administrator and auditor. Then the focus shifted to the suit against Bear Stearns. As year after year passed, the judge appeared to lose track. In July 2004, for instance, he noticed that Gredd's firm alone had billed a total of around a million dollars at two recent hearings, "a very, very substantial amount," as he put it.[200]

The lawyers said the expenditure was mostly related to the Bear Stearns litigation. "Was there a prior award in connection with the Bear Stearns matter?" asked Lifland.[201] There had been "prior awards" related to that matter and the total was more than the "very, very substantial amount" that came to the judge's attention just then.

Gredd acknowledged that the "litigation has been pending for some period of time," but said the application was not "solely for Bear Stearns." She said it included the settlement in the U.S. District Court of the class action. But the class action was negotiated by other lawyers who were paid from the proceeds of the settlement according to their agreement with the investors who hired them. Gredd mentioned also the efforts to get back phantom appreciation from redeemers. But Hirshfield did the work of pursuing the redeemers and his fees were separate from the trustee's own bill that the judge observed was substantial.

At that juncture, the law firm in charge of the creditors' committee, LeBoeuf, came to Gredd's aid. When the judge questioned her fees, a member of LeBoeuf stepped up and declared the expenditures "reasonable".[202]

By choosing to take the Chapter 11 route, Gredd had created this apparatus, providing herself with another party to back up legal bills. Had she agreed to the simpler (and cheaper) bankruptcy procedure that some investors preferred, there would have been no creditors' committee. The committee's attorneys received their appointment thanks to the trustee and were paid handsomely. When there was any question, she rigorously defended their fees. They returned the favor.

The legal rationale for the committee was that it would speak on behalf of the creditors. In practice the LeBoeuf lawyers uniformly supported the trustee who gave them this lucrative job. They told the judge there was no objection to the way she was using the assets. LeBoeuf struggled to find sources of revenue, merging with Dewey in an attempt to gain business. The firm's partners no doubt appreciated the Manhattan bankruptcy money. Later this law firm failed, going bankrupt in 2012.[203]

As for the investors, the protection of whose interests was the ostensible reason for paying a third group of lawyers, no one in bankruptcy court seemed to remember them. The costs were borne by people who were not allowed to interfere with the trustee's use of their money. A more convenient arrangement for the lawyers is hard to imagine, an arrangement in effect provided to them by the Securities and Exchange Commission.

In time, presenting and justifying their own fees and expenses became a job in itself for the groups of lawyers. It was not a simple task. When Stuart and Marc Hirshfield moved to another law firm, they prepared a 121-page bill summarizing the work they had done for the estate until then. They continued to work for Gredd but were required to submit a final reckoning of compensation at the previous firm.

The document filed with the court in December 2002 showed that as the trustee's outside counsel they had collected almost $2.8 million in expenses and fees for less than three years.[204] According to this bill, during the period in question these lawyers assisted and advised the trustee, communicated with various parties and "successfully finalized" the settlement with Ernst & Young, thereby recovering nine cents on the dollar for investors. The fact that other attorneys hired by the investors had in fact negotiated the settlement was somehow forgotten. However, the Hirshfields were on sound ground in claiming credit for getting bogus profits back from redeemers.

By way of defending the fees, Stuart Hirshfield pointed out that the estate had saved $330,000 to date thanks to the 10% discount he gave off his rate of $720.[205] One suspects that the lawyers were perfectly happy to knock a bit off their rate. Had the contract been open to competition, other attorneys would have been delighted to take it on. The discount notwithstanding, the trustee and her various confederates cost investors millions of dollars a year as the suit against Bear Stearns lumbered along.

By the sixth year of the trustee's reign, many of the fraud victims were no longer willing to wait. They gave up on the estate and sold their shares at steep discounts to speculators who take this kind of legal risk. At least one investor talked of suing the trustee. But this was not possible at the time. She had been given wide immunity by court order and any attempt to hold her accountable had to wait for the winding down of the estate and the final accounting of its assets.

To say that the trustee alliance was in no hurry to get to that point is a flagrant understatement. Certainly the investors received plenty of legal services. Nobody could say that the lawyers weren't active. If anything, on the basis of their billings they appeared to be positively frantic in their activity.

Afterlife of a Hedge Fund

There is in the Justice Department a bureau whose responsibility is to prevent abuses by trustees of bankrupt estates. In some prominent cases involving well-connected creditors, this agency has taken effective action, for example forcing Enron's liquidator to cut in half a $25 million fee.[206] In the Manhattan Fund case, the federal overseer repeatedly disputed the payments made from the estate.

Initially the watchdog objected to obvious little items like fax and telephone charges rather than the millions of dollars in legal fees.[207] The judge noticed this and asked that the lawyers provide a better description of their charges.[208] But presented in detail the legal bills could run to hundreds of pages. Scrutinizing these was clearly beyond the capability of the government bureau's modest staff, who confronted three lavishly financed law firms. Ironically, the resources at the disposal of the estate lawyers, given to them by regulators and courts, originally belonged to the people whose interests the trustee was supposed to protect.

The Justice Department watchdog persistently objected to the way Manhattan Fund's assets were spent but did not challenge specific fees. Instead the overseer asked that 15% of the total billed by the lawyers be held back until the outcome of their actions could be seen. This objection did not require analysis of billing details. It was, in effect, a request to make a small portion of the fees contingent on results—a common practice in class action suits. Year after year Judge Lifland refused the Justice Department's request.

Notably, the only bill that ran into trouble in the bankruptcy court belonged to the law firm that filed Bank of Austria's objection to Gredd.[209] This was the one instance when Lifland refused to ratify a payment, despite the fact that the amount was tiny compared to the fees he approved for the trustee and company. The judge suggested that this investor was making trouble, causing an extra expense. Yet the cost of the unsuccessful challenge was insignificant relative to the payments it sought to question. The incident sent a powerful message early in the bankruptcy case: if you get on the wrong side of the trustee, the estate will not pay your legal bills.

Any challengers would have to pay out of their pocket while the Gredd team warding off the complaint would compensate themselves from the ready pot of money (that in principle belonged to the complainants). This financial asymmetry stymied threats to the trustee's authority. After the early years, investors no longer formally challenged Gredd.

In 2007, the estate lawyers submitted yet another round of hefty bills that included the many hours they had spent on paperwork for their own compensation. On this occasion Judge Lifland voiced some annoyance. He said the bills contained "an enormous amount in just reviewing fee applications and reviewing court filing papers."[210] The bills included payment for a barrister hired for Gredd to "to baby-sit" a deposition she took in London, probably of Busson. "Ms. Gredd, you have a lot of baby-sitters," said Lifland.

To show his disapproval, the judge modified his initial order so that now the lawyers would have to pay themselves quarterly – as required by statute – instead of monthly as he had allowed them to do for more than seven years. "It might encourage the parties to really focus on moving this case along, and not with an idea that there's always money around to fuel the armies," he said.[211] But as usual he granted the full amounts they billed.

Lifland turned the fee issue around to the defense counsel. "I recognize that Mr. Davis has a client that may not have concerns about paying his bill, but I think ultimately after seven years even Bear Stearns may question the wisdom of remaining in litigation over this lengthy period of time," the judge said.

Of course, Davis' client had not asked to be sued for so many years. As for defense attorney's bills, the bank had chosen to hire him and agreed to pay his fee. Manhattan Fund's creditors had not hired Gredd to litigate in their name. Indeed, some of them had done everything possible to avoid the process she set in motion. She did what she liked with their property because the government gave her the power, not because the investors wanted her to.

Would the investors have spent so much money on the interminable lawsuit against Bear Stearns if they, rather than regulator-designated lawyers, were in charge? In the class action they initiated themselves, the investors did not shell out all the fees and expenses up front. Much of the payments were contingent — in order to be compensated, attorneys had to win the case or get the service providers to settle. If the investors had chosen to pursue another suit against Bear Stearns, they would have almost certainly made legal fees contingent on the success of the action, at least in part.

After Judge Cote ruled in Bear Stearns' favor, class action lawyers were less inclined to pursue the brokerage because further legal action did not seem likely to bring in money. Attorneys whose main compensation comes from settlements have little reason to engage in suits with a low chance of paying. That was not a concern for the Gredd faction because they paid themselves from the estate's ready cash.

Without the long-defunct fund's money to finance it, the many years of litigation that came after Cote's decision would have likely never happened. Had they already received their property back from the estate, the investors would not have risked it all over again on an expensive, lengthy and highly uncertain lawsuit.

The end of the tale suggests the trustee's litigation against the brokerage was not justified. As expected, Bear Stearns appealed Lifland's decision and the case was returned to district court. There Judge Buchwald decided that a trial was necessary to determine whether Bear had acted in good faith. By the time the trial finally took place, another bubble had burst, the real estate market collapsed and losses in mortgage-backed securities set off a crisis. Bear Stearns no longer existed as an independent company.

Therefore the bank that went on trial was JP Morgan Chase, which acquired Bear Stearns amid the crisis. In the summer of 2008, a jury found that Bear Stearns was not liable for failing to discover fraud at Manhattan Fund and had been diligent in its inquiries during the period in question.[212] For the fraud victims, the many years of litigation by the trustee had been a outrage—committed under the aegis of the Securities and Exchange Commission, which chose the receiver, and the bankruptcy judge who supported the lawyers' alliance around the estate.

Even after that, it took the estate lawyers more than a year to come up with a final liquidation plan for Manhattan Capital and its fund. This document, dated December 22, 2009, for closing down a business that had not operated for a decade, cost the estate additional billable hours. And the process of "liquidating" was still going on in 2011.

So having failed abysmally in its original goal of making money for investors, Manhattan Fund functioned very effectively as a revenue generating vehicle for another group of people. It operated as a hedge fund for less than four years, but for well over a decade it led a twilight existence in the form of pots of money presided over by government-appointed lawyers. This second life functioned so well as a legal fee maker that it provided an alluring model for attorneys, as we will see.

Thereafter, people who knew the Manhattan saga did everything possible to dispense with the voluminous services of a trustee. When futures brokerage Refco landed in bankruptcy court, its creditors fought hard to simplify the bankruptcy process and in particular to avoid the appointment of a trustee. At least one judge agreed that "The appointment of a trustee is an extraordinary remedy," not always necessary.[213]

But victims of fraud typically don't have a choice after the SEC takes charge. For lawyers with the connections to implement the Manhattan estate blueprint, the path to legal Nirvana was clear. What they needed to do was to get the receivership of a defunct fund with sizable assets to recoup – the more complicated the situation the better – and file for bankruptcy in a sympathetic court. Then they could engage in elaborate litigation at fabulous pay, with guaranteed tenure for a decade or more.

CHAPTER SEVEN. Honey Jackpot

Michael Berger was of course right about Bernard Madoff. I will not repeat the familiar Madoff story, since there is much written about it.[214] My purpose here is to look at the sequel — that is, what happened to the investors after the government took over. Despite differences in circumstances, there are remarkable similarities in the fates of the two estates left behind by Berger and Madoff.

    The two schemes were not alike as investment programs or businesses — Manhattan was a real hedge fund whereas Madoff did not run a fund, he supposedly opened brokerage accounts for his clients and traded from those accounts. That aside, Berger and Madoff followed a common pattern into infamy. Both fudged returns and ended up in a Ponzi situation that is the automatic result of claiming fake profits. To keep up the pretense they had to pay those profits to redeeming investors. As a result some clients received money that came from other clients.

    Madoff, a man with a well-regarded brokerage business and high standing, could not have started off with a plan to swindle his acquaintances. Why he did so is not clear. He was not poor to begin with, though over time his legitimate brokerage business appears to have withered. Caught in a vicious cycle, he lied to get money; passed much of the money on to redeemers; and lied again to get more money and pay redeemers, and so on.

A plausible explanation of why he kept up the charade is that he was unable to relinquish the ego trip of having people revere him as a financial genius.[215] This may be a special instance of the bad influence of fame that Tyler Cowen has pointed out as a general phenomenon. A strong desire for reputation can induce people to delude themselves and lie to others — contrary to mainstream economists' view that the quest to protect one's reputation results in good behavior.[216]

In some ways Madoff was distinctive. Berger kept his faith in his investment program to the end, short selling stocks to profit from the collapse of the bubble until he was apprehended. Madoff apparently decided long ago that his strategy did not work – though he described it as doable even after he went to prison – and stopped trying to implement it. He gave himself up; Berger tried to keep going.

But with regard to the role of regulators, there are fundamental similarities between the two schemes. One is the illusion of safety created by government oversight. Assurances from Rader, a regulated broker, bolstered Berger's fabrications and enabled him to trick the fund's administrator and auditor. Madoff benefitted from powerful boosts to his credibility after regulators repeatedly examined him and appeared to find no evidence of wrongdoing.

Then there is the matter of the estates. If Manhattan Fund provided honey pots for lawyers favored by regulators, the sequel to the Madoff con game was a honey jackpot.

Never a Loss

Madoff appeared on the government's radar as a potential problem some 16 years before he turned himself in. His name came up in an 1992 investigation when two people complained to the SEC about investments they made with a firm called Avellino & Bienes. The investments came with guaranteed returns ranging from 13.5% to 20% and were described as 100% safe. Marketing materials claimed that "In over 20 years there has never been a losing transaction."[217]

Upon receiving the complaints the SEC looked into the matter, suspecting that Avellino & Bienes ran a Ponzi scheme. It turned out that the firm invested clients' capital with Bernard L. Madoff Investment Securities. Investors received their money back and Avellino & Bienes was shut down. That satisfied the regulators and they did not look into the Madoff brokerage accounts that held investor money.

In particular, they did not investigate whether the money paid to Avellino & Bienes clients came from other people's accounts. Neither did the SEC alert the brokerage overseer NASD — at least, there is no evidence of a communication regarding this matter and NASD officials said they were not told about it.

Also, regulators could have checked with the independent custodian of brokerage accounts. Had they done so, there was an excellent chance they would have uncovered the scheme in 1992 — so concluded a study 17 years later.[218]

But the SEC found nothing wrong with Madoff. Thus reassured and desirous of the same robust and safe returns, a number of former Avellino & Bienes clients gave their money directly to Madoff. Later 25 investors testified that they knew of and relied upon a 1992 statement from the SEC to the effect that there was no evidence of fraud.[219] One client kept in her files a copy of an article reporting the clean bill of health. "Since we were so sure that all was well if our government had checked we went directly into Madoff Investment Co. from Avellino & Bienes," an investor said.

Berger undermined the private oversight system of fund administrator and auditor with the aid of a regulated broker. In the Madoff hoax, another private control mechanism sprung into action — Harry Markopolos, an analyst working for a competitor, found that Madoff's supposedly safe strategy was a sure way to lose money. Given that the strategy did not work, Markopolos inferred that Madoff's reported returns were bogus.

This check on fraud was undermined by the regulators themselves. Markopolos presented detailed reports to the SEC showing that the returns were suspect.[220] He submitted his first report in 2000 and subsequently added to the analysis and offered expanded versions periodically as he became increasingly convinced that Madoff was engaged in a massive Ponzi scheme. He had conversations with various government agents.

When that had no effect, he spread the word to the press. In 2001, journalist Michael Ocrant published a lengthy expose in an industry journal.[221] Other articles pointed to Madoff's extreme secrecy and his appointment of family members to vital posts at his firm.[222] In addition to the 1992 incident and reports from Markopolos, there were a number of complaints to regulators about Madoff.

Explaining the failure of his repeated attempts to get the government to find the fraud, Markopolos suggests that the SEC was not capable of going after a highly regarded figure like Madoff.[223] It was not just that Madoff was an eminent Wall Street player, part of the establishment, a philanthropist who sat on a university board. Probably more important was the fact that he had numerous high-level government connections. He hobnobbed with top regulators. They asked for his advice on financial markets. When his niece married a former SEC assistant director, several high-level officials attended the wedding. He made political contributions — primarily to Democrats, judging from surviving records.

All that said, Madoff's professional and social standing and government ties did not stop regulators from investigating him time and again. True, he awed the examiners with the names of the SEC higher-ups he knew. They were impressed by his inside knowledge of the next, not-yet-announced SEC chairman.

Inside the bureaucracy, the examiners were tacitly discouraged from getting too aggressive, told that "He is a very well-connected, powerful person." One examiner testified that supervisors appeared to be reluctant to push against influential people.

Nevertheless, they went on investigating him. That is perhaps the most amazing aspect of the story. Different departments of the SEC did separate, lengthy investigations of Madoff. His broker-dealer business was separately subject to the industry watchdog NASD and its successor the Financial Industry Regulatory Authority. NASD and FINRA did routine inspections of the Madoff brokerage at least every other year and investigated 19 complaints. But those complaints were about trade execution problems, not fraud.

Not only did the SEC not tell NASD/FINRA of the fraud suspicions, two separate SEC offices investigated in 2003-2004 without telling each other. They realized this only when Madoff told one team that he had already given to the other SEC team the information they sought. Both groups came across similar evidence that raised suspicion. They found that Madoff was making more money with his secretive investment business than with his well-known brokerage operation.

Bernie the Bluffer

The common excuses that the SEC missed Madoff's Ponzi scheme because its examiners were inexperienced or because there weren't enough resources do not hold up. The agency's own report claims the junior staff failed to appreciate the significance of Markopolos' analysis. But in fact some junior investigators realized there was something wrong and left to themselves would have almost certainly discovered the truth. They were prevented by a senior SEC manager.

A lot of resources were spent on Madoff and at least one team of examiners caught his lies — and left an email trail saying so. One concern was that he was front running his brokerage customers, using information from orders coming to the brokerage to trade for his investment clients. Front running is a serious offense that would have landed Madoff in legal trouble, but the examiners would have done better following the evidence set forth by Markopolos.

What was clear to everybody was Madoff's extraordinary ability to avoid losses. How did he achieve this? To convince regulators that he did not cheat by going ahead of brokerage orders, Madoff trotted out the notion that his trading was automatically driven by a black box computer model. That led examiners to ask questions about the black box. Since he had no "box" he switched to another explanation, namely that he traded on his gut feelings. The SEC examiner who came nearest to calling Bernie's bluff was not convinced.

SEC teams identified inconsistencies in Madoff's replies. To explain why his options trades were not showing up in the market, he said he stopped trading S&P 100 Index options, the instrument his strategy supposedly used. But a large feeder fund, Fairfield Greenwich, showed trading in S&P 100 options for the Madoff investment program. One SEC examiner asked another in an email: "would you have time to take a look at the data to see if I am missing some obvious – and innocent – explanation for this?" The obvious explanation was that Madoff was not telling the truth, and it is hard to imagine how that could be innocent.

This team of examiners was supervised by an SEC veteran with decades of experience. Therefore the claim that inexperience led to mistakes is nonsense: in fact it was the supervisor who told the examiners not to proceed further. He decided against the next step, which was to talk with the feeder fund operators — in effect, Madoff's outside marketers.

The reason for the supervisor's decision appears to be self protection. He mentioned that he was afraid of being sued by Madoff if the feeder funds pulled their assets, but this is not plausible. While any business manager in America fears being sued, a federal agency is largely protected from liability. It is extremely difficult, if not impossible, to succeed in suing a regulator — Landis' generation made sure of that.

And of all people, Madoff was the most unlikely to start a lawsuit. That would have meant being questioned. He was famous for his extreme secrecy, as the SEC staff knew. This was a man who did not want to take questions in private or give information to long-time associates; no way would he subject himself to hostile lawyers in a public courtroom. That may be hindsight, but the fact remains that being sued by Madoff was improbable had the SEC pursued the investigation.

There were other reasons for closing the case — SEC examiners had already spent plenty of time investigating Madoff while brokerage overseer NASD (later FINRA) was the primary regulator of the firm and would in any case conduct additional exams. However, the examiners on the ground were not satisfied. "We still knew and felt that it was highly suspicious," one said later.[224]

The SEC supervisor may have had reasons beyond what was stated for not pursuing the matter further. Madoff was aggressive in resisting investigations into the questionable parts of his story and not shy about raising hell — as long as it did not involve publicity. Had the examiners gone on, he might have privately complained to his high-level contacts that the SEC was harassing him.

From the supervisor's point of view, the options were angering a politically connected man versus saving himself the hassle. Put that way, it was an easy choice. If he is anything like the rest of humanity, the supervisor did not want a lot of aggravation and possible career risk. He took the path of least effort and risk to himself.

A comical upshot of years of examining Madoff's business was that the SEC eventually required him to register as an investment adviser. This meant he had to fill an online form. The filer is instructed to "Complete this form truthfully." Here is Madoff, a hardened impostor, being put through a pro forma process with the injunction to be honest. This was an absurd bureaucratic remedy against a massive scam.

The registration form does threaten bad consequences if a registrant is not truthful: "False statements or omissions may result in denial of your application, revocation of your registration, or criminal prosecution," it warns. But lying on the form was the least of Madoff's transgressions. If he got away with a huge fraud, he would certainly get away with omissions on a registration form.

So he checked off formalities such as business address and hours, listing the latter as nine-to-five. Even that was misleading. In reality most investors were not allowed to visit Madoff, whether during business hours or any other time. Only the operators of feeder funds that raised capital for him had access, and only if they did not ask inconvenient questions. Obviously, the registration exercise in electronic red tape made no difference for detecting the con game or even minor falsehood.

In the Eye of the Regulators

When a money manager is dogged by widespread rumors of fraud or even less drastic legal trouble, most clients typically head for the exit and the manager is forced to close the shop. In a notable example of this, Arthur Samberg, a long-time manager investigated for insider trading by the SEC, shuttered his firm, Pequot Capital, though he faced no charges. Given the critical role of reputation, how did Madoff manage to shake off several published news stories as well as persistent rumors that he was engaged in some sort of scam?

Paradoxically, the more regulators examined him, the better he looked. His business received almost-clean bills of health time and again. Repeated investigations by the SEC and FINRA found only minor infractions, technical issues that were correctable. The examinations must have stressful for the con artist but were blessings in disguise for his scheme.

The regulatory environment would prevent fraud, Madoff himself told a conference audience in 2007. That people believed this helped him. While his persuasive ability sounds uncanny, he could not have kept up the pretense without the assurance the government in effect provided for him. There was no skimping of regulators' resources; on the contrary, they paid him persistent attention. It looked like he'd been vetted through and through, and no fraud was found.

The SEC examiners told each other their suspicions but those were not public. What the investors knew was that Madoff fulfilled the requirements set out by regulators. He was told to register as an adviser and did so. The bureaucratic focus on formalities – going through a checklist as the control mechanism – backfired. He filled the form, the SEC had it in its database where Madoff's clients could check it out, all appeared to be in order. If anything, he looked more respectable as a result.

While an extreme case, the pattern is not unusual. Financial regulators almost never take action until a scheme is near its end and much of the money is already gone. In the meantime, the belief that public watchdogs are there to protect investors reassures people and makes them less vigilant. Government oversight does not prevent or catch confidence games, but it does impair private diligence. The supposed checks by regulators assure investors — perversely creating false confidence that causes people to be less careful.

The Madoff scheme went on so long because regulators in effect sabotaged private control mechanisms and facilitated long-term deception. Had the SEC not undermined skeptics by persistently giving Madoff a pass, complaints by Markopolos and others would have had an impact, at least stopped some investors from putting in money.

Markopolos had a powerful case and generated publicity around it. Admittedly, whistleblowers never have an easy time, whether in private companies or government.[225] Telling disagreeable truths is not the way to make friends and charm people — whereas impostors like Berger and Madoff manage to come across as perfectly pleasant when they need to. Some SEC bureaucrats disliked Markopolos – certainly he did not act like a bureaucrat – and hence were not inclined to pay attention to his complaints.

Given Madoff's long-time success despite all the attention he received from regulators, even those who were not convinced by his investment performance felt that he could not be cheating. Analysts at the hedge fund Renaissance Technologies found reasons to doubt his strategy. But they did not think there was fraud because the SEC looked at Madoff and did not find a major problem. "We felt that he was sufficiently in the eye of the regulators that it was just hard for us to envision that that was the case," a Renaissance manager said after the scheme surfaced.[226]

All skeptics were put on the defensive. One investor who expressed doubts remembered being asked, What makes you so smart? How can you know better than everybody else? Had there been no SEC and the false assurance it provided, the scam would have ended earlier, when the damage was small. In effect, regulators enabled Madoff.

Familiar Venue

The 2008 crisis did what the government would not for 16 years and quickly pulled down the Madoff scheme. People needed money. Some of the investors had loans they had to pay back. Some of the funds that fed the scheme used credit — easy to get in the bubble but impossible to refinance in the crunch. Withdrawal demands spiked while inflows shrank. Since a Ponzi scheme can't go on without fresh money to pay withdrawing clients, Madoff gave himself up.

Thereupon regulators took over and appointed a former regulator as trustee. He filed for bankruptcy at the Southern District of New York. The case could have gone to any one of a number of judges. The new, potentially immense estate was assigned – to my amazement – to Judge Burton Lifland. His courtroom in the handsome old building near the southern tip of Manhattan was apparently just the place for large Ponzi scheme remainders.

By then, the judge's momentous decision backing Manhattan Fund trustee Gredd's claim against Bear Stearns had been overturned. With no more lawsuits left to keep it going, the Manhattan fund estate had absolutely no reason to exist. It looked like eventually any assets left over from the lawyers might actually be distributed to the creditors.

As that case faded, Lifland was again in the limelight, now presiding over the Madoff bankruptcy. His rulings were in the headlines with reporters following the proceedings in the crowded courthouse. This could be seen as the summit of the judge's career.

There was one key difference between the two bankruptcies. The SEC decided that a subset of Madoff investors were brokerage customers and brought in another government entity to work on the debacle. This was the Securities Investor Protection Corp. or SIPC, created by Congress to oversee failed brokerages and protect the interests of brokerage clients.

Calling in SIPC was a surprising choice give the history of the con game. The relation between the legitimate Madoff brokerage and the fraudulent scheme was not obvious. Over the decades the brokerage regulator NASD and its successor FINRA inspected the brokerage with no idea that it held assets for the Madoff investment business — the brokerage examiners were not even aware of the investors.

The SEC knew, of course, but treated the two businesses as distinct. Through its own repeated investigations, the SEC never informed NASD-FINRA that Madoff had an investment management business. Neither did the securities regulator tell the brokerage regulator that there were complaints of fraud. Now the SEC decided that the investment business was part of the brokerage after all.

It would have been very useful to link the two while they were active. Looking at the two operations together would have revealed more than looking at each one in isolation. This might have shown up the fraud. But regulators did not do that; they chose to ignore the connection while the game was going on.

After the scheme was over, some high-level bureaucrats must have decided to use the failing brokerage angle. They did this seemingly so as to get help for the victims, thereby countering complaints about their own role in the deception. Or so I thought at first, failing to realize the full implications of this step until later. Lawyers no doubt figured out those future consequences and the SEC decided that some victims qualified as brokerage clients. The catch was that others did not.

SIPC has a reserve fund, financed with assessments collected from member brokerages, to provide financial assistance to people harmed by the failure of a brokerage. Investors identified as being in this group receive an advance of up to $500,000 not as insurance coverage of losses but rather an up-front advance, to be deducted from what is left in the estate after the customers are made whole, if that happens.

By declaring some Madoff victims brokerage clients, the SEC appeared to obtain immediate relief for them. While typically less than the amount they lost in the scheme, the advance was still a lifeline to people who had suddenly learnt that much of their personal wealth was smoke and mirrors.

Meanwhile, regulators had recommended Irving Picard as the trustee to oversee the liquidation under the law that underpins SIPC. Within a few days of Madoff's arrest, a judge ratified the appointment. A lawyer well known in the small world of regulators and New York bankruptcy courts, Picard had spent many years at the SEC, ending his time at the agency as assistant general counsel.

After that he became supervisor of trustees for the Southern District of New York, the first in a newly created position. Upon leaving the government, he joined a law firm active in the same world, Baker & Hostetler, and built his practice around bankruptcies and liquidations.

He maintained close ties with SIPC and the SEC; he and other members of his firm secured an impressive number of court appointments. He was trustee for 10 or more brokerage liquidations overseen by SIPC, as well as counsel to SIPC-appointed trustees in other lawsuits, and receiver for certain cases where the SEC was involved.

In this long and successful career at the interface of regulators and bankruptcy courts, the Madoff trusteeship represented a sort of apogee. The size of the fraud was unprecedented, attention from the media intense and largely favorable to the trustee. Reporters apparently regarded him as the champion of the fraud victims — though many of the victims themselves objected to what he proceeded to do.

The down side of the SIPC involvement was that it relegated a large group of investors to second-class status. The trustee and regulators agreed that the aid was only for investors who had an account with Madoff in their own name — these were regarded as brokerage customers covered by the SIPC law. But many investors had not invested directly; they had given money to feeder funds that funneled it to Madoff. The feeder funds had accounts with Madoff, not the individual investors. Therefore the latter were not protected by SIPC and the trustee refused their claims. The result was that thousands of victims had no voice or rights in the estate.

In reality the notion of an "account" was misleading. Madoff did not keep proper accounts since he was using the money to sustain his deception. But regulators hewed to the distinction of those supposedly with an account in their own name versus those whose account was in the feeder fund's name. The former were given preferential standing and received help from SIPC.

Feeder fund investors were treated differently even though they had been defrauded just the same and faced similar hardship. They were not directly entitled to SIPC money. The advance was per feeder fund; so the customers of a fund had to share a single advance of at most $500,000.

Madoff was put away for the rest of his life no doubt as a gesture for re-establishing the government's anti-fraud credentials, badly damaged by the spectacular failure to stop him. The 150-year sentence was orders of magnitude longer than time served by rapists and murderers. It signaled an official message. As a practical matter, the sequel in bankruptcy and civil courts was more important for the victims than the prison term meted to the perpetrator.

They looked to the bankruptcy estate and civil lawsuits to get their property back. With the con man settled into a cell, the saga that started with his arrest was no longer his story, any more than the decade-plus-long legal tale that began with the end of Manhattan hedge fund was Michael Berger's. These men set the process into motion, but what came next depended on the government employees who took over when the scheme ended.

Regulators designated the ex-regulator Picard and the bankruptcy lawyers allied with him to take control of the estate. They chose a special legal framework by bringing in SIPC. The particular judge picked from all possible judges had a reputation for being friendly to bankruptcy lawyers and not to creditors — especially not to fraud victims, judging from the Manhattan case. Fate or judicial powers-that-be favored the lawyers. That was an obvious inference.

But the consequences of the SIPC arrangement were not evident at the outset, at least to an outside observer like myself. If you had seen the legal bills for the Manhattan Fund estate, you would suspect what the appointment of a trustee portended in that respect. But the role SIPC played was obscured by technicalities. It took years for the full effects to show up, and even then you'd notice only if you followed closely.

Following Precedent

The mess Madoff left behind was a lawyer's delight. Numerous people and organizations were involved and their involvement took multiple and complicated forms. Most of the roughly $65 billion of wealth investors thought they possessed was in fact Madoff's fabrication. What they really owned had to be determined and thousands of claims investigated.

Another name familiar from the Manhattan lawsuits joined the Madoff bankruptcy case. In March 2009 Baker & Hostetler hired Marc Hirschfield, one of Manhattan trustee Gredd's lawyers. After a decade of experience, Hirschfield knew well the legal tactics used in the Manhattan case. This is clear from an article he co-authored a couple of years later with a colleague, referencing both the Manhattan and Madoff Ponzi schemes, for the American Bar Association Business Bankruptcy Committee.[227]

Clearly, Manhattan fund set a powerful precedent for opportunities available to attorneys in the aftermath of fraud. As a partner at Baker & Hostetler, Marc Hirschfield now joined the team of attorneys who represented Trustee Picard. He was obviously well acquainted with Judge Lifland, having been in the same court for so many years.

The precedent of making investors return to the bankruptcy estate any fake profits they had withdrawn applied. The Madoff clients who took out more than their capital were in for a secondary shock after the first one of realizing they'd been deceived. Even the capital they originally invested was not necessarily theirs to keep — if they withdrew toward the end of the scheme, they could be forced to return some money that was part of their principal.

In the abstract, it seems reasonable not to legitimize bogus profits. After all, the supposed gains came from other people's investments. "By seeking recovery from those entities who received more than they invested, the trustee is able to make a distribution to those entities who received less than they invested," wrote Hirschfield and Klidonas in their 2011 article on the subject. In this way, trustees leveled the playing field. Picard's team sued to get back the difference from hundreds of investors who had redeemed more than they put in.

While legal precedent and logic backed these actions, the problems created for the Madoff victims were far greater than in earlier cases. Other Ponzi schemes did not last as long, therefore claw-backs of fictitious profits were not as disruptive. It can't be fun to be forced to return money you received in the past year and assumed was yours to do as you pleased, as happened to Manhattan redeemers. But it must be a lot less onerous compared to having to return money you received and spent several years ago, as happened to Madoff redeemers.

One claw-back case, against New York Mets owners Fred Wilpon and Saul Katz, became notorious because it forced the defendants to raise funds by selling part of their interest in the baseball club. Others had to sell their homes – in a depressed property market where prices were down 25% or more – and drastically downscale their lifestyle. The claw-backs were a serious setback for retirees who relied on the gains they thought they had made on the investment and had no other source of income for paying the bills.

The trustee instituted a hardship program, primarily for some of the elderly who were in danger of becoming destitute and for people facing bankruptcy or serious illness. Those who qualified as suffering from hardship – as judged by Picard's lawyers – were exempted from having to pay back Madoff's profits.

The trustee reported that of 394 early applicants to the hardship program, 249 were allowed to escape claw-backs and of 128 later applicants, 35 had similar good luck.[228] That left a sizable group of victims who tried on grounds of hardship but could not shake off the claw-back.

At the time of the Madoff bankruptcy, getting fake profits back from redeemers was settled legal practice, well-established by the Manhattan Fund and other cases and affirmed by courts. Therefore it was a routine matter that did not require high-end – meaning expensive – legal skill. Only the hardship program was not routine and hence justified the expenditure of some special effort by the lawyers. Otherwise, the claw-backs were straightforward and brought large sums to the estate.

Thus the trustee negotiated to get $5 billion from the widow of a feeder fund operator, Jeffry Picower, an impressive amount. But this was not a hard case to make because Picower had obviously gained at the expense of fraud victims and his widow was not inclined to contest the claw-back.

In fact she agreed to return another $2-plus billion to the U.S. Justice Department. The Justice Department could have recovered the entire $7 billion in the same action, without the estate lawyers' many billable hours related to this matter.

Had the Justice Department reclaimed the full amount instead of only part and directly distributed it to all Madoff victims, the thousands of indirect investors would have been much better off. As it was, because the trustee and SIPC did not allow them to directly claim assets from the estate, these people had to wait for the bankrupt feeder funds to get the payment and divide it among the investors.

A lawsuit by the New York Attorney General and the U.S. Department of Labor on behalf of retirees and a group of investors brought more than $210 million from a feeder fund complex, Ivy Asset Management, owned by a bank. This suit, filed under New York's Martin Act against securities fraud, also demonstrated the possibility of getting money back and distributing it to the fraud victims without being bogged down in bankruptcy court for an indefinite time. Clients of Ivy feeder funds could directly claim their shares, unlike their predicament in bankruptcy court where they had no standing as claimants.

Thousand Plus Lawsuits

While getting fictitious profits back from the redeemers was a largely successful endeavor, other cases filed by the trustee for much larger sums were another matter. Those actions were taken on the ground that various parties had acted in bad faith and knew or should have known that Madoff was engaged in fraud—in effect, that they were complicit in the scheme.

Thus the trustee sued Met owners Wilpon and Katz not only to recover the estimated $300 million phantom profit they received but also for an additional $700 million in damages. The latter was based on the separate argument that these individuals knew or should have known they were getting money from a Ponzi scheme. While the trustee was on strong ground with regard to the principle of a claw-back, the rest of the $1 billion suit was dubious.

That case and others raised the question of how to establish in retrospect what people "should have known" before Madoff confessed in December 2008.[229]

The shakiness of these charges is obvious from the eventual settlement with Messrs. Wilpon and Katz. After much back-and-forth, the defendants paid back $162 million corresponding to six years' fictitious profits, a small fraction of the $1 billion the trustee originally demanded.

Notable among the many motions in this case was one by the trustee seeking to bar references to his own legal fees—an issue the other side brought up as the possible reason for the trustee's action.

To claw back fake gains, it is not necessary to argue that the recipient was aware of the fraud. Awareness is a slippery argument to make. Maybe someone suspected that Madoff was engaged in fraud, but that does not mean they knew or could have found out—the only entity that could and should have done that was the SEC. No one else had the level of power or responsibility. Nevertheless, the estate lawyers used the "should-have-known" argument to greatly expand the scope of their litigation.

While there were numerous actions for claw-backs, the suits targeting banks and feeder funds with deep pockets were the big ticket items. On the reasoning that these parties should have known of the fraud and stopped it, the trustee asked for huge damages. In this category were a $19.9 billion claim against JP Morgan Chase, almost $9 billion against HSBC, $2 billion against UBS and $19.6 billion against the Austrian Bank Medici, its principal owner Sonja Kohn and affiliated banks and trusts.

All in all, the trustee's team filed more than 1,050 suits. In this respect government-appointed trustees resemble Scheherazade of the 1,001 Arabian Nights. Scheherazade had a secure tenure with the Sultan as long as she kept spinning the fairy tales. Trustees and their associates are in effect guaranteed lavish pay as long as they keep suing. So they spin the lawsuits. The system is like a fairy tale for lawyers who get post-Ponzi scheme jobs. But for many fraud victims, it is more like an extended nightmare.

The case against Bank Medici, Sonja Kohn and related entities asked for triple damages on the basis of a law that is typically used for organized crime, the Racketeer Influenced and Corrupt Organizations Act or RICO. The lawsuit against JP Morgan demanded that the bank pay back the revenue it had received from all Madoff-related activities and transfers, now deemed fraudulent. These came to around $900 million. But the bulk of the claim consisted of another $19 billion in damages for allowing the fraud to continue. The exact amounts were to be determined in court.

This was the second time an acquisition landed JP Morgan in a bankruptcy trustee's sights in the very same bankruptcy court, though the appeals were heard by different district judges. The bank had faced the Manhattan trustee's charges against Bear Stearns after acquiring that company. The origins of JP Morgan's new legal problem went back to 1986, when Madoff opened an account at Chemical Bank. Ten years later Chemical merged with Chase Manhattan and eventually the merged entity became part of JP Morgan Chase, which inherited Madoff's account.

The Picard group's lawsuit made various allegations, the main point being that the bank turned a blind eye to many red flags regarding the account and other aspects of the Madoff operation. JP Morgan had cashed Madoff's checks, allowed money to go in and out of his account without restriction, given him loans and provided credit to one of his main clients who used this to invest with him. The bank had itself invested with Madoff via a feeder fund, despite concerns. A British subsidiary called JPM Securities had helped create and finance investment products for feeder funds that fed Madoff.

The trustee claimed that JP Morgan either knew about the fraud or made a conscious decision to avoid knowing. Hence it was complicit and responsible for $19 billion he estimated as the damage caused by the scheme. From this vantage point, JP Morgan had a duty to stop Madoff but failed to take action and therefore knowingly participated in the breach.

The suit raised the question of whether a bank participated in a breach of fiduciary duty by an account holder by not stopping him.[230] That Madoff violated his fiduciary duty went without saying but whether his banker was complicit in the violation was unclear.

This case brought to mind the charges against Bear Stearns in the Manhattan fund bankruptcy. The matter of fiduciary duty had been at the center of that case. District court judges rejected the trustee's arguments on the ground that the brokerage did not have a duty to its client's clients.

Bear Stearns beat the Manhattan Fund rap in part on the ground that brokerages can't be held responsible for their customers' clients. A similar argument could be made for JP Morgan in the Madoff case that banks are not responsible for the financial well-being of their customers' clients. No doubt aware of the weakness of their case, the Picard team sought to justify the charges as a violation of anti-money laundering requirements and the Patriot Act.

They argued that the bank was required to know its customers and monitor accounts for anti-money laundering purposes. This was of questionable relevance. Anti-money laundering applies to money from illegal sources like drug dealing, whereas the money that came into the Madoff account was originally from legitimate sources and did not need to be "laundered". While Madoff's fraud was illegal, it was a stretch to claim this constituted racketeering by the bank where he happened to have an account.

It was regulators who failed to stop the fraud despite numerous red flags, complaints, even repeated whistleblower reports, but naturally the banks were the ones sued — for the same reason that Willie Sutton robbed banks. The charge of should-have-known could be made against the SEC with much greater force than against any bank. Stopping fraud is what regulators are paid for and equipped by law to do — they are endowed with subpoena power for this purpose. Bankers have no such power. Whistleblowers went to the SEC, not to JP Morgan Chase.

If banks are legally obliged to prevent financial fraud by accountholders, then there is little reason to have financial regulators with broad powers to prevent fraud. Congress could oblige banks and other private parties to do this job, shut down the SEC and save taxpayer money. That may be a better arrangement than the current one, where defrauded investors have little chance in court against federal regulators who did nothing to prevent the fraud.

It would make sense for the investors to sue the SEC in the Madoff case, but the estate lawyers who controlled most of the resources would do no such thing and fought any lawsuits by other parties. The lawyers were not about to bite the hand that fed them – and fed them with remarkable abundance – by suing the SEC.

Like Gredd, Picard received all the rulings he wanted from Judge Lifland. As long as he managed to keep a case in bankruptcy court, it went his way. The defendants recognized this and sought to escape to district court. So many tried to move away that the judge set a deadline for those applications.

Other judges rejected the "should have known this was fraud and prevented it" type charges. Most of the trustee's claim against HSBC was overturned by district judge Jed Rakoff in a ruling with wide implications. Rakoff found that the bankruptcy trustee did not have the standing to make such claims on behalf of the estate. The trustee's "convoluted theories, none of which is ultimately persuasive" made no headway. About one such theory the judge wrote that "To say this argument is a stretch would be to give it more credence than it deserves."[231] Similarly the judge decreed that the trustee did not have the legal standing to pursue racketeering charges against various defendants.

Another district judge, Colleen McMahon, agreed with Rakoff and threw out much of Picard's case against JP Morgan. These verdicts, like earlier district court decisions regarding Gredd's arguments against Bear Stearns, dramatically reduced the trustee's case but allowed the much smaller claims based on fees or profits paid by Madoff.

The developments were widely reported as a reversal for the trustee, who might get back around 10% of the $100 billion he originally demanded in numerous complaints. But it did not really matter for the alliance of lawyers, because they were paid regardless of the success or failure of the cases, just as Gredd and associates were paid regardless of the failure of their action against Bear Stearns. Time was in their favor as much-shrunken cases once again went back to Judge Lifland.

Nearly five years after Madoff bowed out, an appeals court backed the district court decision that the trustee did not have the standing to sue the banks. Picard then asked the Supreme Court to give him the green light. Soon after that, the U.S. attorney for the Southern District of New York threatened JP Morgan with criminal charges for not warning the authorities about Madoff and extracted a total of $2.6 billion from the bank, with $350 million to go to the Treasury Department and most the rest – eventually – to the fraud victims.

The prosecutor's case largely turned on the fact that in October 2008 JP Morgan alerted U.K. regulators about suspicions regarding Madoff but not the U.S. That was just a couple of months before the end came. For 16 years U.S. regulators resolutely ignored warnings from various quarters So what if there was no alert from JP Morgan in October 2008? There would have been no effect anyway. Nevertheless, the bank paid up — otherwise the lawsuit could have gone on for years, hobbling the business.

Out of JP Morgan's payment to avoid criminal charges, the Justice Department routed $543 million to the trustee cabal — who thereby could bill for investigating and "administering" until they returned the money to its rightful owners. In the end the trustee's achievement may be limited to getting claw-backs, but extensive litigation and with it the bankruptcy estate goes on.

In an article, Judge Rakoff argued that the new policy of going after banks and other financial companies – rather than the individuals who committed the alleged deed – is misbegotten on several grounds.[232] Technically, he pointed out, you should not indict or threaten a company unless you can prove that the crime was committed by its managerial agents — but if you have such evidence then you should prosecute those agents, not the company.

But pressuring a bank to settle is the easy way out for prosecutors and other public officials. Companies do not want to have litigation hanging over them for a long time – over a decade in the Bear Stearns case brought by the Manhattan trustee, as we saw – and in any event banks pass through the cost of such settlements to their customers, shareholders and employees. Your pension or 401(k) account pays for part of it.

Activist Victims

While the Manhattan Fund and Madoff estates were overseen by the same judge and run by government-backed trustees pursuing broadly similar legal strategies, the two stories diverged sharply in certain respects. One was how the clients of the two schemes reacted to their plight.

Manhattan Fund investors, mostly wealthy individuals and organizations scattered across the world, had no interest in appearing in American courts and even less in giving interviews to journalists. Only two were willing to testify in the class action suit against the fund's service providers and those carefully avoided publicity. Investors did not make a personal appearance in courtrooms where their lawyers showed up to represent their interest. This desire to remain at a distance meant they could not hope to influence the handling of the estate by appealing to public opinion.

By contrast, the Madoff investors went public. Many of them were well known people. The list of Madoff's clients contained celebrities, philanthropists and political figures — from the owners of the New York Mets to former senator Frank Lautenberg's family foundation. Many lived in the tri-state region around New York City and on occasion were not averse to airing their grievances in person. They talked to the press and complained to their representatives in Congress. Helen Davis Chaitman, an attorney who was also a victim of the fraud, appeared repeatedly in court to dispute the trustee's actions.

Therefore Madoff's victims were eminently capable of putting pressure on regulators and the lawyers who controlled the estate. Manhattan Fund clients could do nothing about the immense legal bills. Had the same exact scenario been repeated in the Madoff bankruptcy, the investors would have resisted with loud protests to whoever would listen, starting with members of Congress.

Given this situation, it was amazingly serendipitous for Picard and his associates that they had another resource.

Since the SEC decided the Madoff investment business would be treated as a brokerage, the legal and administrative expenses of the estate were covered by SIPC. This opened to the estate lawyers the SIPC fund for clients of failed brokerages. Unlike the Manhattan lawyers, they did not bill the estate. Hence the Madoff trustee and his colleagues had a ready answer to any objection to their ambitious litigation efforts and matching fees — the legal bills were going to SIPC and not reducing the investors' portion of the estate, so the investors had no reason to complain.

But the trustee team received SIPC money that could have instead gone to the victims. Picard estimated legal and other estate expenses through 2014 at $1.094 billion and possibly more to come after that.[233] The advances SIPC agreed to provide for the victims came to about $800 million. On that comparison, the lawyers and affiliated professionals received more from SIPC than the victims.

Judge Lifland blamed the law for the large payments to attorneys. Indeed, he had less say in the matter because SIPC defended the expenditures. But in the Manhattan case the judge had approved large legal payments without SIPC involvement.

There are complaints going back more than a decade that SIPC spends too much on bankruptcy trustees and not enough on compensating the customers of failed brokerages as intended by Congress. SIPC tries to save money by excluding people from its coverage. The Madoff victims who were denied assistance fit this pattern of channeling resources to lawyers rather than investors.

SIPC officials defended their payments to the Madoff estate legal team as necessary to conduct the complicated lawsuits that would recover money for the victims. But the claw-back suits, which did result in recoveries, were not complicated. And the "should-have-known" type litigation had less chance of success. The Manhattan Fund-Bear Stearns precedent showed that district courts were likely to reject such arguments.

SIPC officials, in effect the employer of the estate lawyers, always defended and paid the immense legal bills. When questioned by the Government Accountability Office about the payments, they did not mention the fact that the gigantic suits generating astounding numbers of billable hours were not likely to succeed. Impressive as the hundred billion dollars in damages demanded sounded, chances were that the victims would not receive such amounts – or anything close – from those particular suits.

By contrast, the claw-backs brought back big chunks of the money Madoff swindled. This money was recoverable because Madoff had in fact stolen relatively little — mostly he had taken from Paul and given to Peter, and Peter had to return it. Whatever the psychological reason Madoff did this, his strange game allowed the estate to gather substantial assets in a couple of years. By contrast the rest of the litigation was questionable and delayed the final windup.

A group of Madoff victims vigorously fought the trustee clique. Several hundred of them, represented by Helen Chaitman, repeatedly objected to the proceedings. Their efforts were frustrated for several reasons. One problem was that they objected to the claw-backs, but there was strong precedent for these, backed by courts. Another key factor was the defense by SIPC and the SEC of the trustee's legal strategy and its costs.

Given the regulators' position, a judge seriously inclined to limit the payments to lawyers would have had to work hard to find ways of doing so. In any event there was no chance of this happening in the New York bankruptcy court. Judge Lifland had to be the least likely judge in this world to cut estate lawyers' fees. His pattern of favoring trustees and lawyers was clear from the Manhattan case and from bankruptcies that went through his court over the years.[234]

These conditions put dissident investors at a severe disadvantage. The trustee was a quasi-governmental figure supported by other authorities. Regulators chose him, in the main agreed with what he did – indeed, he came from their ranks, was their former colleague – and paid him. A SIPC official appeared in court to indicate regulators' accord with the trustee and Judge Lifland showed his agreement in his rulings.

The trustee and his team turned out to be very savvy at dealing with the media. While certain investors told their side of the story now and then, the estate lawyers ran a persistent and sophisticated public relations campaign. Picard had a spokeswoman to handle journalists and an extensive website, ostensibly to aid the fraud victims but also a platform for messages defending the trustee's actions.

Sympathetic press articles relayed the message that he was seeking redress for people who had been wronged by the monstrous criminal Madoff.[235] Here was an effort to recoup investors' losses and besides, they were not paying the legal bills. How could they possibly object?

Despite these handicaps, the Madoff investors' contacts, political and legal activism and willingness to come forth to tell their stories bore some fruit. The trustee camp did not wait for a decade to start returning the assets as happened in Manhattan case. Qualified investors received SIPC money and the trustee distributed part of the estate after several years.

Even so, many at some point faced the same situation as Manhattan Fund investors. Either you could sell your remaining interest at a discount to speculators willing to wait for the end of the glacial litigation. Or hold on till the lawsuits were done.

At the end of 2010, investors with recognized claims on the Madoff estate were offered 30 or 33 cents to the dollar by speculators. At that time, the trustee had recovered more than $7.6 billion, almost all from claw-backs. This total represented over 44% of the capital lost in the scheme by customers who filed claims.[236] In other words, had the estate assets been distributed at that time, two years after Madoff confessed, the investors would have received 44%.

Madoff clients who heard that Manhattan Fund creditors had to wait over a decade to get money back were more inclined to sell. Indeed, hundreds of investors took the offers from outside parties and sold off at less than their share of the already collected estate assets. However, the victims' protests did push the bankruptcy lawyers to start distributing earlier than they otherwise might have. By late 2013, five years after Madoff threw in the towel, they had returned to victims around half the counterfeit gains clawed back from redeemers.

Picard explained that he could not distribute more money because, one, he anticipated recovering additional assets through litigation and settlements and, two, he needed reserves to deal with appeals and disputes. There was no objection from SIPC officials or Judge Lifland. As long as litigation continued, investors could get only part of the money sitting in the estate.

That the legal team did extraordinarily well under SIPC sponsorship can be seen by comparing the Madoff and Lehman Brothers bankruptcy lawyers' compensation. The Lehman Brothers group liquidated a large investment bank with a variety of businesses employing tens of thousands of people. The degree of complexity and skills required had to be far greater. But the hourly fees did not reflect that. Earlier in the process SIPC paid Madoff estate lawyers an hourly rate ranging from $698 to $742, while the Lehman lawyers' rates went from $529 to $437.[237] A later, different estimate by the Government Accounting Office showed roughly similar hourly rates — the Lehman lawyers averaged $891 and their Madoff counterparts $850.[238]

As with the Manhattan fund case, the benefit went not to a single individual but to an alliance. While Irving Picard was the public face of the legal operation, in fact a large group of lawyers was involved — reflected in the SIPC payments. At the center of the alliance was Picard's law firm, Baker & Hostetler. From the time Madoff shut down shop in December 2008 through September 2012, more than half of the SIPC payments for the administration of the estate went to Baker & Hostetler. The fees paid to Picard personally were a comparatively modest sum — $4.4. million for almost four years of trusteeship. The pattern of billings changed over time but his firm continued to receive the lion's share throughout.[239]

In March 2012 the Government Accounting Office noted that Baker & Hostetler partners charged higher fees than other attorneys; on the other hand, the number of hours they billed had declined. Picard said the partners were more heavily involved earlier in the process because the firm was preparing numerous lawsuits. But the in fact the most amazing thing about the legal bills is how robust they were over time. For the first billing period after the trustee was named, the firm's fees were less than $3 million. Later amounts were orders of magnitude larger.

The drain from the Madoff bankruptcy depleted the $2.5 billion SIPC reserve fund meant to protect brokerage customers. In principle, SIPC could recoup legal fees and other expenses if the estate got back more than the capital investors lost. Once the customers received their original investment, any other money recovered would go to SIPC. But the trustee and Judge Lifland agreed that the estate was unlikely to have enough funds for SIPC to recoup the costs.

That suggests they did not really put much faith into the ultimate outcome of the $100 billion in ambitious lawsuits, even as one led the litigating and the other encouraged it by his rulings.

May Seem Inequitable

Investors in feeder funds that channeled money to Madoff fared especially badly under the SIPC regime, as we know. While the SIPC arrangement created by regulators was fabulous for the estate lawyers, this group of victims were victimized a second time by that arrangement. Not only were they excluded from direct SIPC advances but also had no right to direct payments from the bankruptcy, were not allowed to file separate claims against the estate and in general were barred from taking legal action to get compensation in the Madoff matter except against the feeder funds.

Of course these investors objected, but the SEC, SIPC, Lifland and a district court backed the trustee, citing the definition of brokerage customer in the law under which SIPC operated.

In his ruling the bankruptcy judge wrote: "That this approach may seem inequitable to the Objecting Claimants is not compelling on its own."[240] He pointed out that they would likely get a share of the money the feeder funds received from the estate and they could sue the operators of the feeder funds. Indeed such lawsuits were in progress, "with unpredictable effects on who ultimately will be entitled to current or future assets."

The feeder funds, and not the trustee, were responsible to their clients.[241] But the feeder funds were no longer in operation, the Madoff scandal having destroyed the business. Receivers liquidating the defunct funds would decide what to pay the investors after they were told what they would get from the bankruptcy estate — but the full distribution from the estate would take an indefinite number of years as the trustee's voluminous litigation dragged on. Even after the bankruptcy estate distributed assets and receivers of feeder funds in turn divided the payment among fund investors, the latter were expected to end up with less than the direct investors.[242]

Meanwhile the feeder fund operators and their clients were subject to aggressively pursued claw-backs and other claims. Billions of dollars from this source were gathered for the bankruptcy estate, taking away assets that otherwise would have been available to feeder fund customers.

Under the SIPC structure, the trustee represented the interest of the direct investors against the indirect investors. Thus Picard not only sued the feeder fund operator Fairfield Greenwich Group, but also its clients. Fairfield Sentry, the largest of the funds, had redeemed some $3 billion from Madoff over a period of six years and passed it on to its customers. The trustee sued these investors.

Fairfield Sentry was set up as a company in Tortola, the British Virgin Islands, where a court appointed two insolvency experts to liquidate it. Picard sued them for $3.8 billion. They in turn demanded from the bankruptcy estate $1.2 billion that investors in the fund had lost. To end this impasse, the BVI liquidators and the NY trustee made a deal that substantially favored the estate over feeder fund customers. The liquidators agreed to pay Picard $70 million and reduce their claim from $1.2 billion to net $160 million. In addition, the trustee received most of the proceeds from suits against the Fairfield Greenwich Group and its executives.

Without the deal, the trustee's lawsuits would have left the Fairfield fund investors in an even worse predicament . "The settlement resolves the parties' claims against each other, thereby avoiding contentious, costly and uncertain litigation," said the liquidators in a statement. Nevertheless, the Fairfield clients had little remedy. Most of the fund's assets went to the bankruptcy estate that did not allow their claims.

While the law's definition of brokerage customer had these consequences, there was no real necessity for Madoff investors to be put under SIPC. The distinction came into play only because regulators chose the law for brokerages as the framework for the estate. Turning the investors into brokerage customers was a deliberate choice by the SEC. It was by no means an obvious choice, given that the SEC treated the Madoff investment business as a separate entity while it was a going concern.

That the arrangement would help some people but harm others who lost their money in the same con game must have been obvious to the lawyers. What made things even worse for feeder fund investors was that the trustee camp put severe limits on their ability to get money back from other parties. In effect regulators favored one group of Madoff victims while treating another group of victims as an adversary, to be pursued by the SIPC-paid trustee and deprived of assets they otherwise would have been entitled to.

From a commonsense perspective, the legal distinction between direct versus indirect investor certainly did not seem equitable — all had been equally victimized but the government protected some at the expense of others. Once you go outside the legalism of the particular statute chosen for the bankruptcy, this is arbitrary. It is hard to see how it would be justified if regulators had not imposed the artificial distinction by bringing the estate under the SIPC law.

The net effect of this decision by the SEC is that estate lawyers received a great boon while a large group of victims were left in the cold.

Efforts to Intimidate

In one respect, the Madoff investors were more constrained than their Manhattan Fund counterparts. The latter were able to receive timely restitution by hiring their own lawyers and suing the fund's service providers separately from the bankruptcy estate. By doing that, they got some of their money back many years before the estate paid a single penny to anyone except the trustee alliance.

But Picard's lawyers immediately worked to block any such independent action, arguing that the trustee alone was entitled to sue and distribute the proceeds as he saw fit. Judge Lifland of course agreed with this position. It may have been another lesson from the Manhattan Fund experience: act quickly to preempt competing actions that will channel billable hours to other lawyers. Another law firm started to work on Madoff's personal bankruptcy but Lifland consolidated the case under Picard. As a consolation prize, those lawyers were given the Madoff family assets to look after.

A sizable portion of the trustee's numerous efforts were actions to stop litigation by investors themselves. Within a month of joining the Madoff trustee's firm, Marc Hirschfield was in the news with a letter he wrote to a 22-year-old Brooklyn Law School student.[243] This young man had lost his inheritance in the scheme. In an attempt to recoup some of the loss, he started a suit against Peter Madoff, the brother of Bernie and the chief compliance officer of the business. But Hirschfield informed him that he may not able to keep any money he recovered from Madoff's brother — the trustee would demand it.

There were at least 10 cases initiated by investors who tried legal remedies independently of the trustee, who had not yet gone after Madoff family members. A notable case against the brother was by the foundation of Frank Lautenberg, a long-time Senator from New Jersey, now deceased. The foundation and Lautenberg relatives sued in early 2009 in a New Jersey court to recover their investment from Peter.

Later the trustee team targeted the same Madoff family members. That turned the independent plaintiffs into what lawyers call competing claimants, suing for the same asset pool as the trustee.[244] Picard sought to restrain and ban the independent lawsuits, arguing that these would enable some plaintiffs to recover more than their fair share of the estate while he meant to collect the assets into a single pool.[245]

Lifland ruled that the 10 competing cases could not proceed until Picard's suits seeking $244 million from the Madoff family came to an end. The judge stopped the gathering of evidence for cases in other courts on the ground that the bankruptcy court had exclusive jurisdiction over estate assets.[246]

This meant the investors could not pursue their own cases for years to come and had little chance of getting anything once the trustee took whatever the Madoff family owned. In vain the Lautenberg plaintiffs argued that the brother must have assets that were not part of the brokerage and hence did not belong to the estate that operated under the SIPC law for failed brokerages.

While the trustee's lawyers succeeded in stopping investors from pursuing suits, they faced certain formidable public entities on the same turf. When the U.S. departments of Justice and Labor became involved in settlements, the trustee group had to cooperate. But they aggressively fought attorney generals who used state laws to get back some of the money Madoff moved around.

Investors realized they had not a chance against the trustee group on their own and were certainly not going to get a sympathetic hearing from the bankruptcy judge. So they favored efforts by state attorney generals in other courts. The attorney general of California filed a $270 million lawsuit against a feeder fund manager, Stanley Chais, on the grounds that Chais made money from Madoff's game. Chais had been based in Beverly Hills but died in 2010, leaving a substantial estate. Thereupon Picard sued the attorney general of California.

State laws against fraud are exempt from bankruptcy rules, which suggests the attorney general had a right to sue. Picard argued the exemption did not apply in this case because California's suit had no deterrence value, given that the accused was dead. But the laws are meant to deter all fraud, not just one person. Lifland decreed that the matter be arbitrated by a judge of his own choice.

The trustee group's relentless endeavor to trounce any competing legal action led to a spectacular fight with New York attorney general Eric Schneiderman, who reached a $410 million settlement with feeder fund operator Ezra Merkin. Picard asked Lifland to stop this deal on the ground that it would hinder his own suit to get $500 million from Merkin. The New York attorney general, like everyone else who found themselves pursued by the trustee cabal, went to a district judge and asked that he be allowed to complete the settlement.

Schneiderman told the district court that the trustee "made intermittent efforts to intimidate" him and his predecessors since 2009.[247] Picard had interfered with the attorney general's power to enforce the state's Martin Act and threatened to sue for any money recovered from fund operator Merkin. That's a measure of how aggressive the estate lawyers were in their quest not to allow anyone else to sue when they themselves could do it—they tried to bully attorney generals. One would think the latter are not prone to being intimidated, but apparently that did not stop the bankruptcy estate contingent.

The investors left dependent on extinct feeder funds for recovering assets were desperate for any help. Because the trustee rejected their claims, they could not even sell their interests at a discount as the direct investors with recognized claims could—naturally speculators preferred recognized claims. For this group, the actions by state attorney generals and the Department of Justice offered the only hope.

Thus billions of dollars clawed back by the Department of Justice became available to all victims of the scheme, including the indirect investors.

Unfortunately the U.S. Attorney's office in New York appointed yet another lawyer – a former chairman of the SEC – to dole out the money and this delayed the relief to investors.[248] Most of the payment JP Morgan agreed to make also went to the same fund. It was announced that an all-inclusive distribution would be made but by early 2014 investors had received little.

The New York attorney general, rejecting the trustee's claims, said removing the case from bankruptcy court "will promote judicial efficiency and avoid further delay in making distributions" to investors. Why did the estate lawyers object? Because they wanted to litigate themselves and send more bills to SIPC, judicial efficiency and distributions to victims be damned. That is the obvious implication.

The point is, regulators deliberately set up this structure. Via SIPC they channeled immense resources from brokerages to the bankruptcy lawyers. This allowed the trustee clique to fight anyone who went against their interest, whether investors or state attorney generals. Using the resources provided to them by the government, the estate lawyers stood in the way of investors getting timely relief outside the interminable bankruptcy case.

This alliance of lawyers were guaranteed payments from SIPC as long as they held on to some portion of the estate and engaged in activities related to it. As long as they controlled part of the estate – even as it shrank because they had to distribute some money – and litigated, they would be liberally compensated. This gave them a powerful incentive to not let go for as long as possible.

The Manhattan Fund case had already shown that a Ponzi fraud estate could be kept in bankruptcy for many years. So the lawyers held on to the estate like their fortunes depended on it. The other side of the coin was that investors knew the estate was held hostage for an indefinite time, so if at all possible they tried to get away from the bankruptcy court.

This is as clear a refutation as one can find of the claim that government agents intervene to protect investors. They not prevent the fraud, instead sending deceptive signals that Madoff was above board. Then they created a great situation for the lawyers they favored. The fraud victims did not want a trustee who controlled not only their property but also their right to sue. Having much of their assets tied up indefinitely did not protect their interest. What it did was to create a very valuable income source for a government-connected group.

Shop and You Will Find

Trustee Picard, like Trustee Gredd before him, demonstrated an almost magical gift for landing in just the right place, the court of Judge Lifland. The wide-ranging set of lawsuits, which allowed the long-term extraction of legal fees, could not have gone on for long without the blessing of the bankruptcy judge. And without the pullulating litigation, the clawed back money would have to be returned in full to the investors and the estate wrapped up.

In a previous chapter I cited the work of legal scholar Lynn LoPucki, who argued that certain bankruptcy judges competed for big cases. Following an overhaul of the law in 1978 that established chapter 11 bankruptcy, filers showed a strong preference for the bankruptcy court of the Southern District of New York and in particular for Judge Lifland. In the 1990s Delaware became the favored venue for chapter 11 bankruptcy cases, again with a single judge getting much of the flow.

Finding the right court enables some groups to redistribute wealth in their own favor through tort litigation. However, not all legal analysts agree that this happens in bankruptcy actions.[249] Where there is a choice, it is clear that filers for bankruptcy do pick their venue deliberately. The question is whether bankruptcy judges compete for cases through their decisions and, if they do, whether this process is a form of corruption as LoPucki suggests.

Why would judges compete for cases and implicitly facilitate venue shopping? Elected judges have the same incentive as all elected officials to favor their constituents, so they might go for cases that serve this purpose. Federal bankruptcy judges are not elected but they may have other reasons for wanting to decide certain cases.

"Appointed judiciaries do not have this incentive to 'buy' votes through wealth redistribution, but their insulation from political pressures may instead permit them to pursue their personal preferences and agendas instead of the desires of the litigants and the public," says a reviewer of LoPucki's book.[250] A judge demonstrates those preferences through rulings. New plaintiffs are attracted by a judicial record that indicates they have a good chance in that court.

It may be that the Madoff and Manhattan Fund estates had to be overseen in the Southern District, but that both ended up with the same bankruptcy judge merits attention. The notion that Lifland had experience dealing with the aftermath of hedge fund fraud and therefore was the natural choice for the Madoff estate surely ignores pertinent issues.

Yes, he presided over the ghostly remnants of Manhattan Fund for well over ten years, surely one of the longest cases ever for Chapter 11 bankruptcy by a tiny business that was never a serious candidate for reorganization. You could take that as evidence that Lifland was more experienced in this special area than other available bankruptcy judges. Even so, on a number of counts he was a strange choice for the Madoff liquidation.

Lifland had a reputation for not being particular about the interests of creditors, who in this instance were Madoff's victims. Entrusting their interest to a judge known to favor other parties suggests a lack of concern for the people whose loss was – supposedly – the reason for the aggressive government action. The SEC took control and turned over these people's assets to the chosen set of lawyers ostensibly to protect them. But the reality does not support that claim.

The Manhattan bankruptcy dragged for so many years because Judge Lifland's rulings permitted the tremendously expensive and lengthy litigation against Bear Stearns. There was evidence at the outset that the Bear Stearns lawsuit was unlikely to succeed. Several district court judges disagreed with the bankruptcy court's decisions along the way. At the end Lifland's ruling was overturned and JP Morgan, the acquirer of Bear Stearns, was cleared of liability.

During that time the owners could not touch their property. The fact that many sold their interests to speculators at steep discounts is evidence that even well-off people did not want to be subjected to the decade-plus-long wait. Judging from the Manhattan Fund history, the Madoff victims were in a for a wait as well. From the precedent one would infer that the only parties who would get their money promptly were the trustee and affiliated lawyers. Any fraud victim who knew this story would certainly not want their estate to land in that court.

But from another vantage point, this was the best possible place to be. Any trustee who knew the Manhattan case will absolutely want to have Lifland as bankruptcy judge.

Without Lifland's support, the complex, expensive and lengthy litigation that guaranteed the Manhattan estate would remain under the legal group's control could not have gone far. The judge backed the Manhattan trustee in all decisions and emphatically did not allow investors to pick a simpler, faster bankruptcy proceeding when they tried to go that way. Gredd and her associates got every ruling they wanted and every penny they asked from the Manhattan estate – it is difficult to imagine how they could have been better treated. That they resisted all attempts to move the case to other courts was obvious self protection.

With that record, Lifland's court again became a favorite, this time with New York-based receivers of assets left from financial fraud. The established pattern suggested that the Madoff bankruptcy would go into costly and lengthy litigation enabled by the judge. Picard and his allies, like Gredd and hers, could be counted on to resist efforts to move lawsuits to any other court. This is what happened.

Remarkably, the bankruptcy judge agreed with the Madoff trustee's course of action not just in its broad outline but in almost every single detail. That the perfect convergence of trustee plans with the judge's preferences happened by pure chance is not believable.[251]

Regulators pick and district court judges confirm trustees. Picard was well known to regulators before he became the Madoff trustee. He had worked with them for years. His plans for the estate must have been known by SEC officials at the time of the appointment. It is hard to avoid the conclusion that they knowingly set up the legal structure that under the particular circumstances provided the most benefit to the favored lawyers.

They brought in SIPC, thereby opening another honey pot, one paid for by brokerages. But this was done against the interest of feeder fund investors, who were excluded from the estate and received nothing from SIPC. These victims were made worse off than they otherwise would have been.

———

Enrichment Scheme

Other consequences were less noticeable but still significant. Had the estate paid the trustee team, there would have been persistent resistance from investors. Given their active involvement and political presence, they would have had some impact. With SIPC paying the mounting costs, the estate lawyers had the defense that the customers were not footing the bills.

But of course, the money did not drop like manna from heaven. Someone was footing the bills. The broker-dealers who financed the SIPC fund had to make up for its depletion. While this may sound like a reasonable recourse to help fraud victims, the latter received less than the estate lawyers. There was talk that the SEC might have to go to Congress to bolster SIPC and there might be "dramatic fee increases for broker-dealers." But some regulators did not consider that a problem.[252]

SIPC would assess higher fees and the brokerage industry would be forced to pay—and pass as much of the cost as possible to its customers. So the estimated $1 billion-plus legal bills in effect transferred wealth from the public – those who use brokerage services, in particular pension beneficiaries and mutual fund investors – to congeries of lawyers. In this way SIPC became a means of redistributing wealth to a government-appointed posse led by a former regulator. The skillful legal maneuvering would have awed Tommy the Cork.

Had the brokerage law not been invoked, the victims would not have been divided into two groups, direct versus indirect investors, with their interests at odds. This distinction, deliberately created by regulators, destroyed the investors' ability to act together. Had it not been for the SEC decision to place the estate under SIPC, all Madoff victims would have had the same interest in opposing huge legal bills. The legal format protected the trustee group.

If the trustee had not monopolized the right to sue and undertaken an extraordinarily broad range of suits, investors would have had greater say as to which suits to bring, when to settle, what to settle for. Were they free from the constraints imposed by regulators, no doubt they would have handled the estate differently. The liquidation would be more expeditious and litigation focused on the more promising possibilities.

Even Manhattan Fund investors, not otherwise inclined to come forth, organized to wage an effective class action suit run by lawyers of their choice. There is no reason the Madoff investors could not have done the same. They would be able to pursue the lawsuits they chose, hiring lawyers with agreed-upon terms and fees. If they decided to sue JP Morgan and other banks, they'd do so knowing what they're getting into.

Regulators in effect took away the victims' right to make decisions, including the option to receive early remuneration. If bringing in SIPC was to help the investors, then the best thing to do would be to give them the money and let them decide who they want to sue and for how long. They would certainly have no trouble finding lawyers to hire — there'd be a long line of hopeful candidates looking to take the case.

A key policy choice that furthers the interests of the bankruptcy lawyers is to compensate them for litigating, not for winning cases or negotiating settlements. The Manhattan Fund estate paid legal fees regardless of what that legal activity achieved for the fraud victims. Similarly SIPC paid for hours billed by the group around Picard, whether or not those hours had a useful result. Unlike legal fees in private civil suits, where part of the payment to the legal team depends on their recovering money, the SIPC payments were not contingent.

Privately hired attorneys, paid largely from the proceeds of a settlement, have an incentive not to start litigation unless they think there is a reasonable chance of getting a settlement — as happened in the class action that investors brought against Manhattan fund service providers. But regulators, including SIPC, give no such incentive to estate supervisors, who therefore had all the reason in the world to sue no matter how far-fetched the case.

While the system created and maintained by regulators guaranteed hourly pay at a robust rate, it left the number of hours open ended. Hence it positively encouraged complex and lengthy lawsuits generating numerous billable hours. This depleted the SIPC fund meant for brokerage customers in what looks like a crony lawyer enrichment scheme.

There is evidence that hourly payments result in frivolous or "junk" suits. Thus Helland and Tabarrok investigated the quality of lawsuits under different fee arrangements using data on a cross section of states in 1992. They found that hourly fees encourage the filing of low-quality suits and increase the time to settlement.[253] Conversely, contingency fees enhance the quality of suits and reduce the time to settlement.

Another type of fee arrangement is a conditional bonus — which is tied to winning the case but not to the amount of the award. This does not provide an incentive for lawyers to get larger settlements, but would be better for payers – whether a bankruptcy estate or SIPC – compared to hourly fees with no condition attached. It would discourage unlikely litigation, thereby not only reducing legal payments but shortening the time assets remain tied up in bankruptcy court.

All in all, the system worked beautifully for those who received the legal jackpot. One has to doubt that regulators had fraud victims' interest in mind; but there can be no issue that their decisions served well their fellow lawyers.

CHAPTER EIGHT. Empty Pot

The two schemes we've discussed so far illustrate investors' illusion of safety and regulators' role in encouraging this misperception. In theory financial regulators exist to serve the investing public; in practice the belief that regulators are watching out facilitates the public being deceived. Berger and Madoff may not have set out to exploit this effect, but the perceived regulatory umbrella helped them continue their fraud. A regulated broker covered for Berger. The fact that regulators kept looking at Madoff's business apparently without finding any serious issue reassured investors.

Allen Stanford went one step further.[254] He actively built a network of government functionaries and politicians to protect himself. For years he invested in a web of connections and cultivated office holders in a variety of ways. His political contacts gave him an aura of respectability while the high-level former regulators he gathered around him helped ward off threats to his colossal swindle.

Many – probably most – Ponzi scheme perpetrators slide into fraud because an investment or business idea fails. The initial attempt to make money is honest but once losses show up the manager does not want to admit the failure, hoping to recover the loss. In the meantime he pays redeeming investors with money from new investors. Berger and Madoff fit this common model.

Stanford was different: his idea was dishonest to begin with. It would have been deceptive even if it were profitable, because he never told the customers what he really did with their savings. He ran a criminal enterprise from start to finish, but wrapped up in an elaborate cocoon of legitimacy. Numerous regulators and politicians helped him construct that cocoon. For that reason, the Stanford scheme is especially instructive as to the way government interacts with fraud.

It also exposed regulatory bureaucracies' inner workings more clearly than other schemes. What is more, the sequel make a revealing coda to the Madoff bankruptcy. I don't think I'm guilty of hyperbole when I write that throughout the Stanford affair the Securities and Exchange Commission outdid itself in proving the financial regulatory system a sham.

A Professional Con Artist

You could possibly argue that by not stopping Madoff, the SEC showed ineptitude or a lack of skills. I am not persuaded, given that SEC examiners strongly suspected Madoff and were prevented from investigating further by a high official. Nevertheless you might make a case that the SEC showed itself unable to do its duty, despite the many complaints and even detailed reports about the fraud, due to incompetence in some sense or another.

That argument cannot be made at all with respect to Stanford. The SEC does not come across as inept in the Stanford affair — on the contrary, its mid-level examiners proved themselves to be highly competent and conscientious. As soon as Stanford appeared on their radar, they identified his investment scheme as a likely fraud. They urged that this business – at that time small, with few American clients – be investigated thoroughly. They left a paper and electronic trail marking Stanford as a major potential threat to investors. They did so as clearly as possible. They repeated the warning, again and again, year after year. There is no ambiguity in the matter.

By not stopping Stanford, the SEC itself showed unwilling to do its duty. It was able, but particular decision makers did not want to. No matter how much the examiners urged that the scheme be stopped, higher up in the bureaucracy there was no desire to catch him. The Stanford case has a profound implication for our understanding of how government agencies function: it highlights the motives, not the skills or lack thereof.

The man himself left a long record of misconduct and worse. He was a gym operator in central Texas who overextended the business and went under when the Texas economy was hit by the 1980s oil price collapse and S&L crisis. Pursued by his erstwhile partners who demanded he pay them back, he declared personal bankruptcy. Reports circulated of his drunkenness and multiple arrests.

From that low point, Stanford rose to become a billionaire financier heading a global business — or so he styled himself and was described in the media. He and his father sold a small insurance brokerage founded by an ancestor and took advantage of the local slump to buy cheap real estate. He raised some money from Latin American sources and became a property developer, building townhouses in Houston.

In 1985 Stanford did something one would have never expected from his career up to that point: he established a bank in the Caribbean. He suggested he did this because Latin American investors in his property deals needed a place to put their profits. But there are numerous banks they could have gone to. Why would anyone prefer a brand new bank run by a man who had neither banking experience nor knowledge of financial markets? That is one of the mysteries of Stanford's history.

A plausible explanation is that these were not legitimate investors and the seed capital they gave Stanford for the bank came from illegal sources, possibly narcotics dealing. That money allowed him to get his financial empire going, but suspected links to the drug trade dogged him to the end.

At first the bank was called Guardian International and located in the island of Montserrat. It was under investigation by both Britain and the United States for laundering drug money when the Montserrat bank regulator decided to revoke its license. Among the reasons for this decision was the opacity of the bank's finances, the absence of a proper auditor and Stanford's bankruptcy.

When he learnt that he was losing the license, Stanford moved the bank to Antigua and renamed it Stanford International. Thereby he escaped from the drug money investigations. In Antigua he quickly established close relations with the local government, which was in desperate financial straits and known for corruption. He became its main financial backer and undertook ambitious development projects on the island, building resorts, luxury housing, a fancy gym, even a cricket stadium. He came to own two airlines, two newspapers and a cricket team. Stanford concealed the fact that the bank was the source of the money for all this.

Strictly speaking, Stanford International was not a bank. Traditional banks take deposits, make loans and earn the difference between the interest rates paid on deposits versus earned on loans. The Stanford bank did nothing of the kind. It was not a proper investment bank, either. It was, to put it simply, a way of raising funds mainly to finance real estate ventures without telling people their money was used for this purpose.

The customers were sold a product called a certificate of deposit with the promise that they faced no risk because the underlying investments were extremely safe. The Stanford CDs differed from CDs issued by banks in the United States — his certificates lacked federal deposit insurance. The investors were given the impression that they were protected by private insurance.[255] Of course, his CDs paid higher rates.

These certificates were initially marketed to well-off Latin Americans. To pitch the product more widely, Stanford opened offices in Houston and Miami. These helped sell the product but invited legal trouble. The sales were not licensed, violating banking law in Texas. In 1988 and 1989 the US Office of the Comptroller of the Currency issued warnings that Stanford violated banking laws in Florida and California as well.

After this Stanford kept the business out of America for some years, but his need for more funds pushed him back into the country to peddle the CDs. In 1995 he started his namesake company in Houston, registered with the Securities and Exchange as a broker-dealer of securities and an investment adviser. Thereby for the first time Stanford came under the scrutiny of the American financial overseer, specifically the Fort Worth office of the SEC.

Probably soon after he succeeded in selling the first CDs, he diverted the proceeds from sales not only to property ventures but also to finance his wildly extravagant life style. Over time he used the money to hire former regulators and build relations with numerous politicians, initially in Antigua and later in America.

Possible Ponzi scheme

At the SEC Fort Worth office, an experienced examiner by the name of Julie Preuitt looked at the Stanford brokerage's report and immediately suspected foul play. She and other examiners warned in 1997 of "Possible misrepresentations. Possible Ponzi scheme." They recorded their strong suspicions in the SEC internal tracking system and sent a report to the enforcement division, which can issue subpoenas to get information. But the enforcement division would not act.

The following year U.S. Customs contacted the SEC about the possibility of the Houston broker-dealer being connected to drug trafficking and money laundering. A narcotics investigation by the Drug Enforcement Administration found that the Mexican Juárez drug cartel was passing money through the Stanford bank. An SEC lawyer attended a meeting of law enforcement officers in Houston to discuss this development. A long list of agencies and departments were concerned, from the U.S. Attorney's Office, the Postal Inspector and the Secret Service to the State Department and the Treasury.

In 1999 Stanford handed the Juárez money – $3 million – to the U.S. government. But there was no obvious legal repercussion for him and his business. Another source, the Texas securities regulator, gave the FBI and SEC information about money laundering at the Stanford bank.[256] Neither agency acted on this. How did he get off so lightly? That's another surprising element in his career.

It was reported that he provided information to the Drug Enforcement Administration and other U.S. agencies about his customers in the narcotics trade and flows of illegal funds. Given his extensive international contacts and constant travelling around the world, he probably was a valuable spy.

By becoming a government informer, he obtained protection for himself and his business. Neither he, nor the agencies suspected of employing him as an informer, would comment on this subject.[257]

Meanwhile, the one dogged pursuer of Stanford kept at it. The SEC examiners had a go at the Houston company from another angle. This time they looked at the registered investment advisers employed by Stanford. Advisers have a legal duty to recommend investments appropriate for each client's specific financial needs. But the Stanford investment advisers told the SEC examiner they knew little about the portfolio backing the CDs.

Without enough information behind their recommendations, the advisers were on the face of it violating their legal obligation to customers. "It just smells bad," the examiner concluded. Reflecting the findings, the SEC sent a letter to the Stanford company warning that "Any departure from this fiduciary standard may constitute fraud upon clients…"

The assistant director in the enforcement program at the SEC Fort Worth office, a lawyer named Spencer Barasch, would not start an inquiry after receiving the examiners' "possible Ponzi scheme" report. But his office took action after the money laundering issue was brought to the SEC by other federal agencies.[258] Stanford hired as his attorney a former head of the SEC Fort Worth office, Wayne Secore, who understood how regulators did things and also knew the SEC staff.

He and Barasch met to talk about the inquiry. What transpired between them became a critical question later, but both men claimed to have no memory of it. What's certain is that Barasch shut down the inquiry only three months after it started. He did this knowing that it would shock and disappoint his examiner colleagues. Concerned that Preuitt would not take the news well, he called her and told her the matter was closed due to "some problems with the case."[259]

Barasch said he decided not to pursue the inquiry further after his conversation with Secore, according to Preuitt. As she remembered the call, he said he asked Secore if there was a case against Stanford and Secore told him there was not. Thus reassured by the former regulator, now Stanford's defense attorney, the enforcement assistant director stopped the investigation. No subpoenas were issued to get information about how the money from the CDs was being invested.

Later Barasch denied that he was influenced by Secore in this matter. Given the conflicting accounts, it is not clear why he stopped the inquiry. When the matter was investigated, Barasch and others gave numerous explanations. Among these was the complication that the Antiguan bank issuing CDs was outside U.S. jurisdiction and the investors were not Americans. But the second point was incorrect — the SEC examiners found that the clients did include some Americans by 1998. More important, Stanford was soliciting an ever larger number of American retirees, luring them with his high-paying and supposedly perfectly safe CDs.

In truth, taking on Stanford was tough. Barasch said he had been told by senior SEC officials to focus on accounting problems and there was pressure to bring a lot of cases, which meant a preference for easier targets. Stanford, of course, took care to make himself a difficult target. One way he did this was by hiring Secore, getting the benefit of the erstwhile regulator's expertise and contacts inside the SEC.

Barasch indicated that in 1998 he referred the matter to the brokerage industry self-regulator. No evidence could be found of the referral. NASD and its successor FINRA took no action regarding the possibility of fraud; later brokerage examiners cited the Stanford companies for violations but imposed only modest penalties.

The end of the SEC inquiry meant that Stanford was home free after being investigated by various arms of the US government. He was not charged with any crime, whether money laundering or fraud. He was vetted by the SEC more than once, both his broker-dealer and investment adviser group were examined and he emerged with no serious blemish on his official public record.

By 2000, his headquarters in Houston contained a sizable sales staff. In time he opened more than 20 regional offices in the United States, pushing the CDs to increasing numbers of Americans looking to invest their retirement money. Meanwhile the chasm between the bank's reported assets and actual liabilities kept widening. The value of the investment portfolio was adjusted every year to produce the fantasy returns that supposedly supported the CDs.

Sir Allen Goes to Washington

In 2001, a bill against money laundering made its way in US Congress. It would require offshore banks to report the sources of their funds to American agencies. By then Stanford's Houston company was selling a lot of CDs issued by the bank in Antigua, which would no doubt come under the new law. He quickly hired lobbyists to work against the proposal and a Senate committee shelved it.

Whenever legislation came up in Congress that could lead to greater scrutiny of his businesses in the Caribbean or America, he donated generously to both parties. In 2002 he financed lobbying against a bill that would have allowed state and federal regulators to share details of fraud cases. That bill, too, vanished.[260]

Stanford built a wide-ranging political network of high-level politicians and operatives. He gave millions of dollars to lawmakers across the spectrum, from left-wing Democrats like Charles Ranger and Barney Frank to the Republican presidential candidate John McCain. While he spread the goodies around, in terms of dollar amounts he gave much more to Democrats than Republicans. The Democratic Senatorial Campaign Committee received more than ten times as much as the National Republican Senatorial Committee.[261]

In 2006 Stanford wheedled a knighthood from Antigua and became Sir Allen. So it came about that in June 2008 the *Antigua Sun,* one of the papers he owned, published a photo of Sir Allen with then-Senator Barack Obama. They met in Miami where the presidential candidate was campaigning. Of course Stanford contributed to the campaign.

To his clients, he sent annual reports that contained – besides fake information about returns on investments – pictures of him posing with Senators, Congressmen and other dignitaries. Before he gave to the presidential campaign of Barack Obama, he gave to the inaugural committee of George W. Bush and received a letter of commendation from President Bush, which he included in a report to CD holders.

This was all part of a far-reaching effort to burnish his brand and sell more CDs. The political networking helped him reassure customers, as well as on occasion giving a push in the right direction to proposed legislation he had an interest in. High-end political allies gave him the appearance of legitimacy while protecting his interests to the extent they could.

His top political adviser was a veteran Democrat, a protégé of Lyndon Johnson and a former Lieutenant Governor of Texas.[262] Stanford retained him for years; the payments added up to more than $5 million, to help with various matters in including a tax dodge.[263]

Stanford declared himself a resident of St. Croix in the U.S. Virgin Islands and took advantage of the special low income tax Congress legislated for such residents — in effect only 3.5%. He wanted Congress to keep the rate low and his allies achieved this, though they failed to expand the scope of the favorable tax rate as he wanted. On part of his income he paid no income tax by the simple expedient of not declaring it.

Employing a small army of former regulators and other government officials, he showed a particular liking for attorneys who once worked at the SEC. The more his CDs came under attack, the more regulators and lobbyists he hired. Later on Barasch, having left the SEC, joined the legal team defending Stanford against the investigation that Barasch as a regulator had helped block. This violated rules on federal employees and Barasch had to stop, much to the displeasure of both him and his client.

Stanford then found another old hand from the SEC, a top enforcement counsel from the Washington office who after leaving the agency made a name as a defense lawyer. This former regulator, Thomas Sjoblom, warded off his former colleagues with assurances that Stanford's business was legit, that he, an experienced investigator, had looked into it and no fraud was involved.

The CD sales provided the funds Stanford used to finance his political alliances and hire lobbyists and former regulators. The allies and lawyers, in turn, helped protect the scheme. In this way the fraud and the government connections formed a feedback loop. The more money he took in, the more protection he acquired, which allowed him to go on with the fraud and take in more money.

Without the political connections and the protection, he would not have survived so long. Even more dramatically than Madoff, Stanford was enabled by parts of the government.

All the while, the SEC examiner who first noticed the strange CDs, Julie Preuitt, waged a heroic battle within the bureaucracy for almost 12 years to stop Stanford. She and other examiners investigated repeatedly and issued reports indicating that this likely fraud was spreading. Time and again, they were frustrated.

During this period there were numerous complaints to regulators from Stanford's clients and employees, some of them explicitly describing the operation as a Ponzi scheme. It is hard to imagine any situation where there would a better case for intervention. Year after year investigations by experienced internal examiners indicate something is very wrong, at the same time complaints pile up. How could they leave this scheme to fester for 12 years? The only possible answer is that some higher-level officials did not wish to nab Stanford.

To be fair, the SEC has two defenses in this matter. One, Stanford really was a nasty guy to go after. He appears to have been an evil genius. He concocted an innovative con game that fell through regulators' cracks – since his CDs were not like any other CD and indeed were not real CDs – and spread his scheme across the planet so that every country's regulator saw him as someone else's problem. He obtained extensive protection at highest levels of government. He was defended by former regulators who knew all the angles. They effectively impeded investigations and warded off their former colleagues.

That line of argument is not really persuasive. SEC examiners right away suspected the unusual CDs and noticed numerous red lights about the Stanford operation—they listed these in their reports, leaving clear evidence that his shenanigans were recognized. As many as 30 brokers who worked at the Stanford brokerage complained to NASD and its successor FINRA as well as the SEC that they were pressured to sell the CDs and fired when they refused. Some of them told regulators the CDs were likely fraudulent.

Given all this, there was strong reason to go after Stanford and fight his defenders. That higher level bureaucrats decided not to suggests they are oblivious to the official reason why they exist, namely to protect investors.

However, a second line of defense for the SEC is possibly more credible. As I mentioned, besides befriending politicians and regulators Stanford may have safeguarded himself by acting as a spy for certain government agencies. It was reported that he provided information to the Drug Enforcement Administration and the Central Intelligence Agency. Neither he nor the agencies would acknowledge this, but it is plausible. With his extensive operations especially in Latin America he had many opportunities to gather information and no doubt was delighted to cooperate so as to shield his financial scam.

The SEC may have been under pressure from other parts of the government to leave Stanford alone. To the extent that other agencies protected the fraudster but never acknowledged their involvement, the SEC became a scapegoat. Others told it not to pursue the con man but this was secret—even a member of Congress could not get the full story. So when the scandal emerged, the SEC became the target of public outrage.

While that's a believable explanation, the fact remains that as the main financial regulator the SEC could have forced the issue. After Madoff confessed, the SEC top brass were no longer willing to let Stanford continue because they faced criticism for not catching Madoff. Then they did what that they could have done earlier—they insisted to the Department of Justice that immediate action had to be taken.

Stanford told his top lieutenant that the SEC staff would not be able to catch him because they were not that smart. He was wrong. Once regulators seriously confronted him, the endgame came quickly. Stanford was taken to court and – although he insisted on his innocence and the criminal case was delayed by a beating he took in prison – eventually sentenced to 110 years.

It had never been a lack of smarts that got in the way of pursuing him but rather a lack of willingness. To the very end Stanford acted as if somehow he would get out of his legal travails. Probably this was to an extent self delusion, but perhaps he had reason to believe some government ally would come to his aid because they had in the past. This time they did not. He had become a major liability; his former allies washed their hands of him.

Receiver Wars

A global network is a great misfortune for victims of financial fraud. One government and receiver feeding at the trough is bad enough. When a scheme has global reach, multiple governments, receivers and congeries of crony lawyers lay their hands on the assets.

Stanford claimed to have more than 30,000 clients in 133 countries. These people were left in a dreadful fix. When the SEC stopped the American operation that controlled the far-flung operation, the web quickly unraveled and businesses in other parts of the world were let loose. Various local authorities took over, presenting multiple case studies of what happens to victims of fraud once governments are in control.

Antigua, with jurisdiction over extensive Stanford assets, was a major player in the post-fraud game. As the scandal broke, the Antigua Financial Services Regulatory Commission was still led by a long-time Stanford associate, Leroy King. Only a few days before the SEC took action in 2009, King told an investigating reporter that Sir Allen was "a good corporate citizen" whose customers never complained of not being paid.[264]

At the time a private analyst, Alex Dalmady, had publicized his view that the Stanford bank's returns were not believable. Nevertheless, King said, "we have to stay the course." King was later indicted for complicity in the fraud but at the time he was still Antigua's chief bank regulator.

With the Stanford organization in disarray after the U.S. government took action, King appointed as receivers for the Antigua assets two members of a British accounting firm called Vantis. These insisted on taking Stanford International Bank into bankruptcy and complained of not being paid enough for their services. Eventually they billed the estate for $18 million after having recovered a mere $300,000 in assets.

Vantis was in serious trouble at home. Employees in London, facing criminal tax evasion charges, sued the company. In June 2010 Vantis collapsed and its various components were sold off.[265] Responding to creditors' complaints, an Antigua court removed Vantis from the Stanford estate and appointed another British firm, Grant Thornton. Thereupon the new and former Antigua receivers commenced a public relations battle as they negotiated fee payments.

In the meantime the SEC chose and a Texas court confirmed Ralph Janvey as receiver for the Stanford companies. A lawyer and former government staffer like most American receivers for fraud estates, earlier in his career he was at the Comptoller of the Currency in Washington. Unlike the Madoff trustee he had not worked at the SEC and probably was less connected to that agency.

Janvey and the Antigua receivers proceeded to fight for the control of assets across the globe. At one point the Antiguan Parliament authorized the appropriation by the government of most of the properties on the island but this was challenged in court.[266]

It is hard to pin down the total assets of the Stanford companies at any given time. The numbers Allen Stanford gave news sources were grossly exaggerated. A 2008 *Forbes* magazine profile that accompanied his listing as one of America's richest stated: "Today Stanford Financial manages $51 billion in assets, up 30% from 2007." That is obviously false. In fact at the end of 2008 some 62 Stanford companies listed total assets of $10.6 billion in their balance sheets.

When the business ceased to operate in February 2009, the American receiver identified about $7.2 billion of CDs held by public investors—hence the media typically described the fraud as a $7 billion scheme. If mutual fund sales of more than $1 billion are included, the total is around $8.3 billion. Most of this Stanford lost in grandiose development projects, paid to CD salespeople and redeeming investors, donated to his political friends and frittered away on his flamboyant lifestyle.

Grant Thornton put the value of the property, securities and potential recovery from lawsuits against third parties at $1.5 billion. Similarly the U.S. receiver identified around $1.5 billion in assets all in all and estimated that the victims might get 20 cents to the dollar. Stanford's investments in real estate and private equity had to be sold at immense losses.

A dispute erupted as to which country had the honor of being Stanford's main stomping ground. The SEC weighed in. The Commission came out with a memo arguing for America as the location of the fraud and by implication the right place for the disposition of the estate.

Ironically, one of the reasons SEC officials gave for not going after Stanford was that the American connection was weak. When it came to claiming an estate, though, the agency never let geography or anything else get in the way.

In the many years Stanford operated – and was reported as a possible Ponzi scheme on and off by SEC examiners as well as former employees and some customers – the agency's enforcement staff repeatedly argued they couldn't pursue the matter because the bank and essential information required to take action were in Antigua. For 12 years, they preferred him to be someone else's problem. Only when the scheme ended did it become clear to the SEC that the fraud had happened in the U.S. Then they decided that the American lawyers they named should have control of the estate.

Bank accounts in Switzerland and Britain held $300 million, where the local courts favored the Antiguan receivers' claims. Grant Thornton received permission to spend up to $20 million of some $100 million in assets in the United Kingdom, against the objections of the U.S. Department of Justice and the Texas receiver.[267] Janvey appealed the decision in London but lost. American lawyers must have been apoplectic that others had the assets that could have paid legal fees to themselves and their allies.

The Grant Thornton receivers proposed to use the money in Britain to take legal action to secure the property and assets frozen in Antigua and to develop and sell these properties.[268] The jurisdictional fight continued — with the legal costs eroding the assets that belonged to the bank's clients. One of the British judges noted that the $1.6 million Antigua receivers billed so far was spent mainly to get court permission to spend more of the money. Regarding the turf battles between groups of receivers, Lord Justice Hughes commented: "the lack of co-operation between them has greatly increased the costs at the eventual expense of the victims ..."[269]

His American counterpart in Dallas expressed the same regret for the millions of dollars of Stanford victims' money spent by teams of lawyers in attempts to gain control of the estate. "I'm sadder that the money going to this to pay lawyers is not going to compensate the victims," U.S. District Judge Godbey said.[270]

Despite the concern judges on both sides of the Atlantic expressed about resources spent on the war of the receivers, the battles went on for several years. It was not till late 2012 that the Texas receiver and the liquidators for Antigua reached an agreement, which was then submitted to various courts for approval.

As legal battles raged for control, Stanford's victims had no way to gain access to any assets. People who relied on the CDs for retirement income were left with little to live on. Some of them were blue collar workers who had put their life's savings into what they thought was a safe investment.

No Pot of Gold

While the scheme spawned an immense number of lawsuits, including the usual actions to claw back money from people who benefitted from the fraud, Judge Godbey in Dallas discouraged the Stanford receiver from undertaking additional litigation to recover lost funds. "When the U.S. Justice Department has already checked and there's no pot of gold, then the receiver can stand down," the judge said.[271]

Another point of difference from the Manhattan and Madoff estates was that payment of a portion of the legal fees were held back for a later date. The receiver and his allies got 80% of their bills for work performed and applied later for the rest, when the judge ruled on objections to the payment. By contrast Lifland in New York had refused to hold back the payments to the Manhattan trustee and her associates despite repeated requests by the U.S. Trustee regulator.

The Texas judge demanded that legal fees be proportional to the amount of money the receiver was likely to recover, which was less than expected. Unlike the other fraud sequels, the Stanford estate never went into bankruptcy—though of course it was insolvent. Janvey argued that bankruptcy would be expensive and detrimental to the interests of the investors while receivership is generally more efficient and cost-effective.

So Janvey did not become bankruptcy trustee and remained receiver. As such, he did sue to get back the fees paid to financial advisors who sold the CDs and the fake gains paid to investors, as well as the donations Stanford made to politicians. He did not engage in long-run, large-scale litigation such as the Manhattan trustee's Bear Stearns case or Madoff trustee's cases against certain banks.

But there were complaints about the administrative expenses and the way the SEC chose Janvey as receiver. It was found that the agency violated its own rules in making this decision. The investigation into the matter was tainted by another scandal at the SEC. It was stopped because of an appearance of conflict of interest due to a relationship between the then inspector general of the SEC and a lawyer representing Stanford victims.[272]

From the available record, the appointment appears to have been a surprisingly simple matter. According to Janvey, he was approached in February 2009 – as the agency prepared to go to court against Stanford – by the SEC Fort Worth office enforcement associate director and told that he was being considered for the receiver job.[273] This SEC official, Stephen Korotash, was in charge of the Stanford case.

The SEC neither asked for nor provided any documents before the appointment, Janvey recalled. That suggests a remarkably casual way of naming a receiver for the second largest Ponzi scheme in American history (after Madoff).

Curiously, Korotash was particular about one issue. He asked Janvey whether as receiver he would hire a certain large law firm, Baker Botts, to work with him. The reason the SEC official gave for this was that the size and complexity of the coming receivership required a law firm with diverse and international expertise. No other rationale surfaced as to how and why the SEC came to pick Janvey and Baker Botts for the plum assignment.

A 30-year veteran of the agency, Korotash left the SEC in 2011 and like many regulators joined a law firm. The SEC investigation into the failure to stop Stanford mentioned that he told journalists the inquiry into the Stanford matter started in October 2006, whereas it started earlier. The late date was cited as a defense by the former SEC enforcement officer Barasch, who faced a Justice Department investigation for representing Stanford.

Certainly Janvey and Baker Botts were not the only ones with the qualifications. As usual they gave a discount off their standard hourly rate but almost any lawyer would have done so to get the job. Even without ambitious litigation, there were enough lawsuits on their hands to make a small army of lawyers happy.

Baker Botts turned out to be spectacularly expensive considering the modest amounts that could be salvaged from the wreck Stanford left behind. In the Madoff case claw-backs brought in a lot of money because Madoff had largely transferred assets, not lost them By contrast, Stanford had lost or spent much of the money, therefore it could not be easily recovered.

Even obvious claw-back targets were uncooperative — in particular, many of the politicians who took Stanford's tainted contributions refused to return the money for years.

So the estate remained small and more than half of it was spent on lawyers' fees and other administrative expenses. Although the SEC objected to an initial round of expenses, if it had its druthers the Stanford estate legal group would have the opportunity to make a lot more. We will now turn to this remarkable twist in the story.

A Tale of Two Estates

The Stanford case was unique in giving rise to a court fight between two United States regulators. Stanford's broker-dealer in Houston was a member of SIPC, the brokerage fund operator that financed the Madoff estate. Those who bought the Stanford CDs via the brokerage had reason to think they were under SIPC protection. After the fraud was exposed, its similarity in this respect to the Madoff setup gave the impression that SIPC would provide aid to the Stanford victims as well. In both cases there was a brokerage that channeled money to a fraudulent investment scheme.

As we saw, regulators treated people who invested directly with Madoff as brokerage customers and took the estate into bankruptcy liquidation under the SIPC law. This meant a SIPC payment of up to $500,000 per brokerage customer but more money went to the trustee and Co. for an immense amount of litigation. I've argued above that the arrangement was a great boon for the lawyers while discriminating against Madoff victims who invested via feeder funds and therefore were not considered brokerage customers.

The Madoff case put an unprecedented burden on SIPC. In the 40 years of its existence from its establishment by Congress in 1970, SIPC spent a total of $1.6 billion. The Madoff trustee group's compensation was estimated to top $1 billion and is already close to that, with no end in sight. The fraud victims received around $800 million from SIPC. So the payments to the Madoff estate lawyers and investors used up more of the fund than all previous SIPC aid to customers of failed brokerages.

Since the Madoff estate depleted the SIPC reserve, there was not much left for another such commitment. This did not bother some of the SEC higher ups. A former SEC counsel called the financing issue "a little bit of a red herring." Brokerages would be assessed and pay whatever amounts necessary. Despite the near empty pot, the SEC asked SIPC to take over the Stanford estate as it had the Madoff estate.

But by then the brokerages that would be forced to cough up the money recognized something that neither they nor anyone else – other than the a cabal of lawyers and regulators, presumably – had known earlier. They could be on the hook for open-ended litigation to the tune of $1 billion and counting. That trustee fees and expenses are not subject to reasonable limits and can run for years on end was observable from both the Manhattan and Madoff estates.

The brokerages balked at having to pay gigantic legal bills for yet another team of lawyers. Smaller broker-dealers opposed the SEC demand that SIPC take over the Stanford estate. They said the assessments would become too large for them to afford if SIPC were to cover investment fraud. The result was that this time SIPC would not go along with the SEC. However, reportedly SIPC was willing to provide some assistance to the fraud victims, but without paying the legal fees that it would be liable for if the estate was put into bankruptcy under the SIPC law.

So SIPC proposed a more modest plan to help the Stanford clients — it would pay up to $250,000 per CD holder. Given how desperate some victims were, this would have been a real help to them.[274] But the SEC rejected that plan. While the ostensible reason was to get more money for the victims, the latter would been better off taking the SIPC offer. Instead the SEC went to court to force SIPC and its member brokerages to finance another bankruptcy case — in effect another all-expenses paid legal jamboree.

In response SIPC officials pointed out that by law the reserve fund was to be used in cases of brokerage failure; it was not meant to compensate losses due to investment fraud. But then why were they paying for the Madoff estate? While there were certain technical differences between the Madoff and Stanford schemes, the fact remains that the SIPC fund was not intended to finance ambitious litigation by estate lawyers.

The Stanford victims received nothing instead of the $250,000 SIPC offered. After turning down the offer, the SEC lost the case. A district court decided that the CD holders were not customers of the brokerage but of the bank in Antigua and hence not entitled to any SIPC protection. The SEC appealed, in part on the grounds that SIPC is under obligation to do whatever the SEC demands of it.

Arguably the SEC, as the supervisor of SIPC, misused the fund in the Madoff case. Since so much of the SIPC fund was spent on the lawyers, no resources were left for other victims. Legal decisions may turn on technical distinctions that appear trivial to non-lawyers, but a reasonable application of the SIPC statute would have been to provide some assistance to the victims while limiting the legal payments.

Had the SEC been successful in creating another SIPC-financed estate, there would have been a huge new pot of gold for resourceful lawyers. They could have litigated and billed for a decade to come, with brokerage customers obliged to pay the bills. Pushing for the creation of another SIPC-paid bankruptcy is not really the way to help the victims; it is the way to create a legal boondoggle. Once again, it is difficult to see that regulators have fraud victims' well-being in mind.

NOTES

[90] The official names were Manhattan Capital Management Inc. for the management firm and Manhattan Investment Fund Ltd. for the pool of money it managed. The latter is referred to as MIFL in some legal documents.

[91] Confidential Memorandum for Manhattan Investment Fund Ltd., dated December 1995.

[92] "Market Watch," *Barron's,* November 6, 1995, p .

[93] "Market Watch," *Barron's,* January 1, 1996, p.38.

[94] *Wall Street Notes,* November 5, 1996.

[95] *Wall Street Notes* October 29, 1996.

[96] Waters and Ratner 2002.

[97] *Wall Street Notes* December 10, 1996.

[98] This is the title of Shiller 2000, the notable book that explained the psychology of the stock bubble while the thing itself crashed.

[99] DeLong and Magin 2005.

[100] *Wall Street Notes* December 10, 1996

[101] *Wall Street Notes* September 17, 1997

[102] *Wall Street Notes* October 15, 1997

[103] Miller 2002; p. 11.

[104] US District Court, Southern District of New York, Cromer Finance Ltd. and Prival N.V. vs. Michael Berger et al., Document # 594, Exhibit 75.

[105] *Wall Street Notes*, October 22, 1997

[106] US District Court, Southern District of New York, Cromer Finance Ltd. and Prival N.V. vs. Michael Berger et al., Document # 239, p. 27.

[107] *Wall Street Notes* November 19, 1998

[108] Kurdas 2006a. On that occasion, the question of why the Fed did not prevent the bubble was put to Greenspan directly by the manager of a hedge fund.

[109] The story of LTCM can be found in Lowenstein 2000 and Dunbar 2000.

[110] Birger and Isidore 1998.

[111] Miller 2002; p. 214.

[112] Birger and Isidore 1998.

[113] To use the title of Taleb 2007.

[114] The term is from Biggs 2008.

[115] Berger was by no means the youngest to try out his luck. A 21-year-old New York University history major so wowed investment bankers and movie producers in Greenwich, Connecticut, that they gave him money for a supposed hedge fund— Feuer 2005 tells the story.

[116] US District Court, Southern District of New York, Cromer Finance Ltd. and Prival N.V. vs. Michael Berger et al., Document # 594, Exhibit 84.

[117] US District Court, Southern District of New York, Cromer Finance Ltd. And Prival N.V., et al., plaintiffs, Second Amended Complaint for Violations of the Securities Laws and Pendent State Low Claims, filed July 30, 2001

[118] Quotes from deposition of Peter Gutschow in Expert's Report, Document #593, US District Court, Southern District of New York, Cromer Finance Ltd. And Prival N.V. et al.

[119] The fund made profits 11 months out of its life of about three-and-a-half years. Transcript of hearing held October 31, 2006, U.S. Bankruptcy Court, Southern District of New York, pp. 31, 46.

[120] Second Amended Complaint for Violations of the Securities Laws and Pendent State Low Claims, p. 43. filed July 30, 2001, US District Court, Southern District of New York, Cromer Finance Ltd. And Prival N.V., et al.

[121] Expert's Report, December 20, 2002, at US District Court, Southern District of New York Cromer Finance Ltd. And Prival N.V. et al.

[122] Second Amended Complaint for Violations of the Securities Laws and Pendent State Low Claims, p. 48. filed July 30, 2001, US District Court, Southern District of New York, Cromer Finance Ltd. And Prival N.V. et al.

[123] This 3/18/1999 message is reproduced in document #261 in the case against the auditor Deloitte at the US District Court, Southern District of New York, Cromer Finance Ltd. and Prival N.V. The authenticity of the message was contested by Deloitte's lawyers but it remains in the legal record.

[124] As I pointed out in Kurdas 2009a.

[125] Different individuals' later testimonies about these events varied—October 31, 2006 hearing at U.S. Bankruptcy Court, Southern District of New York, Manhattan Investment Fund Ltd.

[126] Diem Consultants v. Manhattan Capital Management Inc. at The High Court of Justice, Chancery Division, 1999.

[127] Filing with US Bankruptcy Court, Southern District of New York, regarding Manhattan Investment Fund Ltd., Helen Gredd v. Bear, Stearns Securities Corp. April 24, 2001.

[128] US Bankruptcy Court, Southern District of New York, Decision by Burton Lifland, January 9, 2007, pp.23-27.

[129] Quote from FBI agent in Kurdas 2006b.

[130] Schumpeter 1950, p.375.

[131] Tran 2006, p.29, Table 2.3.

[132] Shogren 2000a.

[133] Soros 2003, p. 41.

[134] United States District Court, Southern District of New York. US against Michael Berger, affidavit in support of motion to withdraw plea, document 21, exhibit 5.

[135] Berger repeatedly mentioned this notion to the author in 2001.

[136] Reply Memorandum in Further Support of Motion to Withdraw Plea, November 26, 2001, US District Court, Southern District of New York, US vs. Michael Berger.

[137] Affidavit of Michael Berger, September 1, 2001, US District Court, Southern District of New York, US vs. Michael Berger.

[138] Reply memorandum in further support of motion to withdraw plea, November 26, 2001, United States District Court, Southern District of New York. US. against Michael Berger.

[139] Affidavit of Sanford L. Drob, Ph.D., November 21, 2001, United States District Court, Southern District of New York. US. against Michael Berger.

[140] Memorandum of law in support of Defendant Michael Berger's Motion to withdraw guilty plea, September 24, 2001, United States District Court, Southern District of New York. US against Michael Berger.

[141] Goode 2003.

[142] Bailey 2002.

[143] Government Memorandum of Law in Opposition to defendant Michael Berger's Motion to Withdraw his Plea, Jay Musoff, November 14, 2001, p.69, United States District Court, Southern District of New York, US against Michael Berger.

[144] Decision and Order, Victor Marrero, January 28, 2002, United States District Court, Southern District of New York, US against Michael Berger.

[145] Decision and Order, Victor Marrero, January 28, 2002, p. 36.

[146] Decision and Order, Victor Marrero, January 28, 2002, p. 36-37.

[147] Government Memorandum of Law in Opposition to defendant Michael Berger's Motion to Withdraw his Plea, Jay Musoff, November 14, 2001, pp.49-50, United States District Court, Southern District of New York, US against Michael Berger.

[148] US Securities and Exchange Commission 2002 release, In the Matter of Financial Asset Management.

[149] US Securities and Exchange Commission releases no. 8052, 45224, 2007, and 1485; all dated January 3, 2002. Administrative procedure file no. 3-10670, available on http://www.sec.gov/litigation/admin

[150] This has been found for many countries: see Koellinger, Minniti and Schade, 2007.

[151] This is the cost of excessive optimism: One can be sincere in believing in one's own fantasy, but it leaves one with a weak connection to reality, as a reviewer of books on persuasion and lying puts it: Blackburn 2006.

[152] Barberis and Thaler 2003.

[153] Gilbert 2005.

[154] Taleb 2007 has the best argument, to my mind.

[155] Eichenwald and Wakin 2005.

[156] Cohen, Lucchetti, and Baram 2005.

[157] Bazerman and Tenbrunsel 2011.

[158] Alex Shogren 2000b and c. The SEC official quoted is Bill Baker.

[159] Newman 2003.

[160] "Order Appointing Receiver," signed Denise Cote, January 19, 2000, US District Court, Southern District of New York.

[161] Gapper 2005, Roberts 2005.

[162] Associated Press 2006.

[163] Some experts advocate Chapter 15 in certain cases instead of Chapters 11 or 7. For instance, Lee, Engel and Krys 2007.

[164] "Objection of Bank of Austria AG to Motion for an Order to (1) Appoint a Chapter 11 Joint Trustee and (2) Excuse Compliance with Section 543," filed by Robin Keller, April 4, 2000; p. 3, US Bankruptcy Court, Southern District of New York, Manhattan Investment Fund Ltd.

[165] "Reply to Objection of Bank of Austria AG to Motion Seeking, Inter Alia, An Order Appointing a Chapter 11 Joint Trustee," April 4, 2000; p. 2, n. 4, US Bankruptcy Court, Southern District of New York, Manhattan Investment Fund Ltd.

[166] LoPucki 2006.

[167] Transcript of hearing held September 6, 2000, doc #191, pp. 13-16, US Bankruptcy Court Southern District of New York, Manhattan Investment Fund Ltd.

[168] Transcript of hearing held January 15, 2004, p.15, US Bankruptcy Court Southern District of New York, Manhattan Investment Fund Ltd.

[169] Transcript of hearing held February 19, 2004, p.7, US Bankruptcy Court Southern District of New York, Manhattan Investment Fund Ltd.

[170] Transcript of hearing held December 20, 2000, p.8, US Bankruptcy Court Southern District of New York, Manhattan Investment Fund Ltd.

[171] Transcript of hearing held October 4, 2001, pp.15-20, US Bankruptcy Court Southern District of New York, Manhattan Investment Fund Ltd.

[172] Transcript of teleconference in chambers, July 17, 2002, US District Court, Southern District of New York, Cromer Finance Ltd. and Prival N.V. vs. Michael Berger et al.

[173] Complaint, January 18, 2000, p. 13, US District Court, Southern District of New York, Cromer Finance Ltd. vs. Michael Berger et al.

[174] Affidavit in Support of Objection to the Settlement Class Counsel's Application for Attorneys' Fees and Reimbursements of Expenses, September 20, 2002, US District Court, Southern District of New York, Cromer Finance Ltd. and Prival N.V. vs. Michael Berger et al.

[175] Memorandum of Law of Defendants Bear Stearns securities Corp. and Bear Stearns & Co. Inc. in Support of Their Motion to Dismiss the Complaints, October 20, 2000, p.3, by Schulte Roth & Zabel LLP, US District Court, Southern District of New York.

[176] Opinion and Order, Denise Cote, April 17, 2001, p. 29, US District Court, Southern District of New York, Cromer Finance Ltd. and Prival N.V. vs. Michael Berger et al.

[177] Opinion and Order, Denise Cote, April 17, 2001, p. 30, US District Court, Southern District of New York, Cromer Finance Ltd. and Prival N.V. vs. Michael Berger et al.

[178] Filing for Helen Gredd v. Bear, Stearns Securities Corp., April 24, 2001, pp.20-23, US Bankruptcy Court, Southern District of New York, Manhattan Investment Fund Ltd .

[179] Maiello and Kruger 2001.

[180] Opinion by Naomi Reice Buchwald, March 21, 2002, US District Court for the Southern District of New York, Bear Stearns Securities Corp. against Helen Gredd. Also see Marhedge 2002.

[181] Opinion by Naomi Reice Buchwald, March 21, 2002, US District Court for the Southern District of New York, Bear Stearns Securities Corp. against Helen Gredd.

[182] Transcript of Proceedings, September 12, 2002, pp.19, US Bankruptcy Court, Southern District of New York, Manhattan Investment Fund Ltd..

[183] Transcript of Proceedings, September 12, 2002, pp.8-10, US Bankruptcy Court, Southern District of New York, Manhattan Investment Fund Ltd.

[184] Transcript of Proceedings, September 12, 2002, p. 50, US Bankruptcy Court, Southern District of New York, Manhattan Investment Fund Ltd.

[185] Opinion by Burton R. Lifland, October 7, 2002, p. 6, US Bankruptcy Court, Southern District of New York, Manhattan Investment Fund Ltd.

[186] Opinion by Naomi Reice Buchwald, December 18, 2002, p. 5, US District Court for the Southern District of New York, Manhattan Investment Fund Ltd.

[187] Craig 2004.

[188] Order by Burton R. Lifland, Pursuant to Sections 105, 363 and 503 of the Bankruptcy Code, 28 USC 1781(b)(2) and Bankruptcy Rules 7028 and 9019, January 15, 2004, p. 8, US Bankruptcy Court, Southern District of New York, Manhattan Investment Fund Ltd.

[189] Transcript of Proceedings, January 15, 2004, p. 13, US Bankruptcy Court, Southern District of New York, Manhattan Investment Fund Ltd.

[190] Transcript of hearing held October 31, 2006, p. 24, US Bankruptcy Court, Southern District of New York, Manhattan Investment Fund Ltd., Helen Gredd v. Bear, Stearns Securities Corp.

[191] Transcript of hearing held October 31, 2006, p. 18, U.S. Bankruptcy Court, Southern District of New York, Manhattan Investment Fund Ltd., Helen Gredd v. Bear, Stearns Securities Corp.

[192] Transcript of hearing held October 31, 2006, p. 19, U.S. Bankruptcy Court, Southern District of New York, Manhattan Investment Fund Ltd.

[193] Transcript of Proceedings, January 15, 2004, p.13, U.S. Bankruptcy Court, Southern District of New York, Manhattan Investment Fund Ltd.

[194] Lattman 2007.

[195] Outside lawyers on public record persistently described the ruling as "surprising" or "somewhat surprising". For example, see "Corporate Reorganization and Bankruptcy Update," from the law firm Sidley Austin LLP, February 23, 2007.

[196] Transcript of hearing held February 15, 2007, U.S. Bankruptcy Court, Southern District of New York, Manhattan Investment Fund Ltd.

[197] Transcript of hearing held December 20, 2000, p.17, U.S. Bankruptcy Court, Southern District of New York, Manhattan Investment Fund Ltd.

[198] Transcript of hearing held December 20, 2000, p.15, U.S. Bankruptcy Court, Southern District of New York, Manhattan Investment Fund Ltd.

[199] Transcript of hearing held December 20, 2000, pp.1-2, U.S. Bankruptcy Court, Southern District of New York, Manhattan Investment Fund Ltd.

[200] Transcript of hearing held July 1, 2004, p.15, U.S. Bankruptcy Court, Southern District of New York, Manhattan Investment Fund Ltd.

[201] Transcript of hearing held July 1, 2004, p.16, U.S. Bankruptcy Court, Southern District of New York, Manhattan Investment Fund Ltd.

[202] Transcript of hearing held July 1, 2004, p.17, U.S. Bankruptcy Court, Southern District of New York, Manhattan Investment Fund Ltd.

[203] Marcus 2013.

[204] Eighth Application for Interim Allowances of Compensation of Dewey Ballantine LLP for Services Rendered as Counsel to the Trustee and for Reimbursements of Expenses and Disbursements, Dec. 3, 2002, and related documents presented for a hearing on December 23, 2002, U.S. Bankruptcy Court, Southern District of New York, Manhattan Investment Fund Ltd.

[205] US Bankruptcy Court Case 00-10922, Eighth Application for Interim Allowances of Compensation of Dewey Ballantine LLP for Services Rendered as Counsel to the Trustee and for Reimbursements of Expenses and Disbursements, Dec. 3, 2002, p.18.

[206] Associated Press 2006.

[207] Transcript of hearing held September 6, 2000, U.S. Bankruptcy Court, Southern District of New York, Manhattan Investment Fund Ltd.

[208] Transcript of hearing held September 6, 2000, p.27, U.S. Bankruptcy Court, Southern District of New York, Manhattan Investment Fund Ltd.

[209] See above, section titled "Venue Shopping".

[210] Transcript of hearing held February 15, 2007, U.S. Bankruptcy Court, Southern District of New York, Manhattan Investment Fund Ltd.

[211] Transcript of hearing held February 15, 2007, pp. 23-24, U.S. Bankruptcy Court, Southern District of New York, Manhattan Investment Fund Ltd..

[212] Kary 2008.

[213] Wilchins 2006.

[214] Books on Madoff look to become a minor cottage industry. I think the most interesting account is Markopolos et al. 2011, by a team including the whistleblower whose repeated warnings over the years were ignored by regulators. Details of the scheme and its immediate aftermath can be found in Arvedlund 2009, Kirtzman 2010, Henriques 2011.

[215] Stoffel 2012.

[216] Cowen 2000.

[217] US SEC Office of Investigations 2009b, p. 43

[218] US SEC Office of Investigations 2009b, p. 23.

[219] US SEC Office of Investigations, 2009b, p. 425

[220] This remarkable effort at whistle blowing is described in Markopolos 2011.

[221] Ocrant 2001. Ocrant is one of the authors of Markopolos 2011.

[222] In addition to Ocrant 2001, *Barron's* published a piece by Arvedlund (2001) raising questions about Madoff and *The Toronto Globe and Mail*(2002) published an article critical of nepotism exemplified by Madoff family members who held key positions at the firm.

[223] Hayes. 2009b.

[224] US SEC Office of Investigations 2009b, p. 221.

[225] Kurdas 2011a.

[226] US SEC Office of Investigations 2009b, p. 427

[227] Hirschfield and Klidonas 2011.

[228] Trustee's Fifth Interim Report for the period ending March 31, 2011, submitted to bankruptcy court, Southern District of New York, SIPA liquidation, Bernard L. Madoff.

[229] Sandomir and Belson 2011.

[230] Amended Complaint, June 24, 2011, US District Court, Southern District of New York, Irving Picard vs. JP Morgan Chase & Co. and related entities.

[231] Opinion and order by Jed Rakoff, July 28, 2011, US District Court, Southern District of New York, Irving Picard vs. HSBC Bank plc and related entities.

[232] Rakoff 2014.

[233] Government Accounting Office 2012a and b.

[234] A pattern pointed out by LoPucki 2006.

[235] For instance, Henriques 2011 appears to be written with the help of the trustee group.

[236] Trustee's Fifth Interim Report for the period ending March 31, 2011, submitted to bankruptcy court, Southern District of New York, SIPA liquidation, Bernard L. Madoff.

[237] US Securities and Exchange Commission Office of Inspector General, Office of Audits 2011a.

[238] GAO 2012a and b. Estimates of the average hourly fee vary.

[239] Kurdas 2012b.

[240] "Decision and Order Granting, to the Extent Set forth herein, Trustee's Motion to Affirm Trustee's Determinations Denying Claims of Claimants without BLMIS Accounts in Their Names, Namely Investors in Feeder Funds," Burton Lifland, June 28, 2011, bankruptcy court, Southern District of New York, SIPA liquidation, Bernard L. Madoff.

[241] The ruling was in response to an objection by a group of investors in certain feeder funds and the judge left open the possibility that another group in other feeder funds might be in a different situation. But as of this writing feeder fund clients face a worse outcome than other investors.

[242] Rothfeld 2011.

[243] Jones 2009.

[244] Abrams 2010.

[245] Trustee's Fifth Interim report for the period ending March 31, 2011, p. 45, submitted to bankruptcy court, Southern District of New York, SIPA liquidation, Bernard L. Madoff.

[246] Sandler and Voreacos 2011.

[247] Sandler 2012.

[248] Whitehouse 2013.

[249] Zywicki 2006.

[250] Zywicki 2006, p. 1156.

[251] Judge Lifland could not see the Madoff bankruptcy to the end because he died in 2014, the sixth year of the case, as this book went to press.

[252] SEC Office of the Inspector General 2011b, p.50.

[253] Helland and Tabarrok 2003, also Helland and Tabarrok 2006.

[254] For Stanford's background and career, see Kurdas 2012a.

[255] I've discussed Stanford's CDs in Kurdas 2012a.

[256] Connett and Foley 2009.

[257] Sweeney 2009.

[258] Later the SEC Inspector General found that the enforcement inquiry was likely opened because of the money laundering matter rather than the examiner reports warning of fraud.

[259] US Securities and Exchange Commission Office of the Inspector General 2010.

[260] We don't know for sure how effective Stanford's influence was. He got much of what he wanted on the issues that mattered to him, though not all.

[261] Stanford Financial Group Receiver Janvey's political contributions list as of June 12, 2012. The list changed as political beneficiaries of Stanford's swindle turn in the money.

[262] Ratcliffe 2009.

[263] Ralph Janvey "Receiver's Original Complaint against Ben Barnes and Ben Barnes Group LP," March 15, 2010, US District Court at the Northern District of Texas, Dallas Division, Stanford Group Receivership.

[264] Ishmael 2009.

[265] Singh 2010.

[266] Report of the Receiver, April 23, 2009, US District Court for the Northern District of Texas, Dallas Division, Stanford Group Receivership.

[267] Croft 2011.

[268] Caribbean360.com 2011.

[269] Croft 2010.

[270] Harris and Calkins 2011.

[271] Calkins and Harris 2011.

[272] US SEC Office of the Inspector General 2012a memorandum. Myriad scandals of the reform era are described in chapter 10.

[273] Information about the appointment is from a March 9th, 2012 letter to the SEC Office of the Inspector General from Kevin Sadler, the Baker Botts attorney who represents Janvey.

[274] See Ackerman 2011 ands 2012.

PART THREE. Pretense v Reality.

We saw the case for financial regulation in the first part of this book. On the face of it, the three main arguments for government intervention in the financial sphere – unequal power, conflict, irrationality – may seem persuasive. Then we looked at what regulators in fact do, focusing on the most obvious and widely agreed-upon type of action, taken (ostensibly) to prevent financial fraud and help investors.

A financial regulatory state that is faithful to its three-fold rationale will perform three social functions. It will act as counterweight to the economic heft of big financial players, protecting the individual investor and pension beneficiary. It will impartially referee disputes between groups, thereby boosting efficiency and reducing the cost of doing business. It will enhance rational decision making by market participants, combating deception and delusion.

The regulatory system was set up on the strength of these ideas, versions of which have been elaborated for nearly a century, some simple, others more refined or complex. It is to achieve these ends that financial regulation makes information widely available and mandates sound practices — or at least what are regarded as such. Echoes of these arguments remain prevalent in politics and the media.

But judging from the results, between the abstract case and observable practice is a gulf so immense that there seems to be no connection. Reality diverges so sharply from the reasoning that justified it, one is left to conclude that the justification is apparent rather than real, like returns claimed by con men.

Regulators do not check the financially and politically powerful; on the contrary, they handle such figures with great consideration. Had Madoff and Stanford been small fish, they would have almost certainly been nabbed a lot sooner once people complained to the Securities and Exchange Commission.

Regulators are not impartial umpires; they have their own reasons to favor certain groups and create conflict rather than reducing it. The handling of the Madoff estate is a case in point—government players arbitrarily imposed a legal distinction that divided investors into two groups with divergent interests.

Finally, regulation does not discourage dishonesty and delusion; on the contrary, it makes investors less vigilant and hence facilitates their deception. It does not protect investors' interest; on the contrary, fraud victims are victimized a second time after a scheme comes to light and agents of the state take over. In short, financial regulation does not do what it claims to do.

Perhaps Ponzi schemes are simply not amenable to prevention. Even so, one would think consideration is due to the victims in the aftermath. Yet the bankruptcy estates set up by regulator-picked lawyers serve those lawyers, not the victims.

It is hard to see what the decades-old system has achieved for the investing public. Instead, it redistributes income and wealth from investors to bureaucrat-lobbyists, politically connected lawyers and their allies. As practiced, the cure may very well be worse than the disease—not unusual in government interventions of all sorts, Michael Boskin points out.[275]

What accounts for the corruption of purpose? The next three chapters explain and suggest remedies.

CHAPTER NINE. Statist Mirror Cracks

In 1923, Wesley C. Mitchell gave a lecture at Columbia University, arguing for the redesign of flawed institutions. He possibly went one step beyond his teacher Veblen, but the ideas presented were not original — other institutionalists and legal realists made similar points. Yet this particular occasion was notable. In the audience was Friedrich Hayek, a young Austrian scholar.[276] That day marks the beginning of a systematic modern critique of the view Mitchell expressed.

As Hayek would recall, Mitchell said that since man himself created social institutions, he must be able to change them to meet his desires. This seemingly obvious piece of reasoning puzzled Hayek, who was influenced by the ideas of a fellow Austrian, Carl Menger.[277] From that starting point, Hayek eventually explained the danger of what he termed the rationalist delusion.[278]

More than half a century later, in the lecture he gave on receiving the Nobel prize, Hayek described this menace. Excoriating economists for spawning interventionist policies, he said these are part of "men's fatal striving to control society — a striving which makes him not only a tyrant over his fellows, but which may well make him the destroyer of a civilization which no brain has designed but which has grown from the free efforts of millions of individuals."[279]

His comment applies forcefully to the regulatory state, though at the time he was not talking specifically about that subject.

Limits of Our Knowledge

Social arrangements are the result of human activity, of course. But that does not mean they are the result of human design. While man is a "rule-following animal" by Hayek's definition, society is governed largely by rules that were not deliberately created. Behavior is guided "by rules of conduct of which (people) are rarely aware, which they certainly have not consciously invented..."[280] These are transmitted from one generation to the next. Even where there is deliberate choice, its role is limited.

Social institutions have come about not by plan but through a spontaneous process of cultural evolution, which like biological evolution works through variation. Economic and social practices diverge. The variations may be accidental or initially intended to serve certain purposes but found to have other effects — the latter, unforeseen, overshadow the intended uses. Some rules or a combination of them confers an advantage for social functioning, economic efficiency or likely both. Once the benefits show up, those communities gain an edge and in time others imitate them.

Hayek did not give a full explanation of how social evolution works, in particular how certain institutions get selected.[281] However, one outcome is clear. Social evolution in the West created open societies that depend on markets to meet material needs. In time, the success of these institutions led other countries to adopt them, or at least some subset thereof.

The economic and social order called capitalism was not thought out in advance. It consists of a network of institutions, including the rule of law, private property, competitive markets and the freedom of individuals to make their own choices. These form a system of immense complexity. Numerous people created bits of it but no one deliberately constructed the entire system. Even official laws in the main rely on evolved social rules.

Hayek's central point – put simply – is that no one really can create such a complex order. It is not possible for human beings to foresee the consequences of an institution or to understand how it will interact with numerous other institutions. The full effect became evident only after the order developed.

Early thinkers did not even imagine a capitalist system. From Plato's "Republic" on, ideal societies created on paper by philosophers and political writers revolved around elites.[282] Such utopias were centrally controlled, not made of spontaneously evolved institutions and self-coordinating markets. The essential questions were about the elite, such as how it should be educated.

So the economic system that came to dominate the world by late 20th century was not anyone's vision of the perfect society. It had slowly emerged in a piecemeal fashion. The trading powers Venice and the Netherlands and the industrial pioneer Britain were where capitalism initially showed up. These were relatively free societies — the first two were early republics, Britain a parliamentary monarchy where the monarch became a figurehead. The basic structures were already in place by the late 18th century when Adam Smith noticed that certain institutions, both informal and official, made for a higher level of affluence.

Once capitalism was recognized as a distinct system, one with its own social complexities, critics created alternative blueprints. These had unforeseen nasty consequences no matter how brilliant the creator. Though Karl Marx inspired the Soviet Union, he did not anticipate the result, a police state riddled with gross inefficiency and corruption. "While history runs its course, it is not history to us," Hayek wrote. "It leads us into an unknown land, and but rarely can we get a glimpse of what lies ahead."[283]

Spontaneously evolved institutions tend to be subtle and rely on voluntary action. By comparison the organizations we deliberately design tend to be crude and coercive. This relative crudeness reflects the limits of human intelligence compared to the rich possibilities of historical variation. To be sure, spontaneous mechanisms can't do everything; there is a place for deliberate organization. But to work, interventions have to be consistent with the established values and rules that create order in society and markets.

Best known for his trenchant criticism of Soviet-style centralized planning, Hayek was just as critical of centralized institution building in other settings. The best institutions require no conscious control and get individuals to participate without anyone ordering them around. Blind faith in purposeful intervention poses the danger of replacing spontaneous institutions with coercive arrangements. These destroy not only economic value but liberty, resulting in a society both poorer and oppressive.

We saw that Veblen and Commons had similar ideas as to social evolution. But unlike Hayek, they did not focus on and indeed expressed doubts about the beneficial attributes of spontaneous processes. Commons advocated the creation of new arrangements through state action to remedy the deficiencies in evolved institutions, though late in life he started to recognize the failings of state apparatuses.

Hayek saw institutions as the solution to the fact that our ability to learn is limited. Institutions are

> Successful adaptations to the irremediable limitations
> of our knowledge, adaptations which have prevailed
> over alternative forms of order because they provide
> more effective methods of dealing with that
> incomplete, dispersed knowledge which is man's
> unalterable lot.[284]

For instance, ethical codes or rules of polite behavior make it possible for people to react to situations in a way that other parties recognize and can respond to. Following the rule is sufficient to coordinate behavior among total strangers, as long as they hew to the same code. Hayek's insight can be applied in different ways — to cite one such argument, Young Back Choi (1993) made the point that conventions embody and spread social learning.

A prime example of a knowledge-efficient institution is the market, where individuals pursue their own ends subject to general rules that protect property and enforce contracts. In this setting people use whatever knowledge they have because they benefit from doing so. The knowledge is fragmented and much of it may be implicit rather than explicitly articulated; people do not necessarily put their preferences into words. But they reveal their preferences through actions. Markets work by channeling and coordinating dispersed information that is immensely greater than what's available to the most knowledgeable policy maker.

Like the idea of evolving institutions, the idea of large numbers voluntarily cooperating and self-coordinating was not new. Adam Smith explained how individuals acting for their own purposes with no social goal create a wealthier nation than a central authority pursuing an overarching design. But Hayek pointed to the essential role of knowledge. Free markets make better use of dispersed knowledge than centrally controlled economic decision making.

Among modern students of institutions, Hayek stands out with his insistence that weaknesses in the faculty of reason set limits on not just ordinary people but also those who act in the name of public interest and the state.

From the experience of the first half of the 20th century he derived a lesson in humility: "If man is not to do more harm than good in his efforts to improve the social order, he will have to learn that ...he cannot acquire the full knowledge which would make the mastery of the events possible..."

Hayek's insight for regulation is that it crucially depends on knowledge. The issue is how to avoid the need for knowledge that is not available and provide incentives for individuals to use what information they have. So the key question is: What does a policy maker need to know to achieve a desired goal?[285] Often he needs to know a lot more than he does or can.

To have a chance of success, regulation should not require more knowledge than is readily available to the regulator. For this reason, the goals need to be modest and broadly accepted. Regulation should make use of dispersed knowledge by providing incentives for people to cooperate. To get cooperation, it has to jive with the preferences and understanding of the people subject to it.

That is not how the regulatory state typically operates. Financial regulation in particular has ambitious goals such as counterbalancing inequalities in economic power and correcting irrational behavior. Achieving those ends requires greater understanding than policy makers possess and involves top-down dictates that discourage the pooling of what private individuals know. That is one reason financial regulation fails. But the Hayekian knowledge problem is not the only reason.

Bad Kings

During World War II, the Roosevelt administration imposed price controls. Heading this effort was a young economist named John Kenneth Galbraith, an institutionalist in the tradition of Veblen and a critic of large corporations along the lines of Berle and Tugwell. Galbraith, the so-called price czar, defended price controls on the ground of preventing inflationary expectations.

After the war, he became a well-known advocate for a greater economic role for the federal government, in particular to support the groups who would otherwise be victims of big corporations. He saw this countervailing power as the major new function of government. The measures to check corporate power included the Wagner Act to back labor unions; agricultural price supports and subsidies to boost farmers; and regulations to protect consumers.

Galbraith did not foresee the perverse consequences, such as taxpayers' money being spent on subsidies to "farmers" that in fact are giant agribusinesses — the kind of corporation that the agricultural supports were originally supposed to counter. He ignored the ill effects of interventionist policies and poked fun at opponents, alleging that anti-government people suffered from an ancient bias.

Why did people resist the expansion of public services? The reason, according to Galbraith, was that an old stigma is attached to government. Through much of history, the only service governments provided was security, and this they did badly and at great expense. Kings and princes viciously exploited the population, engaging in "rapacious appropriation of the means of sustenance of the people," in Galbraith's words.[286]

The historical experience created in the collective memory a prejudice against public action, which we – unfortunately in his view – inherited. "Alcohol, comic books and mouthwash all bask under the superior reputation of the market," he wrote. "Schools, judges and municipal swimming pools lie under the evil reputation of bad kings." Truly Veblenian, the half-humorous, half-serious quip puts the blame on a traditional mindset.

Galbraith saw this habit of thought as an obsolete institution that needed to be discarded. Like other decrepit institutions, the archaic bias against government services did mischief in a modern society. We had to get rid of it in order to make better use of our affluence, so as to invest not only in more schools, judges and municipal swimming pools but also regulations.

But why were the old kings and princes so dreadful that their ill repute lived on in collective memory for centuries? It is odd that Galbraith thought this happened in America, a society that has not suffered from a monarch since George III, whose transatlantic impositions were mild compared to what imperial regimes did elsewhere.

Perhaps rulers did not know what to do, lacked an understanding of the consequences of their actions and hence did the wrong thing— a Hayekian knowledge problem. Or, they had no desire to control their rapaciousness and serve their subjects better—a lack of benevolence, which we will call the Buchanan problem, to be discussed later. The third issue is that they did whatever they felt like for the simple reason that they could. Oversight and control over them was weak, at times nonexistent—as a shorthand, let's refer to this as the Schumpeter problem.

Galbraith showed no interest in the question of why past rulers were awful. For him, it was simply absurd to let fear of bad kings taint one's view of modern government. Lessons from long-gone history did not apply. The current political elite was different; modern elected politicians promoted the well being of the population. After all, they are subject to the will of citizens. If they behave badly, voters will boot them out in the next election. It is to the self-interest of elected statesmen to serve the public.

By this reasoning, elected officials will by and large make useful policies and direct their underlings to do the same. By implication, regulators will do what they were put into office to do. If somehow politicians or regulators go against the public interest, voters will sooner or later show their displeasure by changing the guard. Government controlled by the electorate can be trusted not to rapaciously appropriate resources.[287]

If you buy the argument, you may not be terribly bothered by the manifest failures of the regulatory state. These will be corrected, the right policies found and implemented, according to the core logic of the political system. True, thinkers ranging from John Stuart Mill to Isaiah Berlin criticized the "tyranny of the majority" that this viewpoint embodies, but conventional wisdom holds that political differences should not get in the way of good government. A middle ground can be found.

Galbraith was oddly similar to the mainstream economic theorists of the time in putting his faith in public policy, though he criticized them for engaging in useless mathematical exercises. Neoclassical welfare economics indicates – in the abstract – how to promote the public interest as determined by an impartial observer. Taking the vantage point of such an observer, the economist looks to maximize social welfare.

A more recent approach dubbed new or soft paternalism uses the same mental device, though otherwise it differs from neoclassical economics, being based on behavioral findings rather than a mathematically expressed social welfare function.[288] Soft paternalists propose measures to make subjects do what is judged to be good for them.[289] The main national effort along new paternalist lines has been to get people to save more for their retirement by making enrollment in the savings plan the default option.

Like most ideas, the concept of kindly herding the population in the right direction goes back in history. Alexis de Tocqueville in 1840 warned against the danger of a "gentle" despotism in the administrative sphere, the rise of "an immense, protective power" that watches over citizens and claims to provide for them what they supposedly want but cannot achieve on their own.[290]

Tocqueville described the strange paradox this poses in democratic societies: "For the conduct of small affairs, where plain common sense is enough, they hold that the citizens are not up to the job. But they give these citizens immense prerogatives where the government of the whole state is concerned."[291] Democratic despotism infantilizes the citizenry as wards of the state, unable to fend for themselves, yet expected to decide who will run that state.[292]

"It is really difficult to imagine," Tocqueville continued, "how people who have entirely given up managing their own affairs could make a wise choice of those who are to do that for them." In a recent critique of paternalism, Whitman and Rizzo (2007) point out that being under the soft paternalist wing reduces the incentives to learn and self-correct. For example, default enrollees in pensions make no effort to choose investments and hence end up with a low-return portfolio.

For my purpose, the main point is the nature of the public-interest promoting observer, whether a welfare economist, a soft-paternalist law professor or a benevolent despot. His defining characteristic is looking at society objectively, so to speak from the outside, to decide what is in the interest of the people and how best to bring it about. The Hayekian question is what he really knows. Richard Epstein (1998) describes Cass Sunstein, the leading soft paternalist in the legal sphere, as "mistaken in assuming that anyone can climb a perch that offers special insight into the desirability of particular social practices."[293]

In practice, the welfare-maximizing or gentle-paternalist entity corresponds to the impartial technocracy full of public-minded experts envisioned by founding regulators Commons and Landis. But the issues they confronted as they tried to create the right kind of agency are typically ignored in abstract exercises of how to achieve the greatest social welfare.

Despite the differences, various interventionist approaches converge on the promotion of public interest by an entity other than the public itself. Social welfare is to be maximized or behavior molded by policy—because left to itself the public does not or can not enhance its own welfare or shift behavior.

The failure is typically attributed to insufficient rationality. That puts the onus on policymakers to determine the right direction and how to push the public the right way. On the other hand, the same public presumably provides through its votes the mandate for the measures taken. Policy is legitimated by the electorate's approval of what is being done in its interest and name.

So there is a duality embedded in the paternalist vision. It rests on the assumption that the public is incapable of figuring out certain things for itself but capable of voting for a government that will do those things. Any bad king would agree with the first part but would likely not wish to rely on the voting part.

Human Nature in Politics

Schumpeter, the oddball economist famed for his work on cycles of innovation and creative destruction, threw an early salvo against the notion that democratic governments pursue the public good under electoral control. He pointed out a fundamental weakness in voters' supervision of government, thereby showing up the central tenet of policymaking under democracy as a myth.

Schumpeter "is the most radical scholar in the discipline of economics in the twentieth century," one who "still has a great deal to teach us," according to Nathan Rosenberg, an economic historian of technical change.[294] Schumpeter was not radical in the conventional political sense – he was a old-style conservative on most issues – but his ideas were path breaking. Bringing the entrepreneur to the forefront as the primary economic mover was one of his contributions.[295]

Very much a product of turn-of-the-century Vienna, Schumpeter became Austria's minister of finance early in his career. Then he suffered a series of adversities. As finance minister, he was stymied by Austria's economic and political problems in the aftermath of World War I. A ghastly personal tragedy – his young wife and new-born child died – marred him psychologically.

He emigrated to the United States but did not like his adopted country. He taught at Harvard University but found himself increasingly peripheral to mainstream economics after most of the profession espoused John Maynard Keynes' explanation of business cycles rather than his own – as he believed – better explanation. Schumpeter spent the rest of his life smoldering with discontent about the state of economics and the world.

Among his incongruities was a love/hate relationship with, of all things, neoclassical equilibrium theory. From a certain intellectual perspective he admired abstract general equilibrium models that show the supply and demand of everything. On another level, Schumpeter blithely affirmed that this theory was utterly useless for understanding a market economy. It is irrelevant because what makes capitalism tick are waves of technological and organizational innovation, not conditions of equilibrium.

He wanted to develop a theory that would catch the transforming forces and institutions—but better than the old institutionalists, who never developed the deep-reaching, mathematically expressed analysis he aspired to. Thus he commented that Veblen's *The Theory of the Leisure Class* "is brilliant and suggestive. But it is an impressionist essay that does not come to grips with the real problems involved." He wanted a theory that combined insights about institutions with the symmetric elegance of general equilibrium.

Schumpeter never realized this aspiration; he probably set himself an impossible goal. His main contribution to the understanding of institutions, *Capitalism, Socialism and Democracy,* can be described in the same words that he used for Veblen, as a brilliant and suggestive essay. While falling short of his desire to produce a full fledged new economics, it included crucial insights about an aspect of behavior on which the old institutionalists had little to say—human nature in politics, as he termed it.

That people behave differently as voters than they do as workers, shoppers, homeowners or business managers is an obvious but often ignored fact. Schumpeter explained why.

In private transactions, we experience the direct result of our action. We like or don't like a soda we purchase. The price of a stock we invested in goes up or down. Our business is successful or fails. We understand the consequences, bear the responsibility and try to avoid bad outcomes — we pay attention to buying the right soda, picking a good stock, running the business well.

Experience shows us the errors, so we learn; the more experience, the more we learn. "In the ordinary run of often repeated decisions the individual is subject to the salutary and rationalizing influence of favorable and unfavorable experience," wrote Schumpeter.[296]

Human conduct is largely driven by deep-seated emotions, but in the economic realm the rational component is relatively substantial because there one confronts definite magnitudes – income and spending, cost and benefit, profit and loss – that are subject to calculation and purposeful effort. One wills to make more money, keep down spending, reduce costs; seeks the means to achieve those ends; learns from success or failure.

None of these conditions are present for voters in the political realm. There, private individuals do not bear responsibility and do not face consequences in the way they face the result of buying the wrong soda or stock or even making the wrong move in a game of chess. Voters are not grounded in the realities of politics as they are grounded in earning a living or running a household.

Most people have no real experience in politics — the majority of policies and events are at a far remove from their lives, unlike actions they take in the course of daily life. For an individual outside the government and not running for office, politics is to a large extent unreal.

This is especially so because government actions have complicated and long-term effects that are difficult to understand and untangle from other influences, even by experts who study the policies. A conscientious citizen who tries to make informed, independent political decisions would have an extremely hard time.

But most voters don't try, because they have no incentive to be better informed about public policy. It does not pay to spend their time learning about abstruse matters that may affect them little or not at all. After all, the average citizen has no control over political decisions, given that one voter is an insignificant part of a national electorate.[297] A local election in a small town may be different if the population is tiny. But on the national level, a single vote makes no noticeable difference.

An Unworkable Committee

For the typical voter, political ignorance is a rational response.[298] We all have only so much attention, barely enough to take care of family, work, home, health and other concerns. Making informed and calculated decisions requires a lot of attention. In politics, the return to an individual voter for doing this is immaterial; therefore it is reasonable not to devote energy to it, especially in view of how difficult it is to understand policies.

But, as Bryan Caplan argues, ignorance is not the only obstacle to rational political choices.[299] Voters make wrong decisions because they do not know, but they are also vulnerable to emotional influences and biases.[300] After all, voters are the same people who make deluded mistakes in investing; why wouldn't they make mistakes in voting?

Mind you, there are major exceptions to voter indifference and ignorance. Government interventions can have an immediate and recognizable impact on certain groups — those people do pay attention and learn about that particular issue, say a public subsidy that they receive. More generally, if a policy is important to an individual, whether because of economic interest or ideological commitment, he or she may join a group organized around that topic and as a member of the group attempt to influence relevant political decisions.

Schumpeter himself thought voters are rational about short-term, immediate benefits and costs to themselves because those are observable. But they are bad judges of their own long-term interest. They may reject policies that in time would produce satisfactory results and espouse measures that are eventually destructive to their own well-being. Since long-term consequences are difficult or impossible to predict, emotions and biases heavily influence attitudes toward such policies.

As for issues that have no observable and definite effect on themselves, citizens typically pay scant attention. As a result, they are substantially ignorant about public affairs, which does not mean they have no opinion; it means their opinion in grounded in emotion. In short, people tend to be less rational as voters than they are as consumers or producers.

In another way as well political decisions are not like private decisions. Individuals and groups have different values, and based on those values, different goals for the political system. Usually there is no common good that all agree on. In private life, we don't have to agree; we can each pursue our individual goal. But political decisions are about the entire collective.

Only a society that is exceptionally homogenous and consists of citizens who think alike and have similar values can agree on what is desirable. Schumpeter's example is Switzerland in the early 20th century. Otherwise, what emerges from the democratic process is not a program that citizens rationally picked in order to further a unanimously desired public end. Since there is no way to reconcile different beliefs and values, there is no such program. Rather, voters pick candidates who happen to appeal to them emotionally.

The implication for the regulatory state is that voters are unable to exercise effective oversight. The electorate can't really supervise the government; there is no single purpose to be achieved and each voter has little if any information and even less influence. The citizen "is a member of an unworkable committee, the committee of the whole nation, and this is why he expends less disciplined effort on mastering a political problem than he expends on a game of bridge," Schumpeter argued.[301]

However, the electorate does react to major debacles – like wars going bad and obvious economic hardship – by changing the politicians who run the government. Even then most voters may not understand what the new team will do about the problem that's different from what the previous administration was doing. In fact there may be no significant difference in policies. If the situation does not improve to their satisfaction, voters rotate the parties.

When Schumpeter made these points in the 1930s and 1940s, evidence was scant as to how much voters really know. Since then research and data have piled up. Voter ignorance shows up in numerous surveys and about not only specific policies but more broadly the basic structure of government. Majorities of Americans don't know the functions of the three branches of government and the Federal Reserve. Political ignorance has been persistent over the past century despite a vast expansion of formal education and much easier access to information.[302]

Similar ignorance is observed in other societies, including France, despite its vaunted high quality education and political participation.[303] The "pervasiveness of popular ignorance about politics and government," comments political scientist Jeffrey Friedman, "is one of the strongest findings that have been produced by any social science — possibly *the* strongest."[304]

Regarding regulatory issues, only the most extreme situations receive widespread attention, and even then voters know little about the matter and react emotionally. The financial crisis of 2008 is an example — the public was outraged and the majority party (Democrats) decided to take advantage of the situation to implement their pet policies. The electorate wanted something done, something was done. The result was a regulatory onslaught, including a financial law so obscure and complex that regulators themselves can not keep up with all the rules they're supposed to make and several years later much remains uncertain. Electoral anger and ignorance make a potent but unpredictable combination.

Unreasonable Advantage

For a long time – and often to this day – policy arguments ignored the gorilla in the room. The motives of the people who act in the name of the government received no or minimal attention until the later in the 20th-century. But starting in the 1960s, new strands of economics focused on decision making by public officials and politicians. In time this led to a new economics of regulation.

It is the basic assumption of mainstream economics that economic actors rationally pursue their self interest, typically by maximizing their satisfaction. It stands to reason that government agents also pursue their self interest and do what benefits or satisfies them. This is an obvious logical implication—after all, public agents must be at least as rational as the rest of the population. Neither politicians nor bureaucrats are notable for selfless behavior.

Of course, a politician running for office will say he will do what is best for his or her constituency and may indeed do things that are good for some, perhaps many, voters. But that is iffy compared to the certainty that getting elected will be good for her and she will act to achieve that end, whatever it takes. Certainly she will do or say things to get on the good side of the voters she targets, but those choices are made through the prism of her interest in the office.

While no different from the rest of humanity in looking after themselves, politicians have special opportunities to do so. Regulation offers a plethora of such opportunities. A politician can use regulation to redistribute income, to protect some, impose burdens on others—thereby garnering votes or campaign contributions, furthering the political career and developing lucrative job possibilities down the pike.

Agency staffs are in a different situation, but can be expected to similarly use their power to their own advantage in various ways. The Manhattan, Madoff and Stanford cases demonstrate this. We will come back to the subject of agencies in the next chapter.

Bringing up government players' interest is not to say that they never do the right thing, or what they consider the right thing; rather, there is no necessity that they will. The pursuit of self-interest does not mean that people are narrowly materialistic.

Anything that affects a person's sense of well being can be a factor in their choice. If an individual finds satisfaction in contributing to charity or being patriotic, then engaging in charitable or patriotic activity enhances that person's sense of well being. Certainly some officials may get satisfaction from doing what they think is best for the country. This depends on the person and circumstances.

The nub of the matter is that once the element of lawmakers' and regulators' own interest is introduced, it cannot be presumed that regulation will increase public wellbeing, even if there were no knowledge problem. There is no inherent reason what makes regulators themselves better off materially or psychologically will bring about greater social welfare.

One version of the rational regulator argument was developed by economists associated with the University of Chicago, who applied neoclassical modeling to government actors who maximize their own utility — that is, look to enhance their career prospects, income and job satisfaction.[305] The Chicago school investigated whether regulatory income redistribution will be efficient and minimize deadweight losses. While allowing the formulation of precise models, this research agenda may have run into a dead end.

Experience and logic suggest that income redistribution via regulation – whatever its ostensible purpose – benefits a few while imposing costs on many. This was well known centuries ago. "Every new regulation concerning commerce or revenue, or in any manner affecting the value of the different species of property, presents a new harvest to those who watch the change, and can trace its consequences," wrote James Madison in the *Federalist Papers*. Rent seeking is the modern term for efforts to create regulatory "harvests" that benefit oneself while avoiding the cost.

Madison pointed out that this gives "unreasonable advantage" to the enterprising and moneyed few over the mass of people. The more elaborate and numerous the rules, the more bountiful the harvest enjoyed by the well-situated few but created "by the toils and cares of the great body of their fellow-citizens."

The Chicago school's models said little about how this happens. The nature of regulatory redistribution depends on the institutions that shape political choices, which standard Neoclassical models leave open. Resolving the questions requires additional assumptions or a different method of study. "But so far a full analysis of the scope and form of these institutions remains unwritten," according to S. Peltzman, a practitioner who reviewed nearly two decades of mainstream research on regulation.[306]

War of Interests

In the meanwhile a group of scholars went beyond neoclassical models to develop the broader implications of self-interested behavior by government agents. Led by James Buchanan, Douglas Tullock and Mancur Olson, these thinkers focused in particular on innate inequalities in the ability to organize and gain political influence.

Small groups of like-minded people organize relatively easily. Each of the members gets an observable, significant benefit, which gives them a strong incentive to devote resources to this purpose. Labor unions and trade associations fit this description. Once organized, such groups engage in activities to gain power — donate money to politicians, hire lobbyists who know how to deal with government and flacks to shape publicity, offer high-paying jobs to ex-officials. Over time, concentrated groups build extensive networks of influence, which bring them government-mediated gains that the rest of the populace pays for.

By contrast, the largest groups – such as consumers or taxpayers – are at a disadvantage in taking political action. It is difficult to organize numerous disparate individuals who are weakly connected; the common element of paying taxes or buying products is insufficient to make them act together. While the population as a whole may bear a huge cost from a policy, the cost is dispersed across a large number so that each individual bears a small portion. It follows that an individual member would get only a tiny share of the benefit from time or money devoted to organizing the group and advancing its interest.

In short, most members of big, diverse groups do not have sufficient incentive to contribute to political action to protect the interests of the group. It is very difficult for such populations to resist programs or regulations that impose costs on them.

The upshot is that tight, homogenous small groups use political influence to exploit the masses. Large numbers who can't organize and acquire political influence are easy prey. Organized industries gain at the expense of consumers; public unions gain at the expense of taxpayers; a few large, influential companies gain at the expense of numerous small businesses. This is politics as taking, where the Hobbesian war is "transferred to the realm of institutionally organized conflicts," to quote Buchanan and Roger Congleton.[307]

A Leviathan that is party to the war of interests, that takes from the masses to give to small groups, casts a new light on the case Hobbes made for powerful government. It also stands in stark contrast to Commons' vision of regulation as a way to bring about fair compromises reconciling the interests of stakeholders and reducing the transaction costs caused by strife. Instead policy itself becomes a form of strife as groups seek to get government goodies or to escape being the victim in the provision of goodies to others.

Political scientists focus on another aspect of what they call a pluralist system of competing interests. The winners in this system present their agenda as the public interest, legitimized by following democratic procedure. But the focus on procedure ignores the damage. It is not just that policy becomes an exploitative tool to channel resources to the politically organized and connected. It is that government interventions aimed at redistribution cause the economic pie to shrink. The cost of doing business increases, discouraging economic activity. Resources that could have been invested in productive enterprise are spent on the political war of interests.

Instead of making cheaper or better mousetraps, a producer can get the government to impose costly regulation on competitors while exempting his mousetrap. Or he might get a subsidy or tax exemption for his business. As long as the value he receives covers the cost, he'll be willing to compensate politicians and bureaucrats, whether in the form of campaign contributions or high-paying jobs, and hire people with the requisite political connections and skills to influence policy.

On the losing side, consumers end up with expensive and shoddy products while taxpayers are forced to foot the bill for numerous subsidies and tax exemptions. But this is not just a matter of winners and losers. Once political rent extraction becomes the accepted way to get a high return, it drains away scarce talent and other resources. It discourages saving and investment by creating uncertainty as to what politicians and bureaucrats will do next. It reduces the incentive for innovating and investing — instead entrepreneurs focus on politics to get government bounties.

As economic life becomes increasingly subservient to politics, material well-being is eroded. "There is a vast negative-sum game in which people with high natural talents, who are willing to work hard, can get very large returns while generating a social loss," wrote Buchanan, Tullock and Tollison [308]

Attempts to either gain from regulation or evade it lead to special provisions and exceptions, so that the rules become more numerous and cumbersome. Olson explained that complexity, in turn, creates an ideal environment for special interests, which are more likely to succeed in manipulating detailed or complex rules rather than general and simple policies. In a vicious spiral, manipulation increases complexity; complexity raises the return from political manipulation and therefore leads to more complexity.

The more elaborate the regulations, the more need for specialists like lawyers and government relations consultants to deal with the rules. These specialists themselves become a vested interest that favors complexity against simplification. As the rewards for work, innovation and investment decline, the rewards for lobbying grow. Olson puts it in a nutshell: "The incentive to produce is diminished; the incentive to seek a larger share of what is produced increases." [309]

A key difference between a free market and the politicized economy is the latter's ability to inhibit competitors. When market entrepreneurs create novel products that allow them to reap extra profits over and above what they would get in another line of business, this acts as a signal. Other people start to offer similar products and in time the rents are competed away. The excess returns from innovation are temporary, as Schumpeter pointed out. Established industries are challenged in innovative cycles of creative destruction, but society as a whole becomes richer over time.

Unlike entrepreneurial returns, the rents extracted in the political game are not competed away as long as the recipient has inherent advantages in organizing and acquiring political influence. A politically favored player can use this influence to destroy competitors and set up barriers to newcomers—such as the high cost of useless but elaborate regulation. Thus political rent seeking replaces economic dynamism and growth with stagnation.

It is a sad irony that the great Louis Brandeis, like other idealistic inspirers of centralized utopias, helped set up the conditions that in effect destroy what he wanted to preserve. He regarded free competition as valuable and wanted to protect it. That was the reasoning behind his rejection of the Roosevelt's National Recovery Administration. Yet the regulatory state that owes its beginnings to him favors politically influential large entities, whether unions or big companies. It discriminates against small businesses, reducing competition.

Interventionists twist this argument around to fault business interests for lobbying. Thus President Barack Obama suggested businesses cause the negative-sum game —even as, like most politicians, Obama takes money from business interests. He even received a donation from "financier" Allen Stanford and posed with the thug for a photograph, both of them smiling widely. You may say that's the way of the world, a politician can't avoid special interest contributions if he or she wants to win elections.

But the same argument can be made for business people— they can't avoid paying for political protection in an economy ruled by political influence, which is what the regulatory state is. It is the political class that is creating a system in which the obvious way to get ahead and do well in business is to acquire political influence. And it is the political class – broadly defined – that is the prime beneficiary.

Regulation is a key tool for political extortion, though not the only one, as the diverse examples provided by Schweizer (2013) demonstrate. The expanding regulatory state creates numerous openings to benefit from political influence. The only real solution, as Buchanan argued, is a limited government in which there aren't opportunities for the politically powerful to exploit the rest. Otherwise, the system of endless economic interventionism will continue to breed influence seekers like a swamp breeds mosquitoes. The argument for limited government is an argument for draining the swamp.

Certainly the problem is not new. Early Americans, among them Thomas Jefferson as well as Madison, were familiar with the menace of public officials serving themselves by helping a few to largesse taken from the many. John Calhoun, a 19th century politician, was a precursor of what came to be called public choice economics. He distinguished those who get a net benefit from state activity versus those who pay the cost. Tabarrok and Cowen (1992) found that Calhoun anticipated Buchanan's point.

Given the precedents and the importance of the topic, it is strange that modern economists did not even study these issues until the second half of the 20th century. The regulatory state was originally developed with scant attention paid to the behavior of public actors. A sprawling system was created in the name of achieving equity and efficiency but it turned out to be a great boon for organized special interests. Truly a venture into the Hayekian "unknown land" with dreadful consequences, both political and economic.

New Institutionalists: Private Orders

Veblen thought Americans were inclined to chicanery because the culture is centered on money making to the exclusion of other considerations — it makes individuals aspire to be rich through whatever means, whether honest or not. The social norms that shape people's thinking can prevent fraud, but he believed American values encourage it.

This view may be at best too narrow. By all evidence Americans' informal values are strongly against deception in financial dealings. When a scheme becomes known, the public's inclination is to condemn and indeed ruin the perpetrators. Madoff's family faced social ostracism aside from legal prosecution — the fact that his son committed suicide upon finding himself surrounded with hostility gives a sense of the social reaction.

Regulation hinges on the proposition that the state can improve the outcome when private sanctions fail to restrain bad behavior. Commons argued that government coercion is necessary because private sanctions are weak. A danger particularly germane for the regulatory state is that legalities replace informal norms to the detriment of social wellbeing. Bottom-up legal reasoning – discussed by Rizzo (1999) – builds on social custom rather than replacing it. This may preserve the civil institution.

But top-down interventions dominated in the past 80 years, in effect bulldozing the social landscape and replacing it with official apparatuses. "Modern regulators, typically underestimating the importance of ..institutional and reputational sanctions, often insist on direct state-imposed sanctions," wrote legal scholar Richard Epstein (1998). He describes understanding the relationship between law and social norms as a lesson in how to avoid doing harm.

Heavy dependence on governmental rules causes the role of civil society to be ignored or forgotten. I would guess that the extreme social disapprobation faced by Madoff's family is a stronger deterrent against fraud than any action by the Securities and Exchange Commission. But the emphatic message from officialdom and the media was the need for more regulation — culminating in the mammoth 2010 Dodd-Frank Act.

In making financial rules there is some procedural attempt not to violate - at least not too cavalierly - industry practices. The SEC asks interested parties to comment on new policies and may revise rules so as to reduce industry opposition. Nevertheless, it is fair to say that financial regulation would be a different animal if it had been based on existing practices. Almost certainly it would be less convoluted, as most people don't like to tie themselves into knots and left to their own volition gravitate to simple rules of thumb.

An intriguing set of ideas came from Elinor Ostrom, a political scientist who was the first (and to date only) woman to win the Nobel prize in economics. Ostrom found that communities have diverse social systems for managing communal resources. The common resource may be a fishery, grazing ground, clean air or water. Without social control, every user will exploit the resource as much as possible and it will be depleted. The problem is solved by agreeing to restrict the use, often by simple rules that work through subtle social interactions.

The social arrangements Ostrom and her followers studied are an alternative to both government and market. By contrast, centralized state control of common resources often fails, foiled for instance by lack of accurate information — though the government may enforce bottom-up rules arising from the community. Neither does privatization and market competition work well in these situations.

Applying this perspective to fraud, social rules that promote honesty protect the communal resource of trust.[310] But not all communities can agree and act on effective rules — if they could, there would presumably be less call for regulation. Why does a community fail in this respect?

Another Nobel-winner, Ronald Coase, highlighted the key role of transaction costs.[311] If the cost of negotiating and enforcing an agreement is too high, then no agreement will be forthcoming. Unless a way is found to prevent opportunistic behavior, the rule is useless. Ostrom focused on small communities where people know each other for a long time and want to preserve friendly relations. Legal scholar Aviram (2011) examines social forces such as common religious belief as mechanisms that make individuals cooperate.

In a large and diverse society, there may be no practical way for informal institutions to prevent certain violations. Hence Commons' argument that the state should reduce transaction costs by turning informal rules into enforceable laws. But if applied widely, that raises the specter of government control replacing and weakening social institutions, increasingly encroaching on freedom and economic activity, causing greater inefficiency than the private arrangements it was supposed to correct.

Taken to its ultimate logical conclusion, this vision leads not only to stagnation but to fascism. Not for nothing that Commons, dedicated though he was to American democracy, at one time looked to Mussolini as a regulatory avatar. After all, who better to control unruly spontaneous institutions but a seemingly benign dictator?[312]

New Institutionalists: Competitive Polity

That regulation should facilitate market transactions, making them efficient and cheaper, remains an agreed upon goal. The economic historian Douglass North, arguably the foremost figure in the new institutionalist resurgence, observed that while some rules do indeed lower transaction costs others "such as rules that restrict entry, require useless inspections, raise information costs or make property rights less secure – in fact raise transaction costs."[313]

Is there a political and social mechanism to get rid of rules that make transactions more difficult? As far as financial regulation goes, it would seem that there is no effective mechanism to remove transaction cost-raising interventions. Rules have accumulated and become more costly, not less so. Their benefits remain unknown. Around each regulation are organized and politically connected groups that gain from it, notably lawyers. These groups are effective in protecting their interest while the public as a whole is not.

For Commons and other early institutionalists, the jostling of interests was just the way democracy works — competition in the political realm, to match competition in markets. In taking this rosy view, they ignored the advantages some groups have over others in gaining political influence. It is those special advantages that push the regulatory state to provide benefits to some at the expense of others. Moreover, the larger the government and in particular the greater its economic powers, the more potential loot there is for the politically influential.

Still, some scholars as well as voters hew to the belief that state oversight is largely benevolent — or at least can be so in a democratic society. So argue new institutional economists who see a trial-and-error process that in time does solve policy problems, as Commons hoped.

Thus North, John Wallis and Barry Weingast (2009) recognize that much policy making creates privileges and rents for organized interests. But they nevertheless point to the efficacy of political competition and experimentation to limit bad outcomes in government. "This experimental process is imperfect, in part because of the fundamental uncertainty about the nature of the problem and in part because of voter ignorance," they write. "Nevertheless, experimentation provides the best opportunity for open access orders to persist."

North and his co-authors disagree with Buchanan, Olson and Tullock about the impact of rent seeking. They argue that in a society like America, because the system is open to political competition, destructive interventions instituted to benefit special interests are gradually weeded out. If established politicians will not change, then newcomers challenge them and bring about a new administration. After all, free markets have survived — at least to some extent.

This scenario postulates a selection mechanism that favors better policies and politicians. In time good policy replaces bad policy; ideas and leaders that fail to solve problems fade away from public life. But for failed experiments to disappear, the electorate has to recognize the failure, identify the particular policy or rule that caused it and make government players get rid of that policy. North, Wallis and Weingast do not explain how good policies will be selected when there are knowledge gaps about policy consequences.

Of course, voters do replace politicians and parties because of large-scale obvious problems such as high unemployment or a disastrous war. But many policy areas, among them financial regulation, are arcane and known only to a few people. The effects are indirect and long-term, almost impossible to trace. Most of the population does not know what the rules are and what consequences these have over time.

Therefore voters can easily pick politicians with bad policy ideas and never connect long-term consequences to those policies. In other words, the electorate will likely not recognize failed experiments. For bad policies to disappear, the political elite has to identify and lead the way in getting rid of them, even if there is no mandate from voters to do so.

This is plausible if a policy harms a significant part of the elite. If that is not the case and a wide swath of the public is harmed but is not aware of the destructive effects of the particular policy, it is risky for a politician to try to stop it. Opponents can easily blame problems on other policies and paint as an extremist the politician who challenges established practice. The policy and its effects may be too complex to be turned into an appealing political cause.

Also, members of the elite may be as unaware as the public of a policy's true consequences. The effects of regulation are typically not known for decades, if ever. A study on the results of the 1933 Act Corcoran pushed through Congress was published in the 1980s, some half-century later. It reported that investors gained little from the law.[314] That's just a single and simple example. There are thousands of financial rules with unknown effects.

When empirical studies of various types of regulation are done, the conclusion is often that the supposed correctives to market inefficiencies themselves failed. After reviewing evidence from diverse fields, C. Winston concluded: "Given that government has consistently failed to correct market failures, it is unlikely to start being more successful now, particularly when it is facing more difficult problems."[315]

One might expect research findings to be incorporated into new efforts to correct for problems that showed up in the past. But policy makers are necessarily impelled by their current political needs, not the lessons from historical failures. If someone wants to impose new regulation because this is politically advantageous, they do not talk about past regulatory fiascoes. That would not make for good public relations.

Considering all this, the early 20th century grand quest to improve the world step-by-step through rationally designed rules and experimentation appears to be unrealistic. The follow-up by North and others, relying on political competition to correct mistakes, is not persuasive. The Buchanan interest, Hayek knowledge and Schumpeter oversight problems are powerful barriers. The paucity of knowledge as to policy results, lack of public oversight and the interests of the political players conspire to block any correction mechanism.

Commons' notion of disinterested arbitrators who reconcile conflicting interests is not credible in a polity where those who hire top former officials get the better deal. And wearing blinders as Corcoran advised can't be the way to correct past mistakes in regulatory design. On the contrary, the business Corcoran exemplified depends on taking advantage of those mistakes and keeping them on the books to serve the client's interest. Regulatory utopia in reality is something other than what it promises—just as collectivist utopias turned out to be something else.

CHAPTER TEN. Feral Surrogates

One word haunts the regulatory state like a dirty secret. Advocates were careful not to use this word in public, as if it were an obscenity.

When open-minded observers pointed it out, they often did so with a sense of its inevitability. "Even in democratic America I see how quickly a private citizen, when elected or appointed to public office, becomes a bureaucrat," Commons wrote in his memoir. He recognized the behavior for what it is, though while he was making policy he may not have worried much that the state apparatus he helped create could be nothing other than a bureaucracy.

All regulatory effort requires some sort of organization to formulate, clarify and enforce rules. Any organization beyond the smallest consists of a formal hierarchy, otherwise known as bureaucracy. Like Commons, Felix Frankfurter and Roscoe Pound must have recoiled when they saw these entities in action. Thereafter Pound tried to check the growth of the regulatory state and Frankfurter as a Supreme Court justice disappointed interventionists.

Proponents of regulation such as Landis avoided the word and employed the positive-sounding terms "administrative agency" or "public administration." These substitutes are free of bureaucracy's bad connotations such as inertia and corruption of purpose. If you are out to build or defend a boundless network of the same, you had best avoid the B-word and use innocuous substitutes. It would have been hopelessly bad rhetoric to propose the building of vast congeries of bureaucracies. So the public organizations created in America under the auspices of regulating away the failures of capitalism, foremost among them the Securities and Exchange Commission, are usually referred to as agencies.

Whatever term you use to describe it, the system is supposed to be subject to two levels of oversight: the electorate's say over its representatives and the latter's supervision of regulators. Legitimacy, following oversight, is transmitted in two relays, the first from voters to lawmakers and the White House; and the second from the elected officials of Congress and the Executive to regulatory agencies.

Besetting this system is a two-fold Schumpeter problem. We've discussed one part. Voters pay little attention to regulatory policies, have only the scantest knowledge outside what directly affects them and lack a single view of how to boost general wellbeing. Therefore the electoral mandate indicates neither clear goals or policies nor informed consent for an agenda. The electorate can't really supervise its representatives, though of course it will change them if there are noticeable bad developments.

That's an age-old aspect of democracy. By contrast the second oversight issue has more recent roots. A remarkable feature of the growth of the U.S. regulatory state is how it undermined governance by elected representatives. The surrogates who make most decisions are not elected; they are appointed. Inadequate electoral control has been compounded by the weakening of elected politicians' control over public bureaucracies.

This chapter is primarily about the latter, a topic that is impossible to avoid in examining the regulatory state yet gets hardly any attention when new regulations are proposed.

The Anointed

Weak democratic control boosts the power of the political-policy elite. This is good or bad depending on which one of two visions, rooted in conflicting views of government, you espouse.[316]

The interventionist elite – Thomas Sowell labels it "the anointed" – has faith in its ability to solve socioeconomic problems by relying on the special talents of the few. In this view, what matters is expert knowledge, which policymakers will use to bring about a more egalitarian and just society. Early 20th century institutionalists, legal realists and New Dealers – but also much of the policy establishment today – holds some version of the expert-centric ideal of governance.

Commons and Landis were leading examples. They set their hopes on a well-informed and well-intentioned social strata specialized in policymaking. Bright surrogates would mind the interests of the – less bright, less knowledgeable or simply uninterested – many. While politicians are part of the elite, the main proxies for the public in federal policy making are department and agency staffs.

Once you put your faith in the policy elite, whether or not voters fully understand what they're getting seems less important. Of course politicians should explain, in suitable language, what's being done. But it's the policy experts who have the skills to decide the best course of action. By implication, the more power to them, the better. This faith in smart bureaucratic proxies must be extraordinarily strong – How else to explain its survival after numerous regulatory and other policy debacles? No matter how many time they fail, hope springs eternal that bureaucrats will succeed with some new interventionist project.

Blind inconsistency is often part of the faith. Thus New Dealers held a blatant double standard. On the one hand they had a low opinion of the men who ran corporations. It was not just that business executives were immoral; in addition they were ignorant, unrealistic and short-sighted – yet somehow had succeeded in achieving the record levels of productivity that impressed Berle and Tugwell. After all, these two were of the opinion that the modern corporation was the epitome of technical efficiency.

At the same time, Tugwell seriously believed that federal bureaucrats sitting in Washington could know more about an industry and how it worked than the people who ran the companies and brought about gains in productivity. When the New Deal scheme to have Washington fix prices and wages failed, he could not really fathom why. It did not seem to occur to him that he was applying a double standard, recognizing shortcomings in corporate managers while glorifying government bureaucrats. For his industrial planning proposal to succeed, it would have to be run by near-omniscient beings who glimpse from afar what people who spend their careers in an industry fail to see.

In the opposite camp are proponents of what Sowell terms the tragic vision, who range from Adam Smith and Edmund Burke to Schumpeter, Milton Friedman and in our time Sowell himself.[317] From this view, the cognitive resources of any one individual is severely, inherently limited and that goes for the policy elite as well as for common folk. Despite the trappings of civilization and reasoned discourse, humanity contains the potential to descend into barbarism because our rational capabilities and control can be overwhelmed.

Therefore we need to rely on inherited institutions that have proven to work relatively well, such as moral precepts and respect for private property. These embody implicit knowledge from the past, to supplement our present knowledge and reason. The other way to supplement rationality is to rely on the combined wisdom of large numbers in markets that combine the knowledge of many. Following Hayek, Sowell pits the "power of unarticulated social processes to mobilize and coordinate knowledge" from numerous individuals against the articulated rationality of the elite.

Sowell's comparison of the American and French revolutions illustrates the sharp contrast between the two visions regarding confidence in political actors. While America's founders carefully devised a government of checks and balances so that none would have great power, "the French revolution concentrated vast powers in its leadership, so as to allow those who were presumably wise and benevolent to effect sweeping changes with little hindrance."

In the tragic vision, nobody is that wise and benevolent; nobody can be trusted with unchecked authority — not politicians, not judges and not regulators.

Old institutionalists would have agreed with part of the tragic vision. Certainly Commons would concur with Burke that the "contrivances of our reason" are "fallible and feeble" and long-established institutions fortify our frail rationality.[318] But Commons did not appreciate that the discipline of the marketplace also plays this role. And he kept trying to use policy to create better social arrangements — realizing too late that the new rules he so thoughtfully designed did not work as intended.

The two opposed views have dramatically different implications as to what regulation can achieve. To start with the Hayek problem, the staffs of government agencies don't have the right knowledge. Obviously experts possess knowledge in their specialized areas, whether in their minds, books or computers. But that is not the issue.

The real question is whether policy makers know how to make the public better off, in the sense of a net gain in overall satisfaction across the population. Even on the simplest individual level, it is easy to achieve one goal - to drink less soda, say - at the expense of another — to eat less candy, sabotaged by the soda restriction. To achieve a net gain overall, policy makers have to understand and factor in myriad tradeoffs. But regulation is piecemeal, each piece about one aspect of life, not the innumerable other matters also affected by it.

To really make the public better off, it is necessary to achieve the right tradeoffs, giving up what matters less to get what matters more. This requires the unique and widely dispersed private information that individuals possess as to their own wants, capabilities and priorities. Government agents don't know the relative importance people assign to myriad different wants and have no way to reconcile numerous priorities across society. Specialists know certain things better, but not the preferences of other people.

Everybody is ignorant, only on different subjects, says a succinct summary of the tragic vision — it so happens, in a message found in Chinese fortune cookies. To further the public good as a whole – or even to define it – the narrow knowledge of experts is comically insufficient. Sowell makes the critical point: no one group has general superiority in deciding what is desirable.

In the political realm, what the cognitive elite in general knows better turns out to be ideology, in the sense of a system that tells you what position to take on a given issue. Because they rely on ideology as a guide, professional observers have well-developed views. But they cannot judge the validity of the guide itself. J. Friedman's conclusion is persuasive: "it is not at all evident that we would be (or are) better ruled by the knowledgeable but doctrinaire elite than by the ignorant but eclectic population."[319]

To Enforce or Not to Enforce

Leaving aside what they know, the more power surrogates have, the more good or bad they can do. Classical legal doctrine prescribed a democratically accountable administrative system. Public bureaucracies were set up to perform certain narrowly specified functions. They were tools for Congress to achieve its purposes, organized to put into practice an agenda set by elected representatives and kept in line by Congressional directives.

That notion might not have been fully realistic, but it was achievable to some extent because the number of government departments was small and their functions limited; a member of Congress could examine and more or less understand what a department did. The public might not pay attention but its elected representatives could look over the shoulders of regulators, providing a secondary source both of oversight and legitimacy

In the past century that picture lost all relevance. This was deliberate. Landis and other reformers argued that lawmakers should not keep close watch over regulators but rather give them broad mandates and let them follow these according to their own judgment. That indeed is what happened.

Public agencies staffed by highly educated men and women were considered a bulwark against politicians who would otherwise meddle in administrative decisions for corrupt ends. An independent bureaucracy would act as an impartial minder of public interest, it was believed. On this ground, it became established policy to shield agencies from the demands of elected politicians as much as possible and leave them alone to do their job. Civil service laws and public unions have so many rules to protect agency personnel that it would be hard to count.

The doctrine that Congress should leave the specifics to agencies had defenders on both sides of the political spectrum. Thus Schumpeter thought it was desirable for appointed functionaries to be autonomous. The elected government becomes a general contractor; it grants the powers to agencies, where staffs decide what to do.

This would work tolerably well under certain conditions, according to Schumpeter. There has to be a well trained bureaucracy of good standing and long tradition of public service. It has to be efficient in administration and competent to give advice to politicians, guiding them when needed. To be able to do this, officialdom must evolve principles of its own and be independent enough to assert them. It has to be relatively immune to political strife.

"It must be a power on its own right," Schumpeter argued.[320] The independent power base cannot be created in a hurry. It requires a social group, such as an intelligentsia possessed of sufficient prestige, that sees civil service as its mission. If those conditions are present, then the public bureaucracy can run a country well enough, he believed. That does not mean he saw the bureaucratic state as panacea. Just that it would "display no inefficiencies other than those associated with the word bureaucracy."[321]

This trend of endowing regulators with wide discretion, intentionally encouraged by legal and political writers, gained further momentum for a practical reason. It had always been hard work for elected officials to oversee the regulatory system. But as the system grew in size and complexity, it became impossible. Not only Congress but the executive branch lost the ability to follow what goes on inside agencies.

Schumpeter pointed out the problem. Politicians' competitive advantage is to create a brand that gets votes. A successful politician has demonstrated the ability to campaign for and win political races, but not to run the government. For the latter role the elected have no qualification — having won thanks to a very different skill set. As Schumpeter put it, "the democratic method creates professional politicians whom it then turns into amateur administrators..."

Somebody else formulates policy and make rules. It is now accepted practice that agency staffs do this. There is no longer a serious claim that they simply implement policy handed down by Congress.

A particular inefficiency inherent in bureaucracy is the inability to take advantage of individual initiative — or even to allow it to exist. Schumpeter surmised that besides causing a sense of frustration and futility among the officials themselves, the smothering of initiative would likely result in a stagnant economy. But he saw no alternative. From the vantage point of the besieged capitalism of the early 20th century, he predicted the coming of some sort of socialism, likely in the form of gradual bureaucratization.

Writing around the same time as Schumpeter, Ludwig von Mises offered a different view. In Europe, government bureaucrats had long formed an integrated group with its own culture and interests. This class lorded it over the rest of the population — "the officeholders are no longer the servants of the citizenry but irresponsible and arbitrary masters and tyrants," Mises wrote.

The reason this happened was the government's increased meddling, which necessarily leads to a growing and more powerful apparatus to handle the interventions. Increased bureaucratization is an unavoidable consequence of interventionism.

"Those who criticize bureaucracy make the mistake of directing their attacks against a symptom only and not against the seat of evil," Mises warned. It was a mistake to attribute the failures of European bureaucratic states to intellectual or moral deficiencies of personnel — "Many of the most gifted and lofty members of the intelligentsia served in the bureaus."

The problem was more fundamental. Subjecting economic matters to government decisions inevitably results in a country becoming dominated by bureaucracies. "The system is bad, not its subordinate handy men," Mises said. A parliament does not have the time or ability to implement policy; there is no choice but to turn the tasks and power over to bureaucracies.

Mises held up Germany in the late 19th and early 20th centuries as the country most advanced in bureaucratic regimentation. He quoted a Rector of the Imperial University of Strassburg. ".. No kind of rule is endured so easily or accepted so gratefully as that of the high-minded and highly educated civil servants," the man had declared in 1891. "The German State is a State of the supremacy of officialdom — let us hope that it will remain so."[322]

That "supremacy of officialdom" ended with a bad reputation after the country suffered the horrors of World War I. But Mises' point is that the bureaucratic ascendancy in Germany was a result of the state's abrogation of powers. The latter led to economic stasis and political corruption. It would have done so even run by a class of high-minded scholar-administrators.

Mises' stylized description of German history offers a dire lesson. With government bureaucracies dominating economic life, citizens focused on getting benefits and protection. People courted high officials and spent resources on winning their favor.

So the expansive bureaucratic state degenerated into racketeering. Bureaucratization, itself a result of state expansion in the economic sphere, brought not only stagnation but corruption. Impoverishment and social unrest followed.

As Mises saw the German experience, the bureaucratic state robbed citizens of their money and liberty while appearing as their benign protector. "You could revolt against a Bourbon King," he wrote. "But you cannot revolt against the Good State and against his humble handy man, the bureaucrat."

A similar trend is noticeable in other countries. In America, as regulatory functions and powers expanded through the 20th century, so did the bureaucracies to yield the powers. As regulatory laws piled up and became more complicated, Congress could not possibly specify the details or keep a tight rein on what the agencies made of its directives. So it was not just arguments such as Landis' but necessity that gave increasing control to bureaucracies. As a practical matter, the regulatory state is the bureaucratic state.

When it comes to fraud, bureaucrats' historic record is abysmal. Government interventions track Ponzi schemes in reverse — fewer interventions when schemes are rife in good times; more when schemes become rare in slumps.[323] This is the exact opposite of what you would expect from an effective prevention program.

In a boom people are overly optimistic and willing to believe extravagant claims. Gains from fast-rising markets encourage investors to be over-confident and ignore evidence of malfeasance. Schemes prosper — as did the Manhattan, Madoff and Stanford con games. Regulators should be more active in booms if they are to dispel delusions. But in fact they tend to be perversely quiescent at such times.

Typically they take action after the market comes down and schemes collapse. In the aftermath of the 2008-2009 crisis, the Securities and Exchange Commission appeared to prosecute anyone it could collar for whatever reason. Having failed signally to prevent the big swindles of the boom years, the SEC and the Justice Department came up with a rash of insider trading and other charges.

Why do bureaucrats fail to intervene and deter schemes in strong markets?[324] Possibly they get caught in market euphoria like everybody else. They are not more cogent or better informed than market players and fall into the same delusion. If regulators are as muddled as private parties, they will not do any better in catching fraud — in fact they will do worse because they have less incentive.

In that case there is no real argument for financial regulation for correcting the population's cognitive failures and preventing fraud. Possibly it can be defended on other grounds. Protecting the economically weak – like small investors – may make a politically appealing rationale, but that also requires regulators to understand what's going on in the market.

The alternative explanation for the cyclical pattern in interventions is that government agents' goal is not what it is claimed to be. How they apply the rules depends on what they want to achieve, which is not the officially avowed mission. In other words, they do not try to catch fraud in good times because that is not in their interest. The Madoff and Stanford schemes provide evidence for this.

Regulatory cycles provide a clue as to how bureaucracies act. Whether or not they are better informed and capable of sound judgment about market bubbles and schemes, they have reason not to act during booms. Raining on people's parade with interventions aiming to disabuse them of their excessive optimism would be unwelcome. By contrast in difficult times it is politically expedient to appear to solve problems, hence regulators go into frantic motion.

To the extent the bureaucrats know what's going on in markets – an open question – their choice to enforce or not to enforce existing rules reflects their interest. Given the lack of oversight by the public and its representatives, agency staffs will go by their own preference until a crisis forces them to pay more attention to public relations and look sharp for a while.

The Most Rational of Men

Increased bureaucratization was inevitable, Schumpeter believed, because economic life in general was already to a large extent bureaucratized. Large hierarchical organizations spread in tandem with modern economic development and the growth of democracy. The trend would no doubt continue. "Its expansion is one certain thing about our future," Schumpeter predicted.[325] Bureaucracy was like death and taxes.

This was – and probably is – a common view. It is not just public agencies that proliferate; similarly large business organizations run by professionals dominate the economy, as Berle and Means demonstrated. A substantial portion of the private economy may be as bureaucratic as the federal government.

Except that there is catch, a crucial difference, as Mises pointed out: businesses have to meet the market test.[326] Their product has to appeal to customers who are willing to pay a price high enough to yield at least a normal profit. A business that is not profitable sooner or later disappears. But government organizations persist indefinitely even if they produce nothing of value or, worse, destroy economic value.

Indeed, objective valuation of their output is practically impossible; any estimated value is essentially arbitrary. The resources they use up can be measured, but assigning the product a price is guesswork. Often it is not even clear what exactly the product is. Being outside the cash nexus means that government organizations do not have real valuations to evaluate performance. Emphasizing the distinction, Mises reserved the word "bureaucracy" for public organizations alone.

Specific directives from Congress could at least provide meaningful benchmarks for performance but agencies no longer have such directives. The laws are too broad to play this role. Consider the vague mandates of the 2010 Dodd-Frank Act, still in the process of being turned into numerous rules by financial regulators, who will then implement the rules they made. Their performance would have to be measured against the rules they created themselves, in so far as it is measured at all. The sprawling but fuzzy law that came from Congress lacks the specificity to be a practical yardstick.

There being no external criterion for assessing the specific work being done, the internal relationship between subordinates and superiors becomes all important. Most civil servants are committed to a career of finding out what their superiors want and doing it, as Tullock puts it.[327] This means that in the main information flows from top to bottom — the superior informs the subordinate. Since going against the flow would hamper the subordinate's career, facts that are inconsistent with the superior's viewpoint are ignored or shelved.

While the resulting disconnect from external reality may have the appearance of bizarre irrationality – for which the term Kafkaesque was invented – each individual official acts to advance his or her own interest. If they fail to do so, they do not move up in the bureaucracy. "Those who rise in a merit-based hierarchy will be among the most rational of men," Tullock notes. To rise, they have to be.

Agencies' growing powers and the waning of Congressional and executive ability to control or even know what they do makes regulators to a large extent self-governing. Bureaucracies are run in accordance with internally generated rules and the preferences of those high in the pecking order, on whom there is little or no independent check. This results in a certain mindset. Thus the old-world bureaucracies of Europe developed a peculiar character that Mises described: "Their intellectual horizon was the hierarchy and its rules and regulations. They fate was to depend entirely on the favor of their superiors."

As for the U.S., the political scientist James Wilson studied various agencies, including the FBI.[328] He found that public bureaucracies define their mission not by the goals they were given by Congress or the White House but by the nature of the work and the particular situation they find themselves in. An organizational culture develops and leads to behavior that may not be reasonable for pursuing outside mandates but makes sense for the bureaucracy itself.

Interestingly, the real power tends to reside not at the visible tip of hierarchy – the political appointee who is the public face of the agency – but on the rungs right below the top. Wilson observed that the high officials who make policy tend to be disconnected from those at the lower rungs who put the policy into practice. The man or woman who appears to lead the agency and represents it to Congress, the White House and the public often has limited power to shape what the bureaucracy does.

Generalizations may seem unwarranted because public officials are not all alike. The two SEC regulators who faced off for years on the matter of pursuing Stanford, Julie Preuitt and Spencer Barasch, were almost complete opposites. Given any situation, individual preferences and as a result individual responses, vary.

But bureaucrats tend to be more alike than not. They have similar backgrounds, are self selected on the basis of similar priorities such as job security and face similar incentives.

They are alike in education — during the years the three Ponzi schemes took place, almost all high-level officials at the SEC were lawyers. They work under pressure to conform to the collective culture and please their immediate superiors in a hierarchical organization. Those who do not fit the group think don't do well. Preuitt was an outlier in the SEC, had great difficulty getting the decisions she argued for – despite presenting strong evidence – and was punished, in effect, for not fitting in.

These features encourage bureaucrats to act together to protect the collective interest of the group. Well aware of how to enhance their standing and capable of running sophisticated public relations campaigns with the resources and powers they possess, public bureaucracies form a potent vested interest.

They "make a significant contribution to rent seeking and to the dissipation of wealth in society, taking full advantage of their status as small, privileged, homogeneous special interest groups, empowered by their ability to coerce members and thus to overcome the free-rider effect," Tullock pointed out.[329]

Public Policy Could Become Captive

The fundamental question about the independence of public bureaucracies was posed – though not answered – by Stephen Breyer, arguably the most distinguished successor to Frankfurter and Landis as administrative law professor at Harvard. If agency decisions are not controlled by Congress and are not scientifically determined, then what right does an agency have to make policies?

Breyer asked: What makes the decision legitimate?[330] Given that the outcome of a policy initiated by Congress or the executive depends so much on the bureaucracy empowered to carry it out, is policy making really democratic?

Writing about measures to make policy more responsive to democratic control, Breyer pointed out that a regulator can evade the spirit of laws requiring openness and consultation, thereby remaining "vested with nearly uncontrollable discretion, unelected, freed by wide statutory mandates from close judicial scrutiny and unchecked by professional discipline."

What I've called the second Schumpeter oversight problem is an often ignored aspect of the rise of regulatory officialdom. Public employees are in unionized civil service jobs, well protected even when they engage in egregious wrongdoing. By contrast, elected officials come and go. Bureaucrats are still around after a politician moves to other issues, loses an election or metamorphoses into a lobbyist. The sponsors of the Dodd-Frank law, Christopher Dodd and Barney Frank, both veteran politicians, left Congress long before the regulations took final shape. An army of bureaucrats decided, according to their own lights, what to make of the law.

When Congress demands that regulators promote a goal, the bureaucrats may like or not like the task. Their decisions as to how to handle a Congressional edict range from aggressive implementation to deliberate neglect. On occasion they choose to ignore a direct order from Congress. Thus an SEC Chairman decided not to do much about a 1975 law to promote competition in securities markets. He said the required measures would disrupt trading.[331]

Was he worried about trading or about political risk to the agency? Promoting competition meant going against powerful financial interests. By disregarding the 1975 law, did regulators do what was best for securities markets or did they do what was convenient for themselves? There's no way to answer such questions. The fact remains that the agency did not do what lawmakers wanted and members of Congress did not or could not force the issue.

The notion, often expressed in the press, that deregulation caused the 2008 financial crisis confuses the behavior of government agents with their legal powers. Regulators choose not to apply or enforce certain laws and rules, using the vast discretion they possess. That the SEC chose not to stop Madoff or Stanford demonstrates the license such bureaucracies have to act or not, as they wish. It is not the SEC lacked authority or tools to tackle the con men.

Another example is the Federal Reserve's choice not to discourage the 1990s stock market bubble or 2000s credit bubble—by keeping interest rates unusually low for several years, as John Taylor (2009) shows. It is not that the Fed lacked the power to discourage market exuberance; the bureaucracy – or its at least higher echelon – decided not to.

Federal agencies have long possessed ample legal authority; that has not changed. But measures that are not to the bureaucrats' liking or advantage get short shrift. This is glaring in their handling of financial fraud. Sharing information across regulators could inhibit fraud. But even groups within the SEC are not always willing to share information with each other, let alone with another organization.

The industry overseer FINRA inspected the Madoff brokerage numerous times yet was never told about the series of complaints the SEC received regarding the firm.[332] At least part of the reason was that heads of departments wanted to protect their own turf. The investigation into the treatment of Madoff quotes an official that the head of one of the SEC offices "was particularly protective of … his territory and …was very political."

Typically a member of Congress has little knowledge of what a bureaucracy did about a certain matter and though he can demand information, he remains dependent on the bureaucrats. If the result of a policy is not what politicians wanted, correcting the implementation is an uphill battle that requires identifying what went wrong and getting enough backing in Congress to force the responsible bureaucracy to change its approach.

Politicians have neither the skills nor the time for such work. After all, their comparative advantage is electioneering, not the details of policymaking. They can reduce an agency's budget, but this does not necessarily make it behave better. Time is on the side of the bureaucracrats. This year's budget cut can be more then compensated for by next year's budget increase.

The executive branch is in a similar position of relative weakness against established bureaucracies. The White House can replace the head of an agency, but this is politically risky and in practice tends to be limited, happening at the start of a new administration. More important, even if a new appointee wants to do something different, he or she faces bureaucratic inertia that takes special efforts to overcome and given the rules may not be possible even for an energetic new chief.

As I've described, the independence of agencies was long seen as highly desirable. Neither the New Dealers nor well-informed observers like Commons and Schumpeter recognized the danger in creating a autonomous administrative realm. They gave little thought to the downside of a power that uses legal authority to reshape parts of society and the economy but is not elected and is subject to minimal – if any – control from the outside.

A few statesmen recognized the implications. President Eisenhower in his January 1961 speech in which he warned against the military-industrial complex – probably the most quoted Presidential farewell after George Washington's[333] – also warned more broadly about the policymaking elite and the "potential for the disastrous rise of misplaced power."

In particular, Eisenhower highlighted the "danger that public policy could itself become the captive of a scientific-technological elite." As perceived by proponents of interventionism, he's referring to surrogates who are minding the public's interest. With his long experience inside the government, Eisenhower knew how different real elites are from idealized surrogates.

Real Surrogates: Judges and Their Friends

The judiciary is probably the most rule-bound and transparent arm of government. By the same token, there is no clearer demonstration of independent government agents' immense potential for mischief than the spectacle of judges gone bad.

Judges have been examined and analyzed more extensively than other public officials. Epstein (1990) argued that the American constitutional structure channels judges' self-interest in desirable ways but some constraints against obvious abuse and misbehavior are justified.

Posner (2008) developed a model of judicial behavior as utility maximization, but with greater weight to non-monetary factors such as prestige, power, influence and celebrity. Posner describes as defensible realism his view that judges – like other human beings –are influenced by costs and benefits to themselves, with political, sentimental or other personal factors coming to play in that assessment.

But those factors do not entirely determine judges' decisions, which are constrained by professional and institutional rules and expectations. An empirical test of this model suggests that judges at higher courts tend to be more politically motivated than those at lower courts, who deal with routine cases.[334] It seems that the more discretion a judge has, the larger the influence of his personal beliefs and preferences.

Despite numerous formal safeguards and a professional culture that goes back centuries, some judges do engage in egregious misbehavior. In some instances the motive is obvious financial gain Thus two judges in Pennsylvania received millions of dollars in kickbacks for sending children to a certain private detention center. Youngsters were shackled and taken to jail for no good reason over five years, starting in 2003. One 11-year-old called the police when he was locked out of his home and was immediately incarcerated at the facility that paid off the judge.[335]

Eventually these judges themselves ended up in prison on corruption charges. One can regard them as two exceptionally bad apples among thousands of honest men and women. But many officials, including other judges and prosecutors, could have taken action to stop the abuse of authority. Most did nothing as children were used to boost detention center revenue and judges' incomes.

In other situations a judge may be influenced by the non-monetary factors Posner emphasized. The Chicago school of economics Posner belongs to typically casts the desire for reputation as a beneficial influence that promotes good behavior. Judges concerned about their reputation should make decisions that other judges are likely to approve of, hence acting in accordance with professional norms.

But that is a partial view. I've referred above to Tyler Cowen's point that reputation is a double-edged sword.[336] The pursuit of fame can encourage false claims and socially damaging behavior — Madoff's desire to protect his legend as money manager may have been impelled him to start conning people. Judges who seek public acclaim can make decisions that get their names into the news but are bad decisions. As we saw, certain bankruptcy judges attracted attention and cases by favoring debtors and bankruptcy professionals. Their rulings were biased in a way that diverged from the norm.

As for the subject I've tackled in previous chapters, namely estates, a long-running scandal in Brooklyn, New York, confirms the problems that arise in that area. This story goes back to 1996, when a judge who decided on scheduling trials for Brooklyn Supreme Court civil cases was found to have received large campaign contributions from lawyers whose lawsuits depended on his rulings. These were mostly personal injury claims, potentially very lucrative for the lawyers, who stood to lose or gain a lot from the case the judge sent to trial or arbitration.

Early in his long career, the same judge, Michael Feinberg, got a black mark for failing to obtain an accounting of money he contributed to the Kings County Democratic party for his own political campaign. Nevertheless, he was a civil court judge for 10 years and since 1990 was on the Brooklyn supreme court. In 1996 he ran for a new position, the Brooklyn surrogate court judgeship.

Despite adverse publicity about the contributions from interested lawyers, he easily won the Democratic primary and the general election. Many voters probably did not pay attention to surrogate judge slot. No doubt they voted for him because he was on the Democratic Party ticket; Brooklyn is heavily Democratic and dominated by the local party machine.

So Feinberg became responsible for overseeing the estates of people who died without a will or whose heirs are unwilling or deemed unable to handle the estate. His job included the supervision of the public administrator office, which directly handles the assets of the estates, and the counsel to this office. His old law school chum and political supporter, Louis Rosenthal, knew well how this office worked. Years ago, Rosenthal's father had been the public administrator.

During the campaign for the surrogate judgeship Rosenthal gave Feinberg advice and solicited support, votes and money for him. When Feinberg won the primary, Rosenthal told his friend that he wanted to be counsel to the public administrator. As soon as he took office, the judge dismissed the law firm did this job for many years and appointed Rosenthal.

The previous law firm had an agreement with the attorney general of New York to charge no more than 6% of estates up to $300,000 and no more than 5% for assets beyond that. This was in keeping with surrogate legal fees in other New York counties. In 2002, the *Daily News* reported that the surrogate judge regularly awarded large fees to his friend – 24% of certain estates over $100,000 – for unspecified services. Rosenthal wrote the fee he wanted on a Post-It note and Feingold let him have that amount without requiring him to document or even identify the services for which he compensated himself from estates.

Eventually the state commission on judicial conduct investigated and found that the fees came to 8% of the gross value of the estates. The public administrator took another 2% of the gross for its services, although the office was staffed with salaried public employees. This way of calculating fees meant that public officials took about 10% of an estate before the payment of debts, taxes and other expenses. If an estate included a house with a mortgage and a car with loan payments, court officials creamed 10% off the total without subtracting the liabilities. Then the mortgage, loan, other debt and taxes were paid and the net remainder eventually went to the heirs, who in some instances received less than the lawyer.

The state commission on judicial conduct found that Rosenthal's $9 million in fees as counsel for the public administrator was excessive compared to what other lawyers received for similar work and what he was entitled to according to the agreement with the attorney general. The commission estimated that $2 million in fees were unwarranted. The surrogate court judge was removed in 2005 and disbarred in 2008, twelve years after his corrupt campaign financing first hit the headlines.

Initially the New York attorney general was unwilling to try to get the money back from the lawyer — he blamed the previous attorney general for failing to stop the payments to the judge's crony. The previous attorney general was Eliot Spitzer, who by then had resigned his position as governor when it emerged that he patronized prostitutes. Needless to say, the lawyer fought all efforts to make him pay back the excessive fees.

It is easy to dismiss established abuses as an exception, but what came to public attention is likely the tip of the iceberg. Brooklyn surrogate judge Feingold had two defenses. One, he did not know that payments from estates to lawyers required affidavits showing services rendered. Neither did he know about the agreement with the attorney general that set a ceiling to such payments.

The commission investigating him found this explanation unacceptable on the principle that judges are supposed to know applicable law and precedents: "A judge's misconduct cannot be excused by inattention or oversight."[337]

Two, Feinberg defended his actions as the norm in the court system. All the judges and lawyers did the same thing, he claimed. This is the most intriguing part of the affair. In reply to Feinberg's contention, the commission acknowledged the widespread problem: "We are mindful that within the existing system there has been too much opportunity for lucrative fees to be doled out by judges to their friends and political associates. However, the conduct of other judges is not before us."

That suggests Feinberg was unlucky in becoming the subject of unflattering news stories and thereby ending up in front of the judicial conduct commission. Had he managed to stay out of the (adverse) limelight, he could continue what he was doing, like the other judges. Pervasive sleaziness is the overall impression from the story.

However, the commission pointed to efforts at reform: "We note that the court system has focused on patronage-related problems, initiated certain reforms and appointed an Inspector General to investigate abuses. These efforts are continuing."

What's truly notable is that despite those efforts and much publicity, the Brooklyn grave robbery did not end. In 2009, the public administrator was found to have mismanaged estates and sold assets in shady deals. The New York City Comtroller who audited the office found it necessary to issue a warning to the public: Make out a will as soon as possible to avoid falling into the hands of the public administrator (and the surrogate court).

Nationally, the process for settling wills is so burdensome that there is a cottage industry giving advice on how to steer clear of the probate procedure and the surrogates who oversee it in some states — books with titles such as "8 Ways to Avoid Probate."[338] Many people hire a lawyer to set up their estate so that their heirs may stay out of probate, which in theory is supposed to protect the public interest, like all regulation.

Gordon Tullock argued that the complex and costly procedure is unnecessary. He suggested replacing it with a law that treats inheritance as a deed of gift, a reform that would benefit everybody except for probate court personnel and attorneys. But the latter clearly have the upper hand — Tullock wrote about this matter in 1971; probate attorneys and surrogate courts continue to grind away at estates in 2013.

This is an instance of the public knowing its interest is easily traduced in the courts – which are open compared to other arms of the government – and spending resources to avoid it. Judges are exceptional in being in the public eye and having their actions second guessed by judicial experts who are not always their cronies.

Other public agents are not subject to such safeguards. Most government functionaries are watched only by their own colleagues in the same organization, behind closed doors. If court officers can grossly abuse their authority with impunity for prolonged periods as the above examples show, other officials such as regulators, who are not subject to the same kind of control, have ample opportunity to do so.

The two-fold Schumpeter problem gives regulators a freedom of choice that no one else possesses. Hence the old adage that power corrupts applies forcefully to regulators. The following selection from the recent mishaps of the Securities and Exchange Commission indicates the extent.

Real Surrogates: Reform Era Scandals

In the aftermath of the 2008 financial crisis, the SEC emerged as a problem child. Landis's iconic agency, the great success of the regulatory state, had become a symbol of failure. Congress investigated – among other matters, the Stanford and Madoff schemes – and ordered the SEC to get help for reforming itself. Faced with the need to assuage public anger, lawmakers (or their staffs) clearly felt something had to be done — but lacked specific suggestions as to what.

The result was a provision in the Dodd-Frank law requiring the agency to commission a study on its organizational problems and apply the recommendations. The Boston Consulting Group was hired and came up with a 263-page report with the unremarkable message that the SEC had opportunities to make better use of its existing resources. If that did not satisfy Congress, then there were two choices, according to the consultant — either more funding or a role change to fit the budget. Thereupon the SEC started to issue periodic reports on the reforms being implemented.

Meanwhile President Obama appointed as SEC chairperson a career regulator, Mary Schapiro. This did not inspire confidence in the message that a brand new improved SEC was in the works, given her previous tenure at FINRA – and its predecessor NASD – where brokers who complained about Allen Stanford's fraud were persistently shown to the door and left to suffer payback from the thug. Even so, nobody predicted that the SEC would be racked by scandal after scandal in just about every possible area.

Schapiro appointed as general counsel and senior policy director a lawyer who had gone through the revolving door, as per SEC custom. David Becker first joined the agency in 1998, became general counsel, left to work for a law firm.

In the press release announcing his return to the agency in 2009, Schapiro praised Becker's "wisdom and careful judgment" and said he would "help shape the SEC's future as an ever-stronger regulator." In addition to his other roles, Becker became the alternate manager of the SEC ethics program.

As luck would have it, Becker and his brothers had inherited an investment with Madoff and redeemed it several years before the end of the scheme, taking home $2 million that naturally included fictitious profits. Therefore they were subject to claw-back by the Madoff trustee, who demanded they pay $1.5 million to the estate. This in itself was not an impediment to Becker functioning as SEC counsel. But he did the one thing he should have known to avoid, especially as he was the alternate manager of the ethics program. He became closely involved in SEC decisions concerning the Madoff estate and in particular the claw-backs.

To start with, Becker pushed for a certain method for calculating an investor's equity. He favored recognizing the last account statement from Madoff to determine what an investor could claim as his or her own. This would legitimize fictitious profits and, as the trustee pointed out in objecting to the idea, eliminate the possibility of claw-backs.[339] The SEC general counsel abandoned that notion for another one that again favored those facing claw-backs, including himself and his brothers.

The idea was to correct the original capital for inflation so that the recognized equity became larger — reducing the amount that could be clawed back. Becker worked to persuade the SEC commissioners to support the inflation-adjusted equity approach, contrary to the position the agency took previously and against the objections of the Madoff trustee and SIPC. This would reduce the claw-back he and his family were liable for by about $140,000.

Several SEC lawyers, including ethics officers, as well as Chairwoman Schapiro, were aware of Becker's Madoff connection but did not suggest that he stay out of Madoff-related decisions — as staff with any link to Madoff were expected to do. However, when he was about to testify to Congress, higher ups in the agency had someone else testify instead on the ground that the disclosure of Becker's Madoff interest might be a "distraction" in the political setting.

There is an obvious conflict of interest that a man whose fake gains from a Madoff account were subject to claw-back advised SEC commissioners on how the fake gains should be calculated. Other than Schapiro, the SEC commissioners did not know that the general counsel whose opinions they relied on had such an interest and were astonished to see news stories about it. Becker left the agency in 2011.

Numerous other troubles beset the SEC. A 2010 investigation showed that some employees, among them several high-level lawyers, looked at pornographic websites while at work. One spent as much as eight hours a day on his porn habit, downloading contents to DVDs he stored in the office. A year later, despite the loud public outcry, SEC personnel were still accessing porn sites.[340] They did not seem to be too concerned about the outrage in Congress, probably because civil service and union rules made it difficult to fire culprits and in any event many staffers planned to go through the revolving door to the booming lobbyist industry.

In 2011, it emerged that the agency had taken a 10-year, $550 million lease on high-end office space it did not need and subsequently relinquished. It made no attempt to get competitive bidding for the contract.[341] This followed the so-called "restacking project" in which the SEC spent about $4 million to move the desks of 1,750 employees, with much waste of tax dollars according to complaints.

In 2012, a major scandal erupted at the SEC watchdog, the office that had investigated the Stanford and Madoff failures, porn surfing and numerous other questionable incidents. The aggressive head of the watchdog, a man detested by many because of his sharp criticisms of the bureaucracy, left. He was accused of having affairs with colleagues and with lawyers connected to matters investigated by the watchdog.

The accusations came from the chief investigator of the office, David Weber, who subsequently was himself fired. He then sued the agency and chairwoman Schapiro. Weber claimed they retaliated against him because he informed Congress of his former chief's misconduct and that SEC employees exposed sensitive stock exchange data to international hackers. The SEC settled with Weber, paying him $580,000 to drop the lawsuit.

Breakouts of organizational dysfunction and irresponsibility did not end. The second Obama administration replaced Schapiro with another revolving-door lawyer. Of course Schapiro herself went through the same very active door to the other side.

Most remarkable were the multiple failures caused by attempts to make the agency perform better. One such incident unfolded over six years. The SEC has a program to inspect the technologies and operations of stock exchanges and brokerages. In 2005, the Government Accountability Office recommended that SEC staff acquire expertise in technology, especially with regard to information security, in order to enhance the effectiveness of these reviews. In response the SEC created a computer security lab to acquire, test and understand technologies used in the financial industry.

To aid the inspections, the exchanges were asked to provide proprietary information to SEC staff. It was this information that was on unprotected SEC computers taken by staff to a hackers' conference and connected to unsecure wireless networks at various locations. At the IT security lab itself, they used the network unprotected from intruders while the firewall was down, among other activities to visit gaming sites.

Despite the mission, most of the IT lab staff did not have financial industry technical skills. They were given training at the expense of the agency but were not required to stay there afterwards — one employee left after receiving $50,000 of training. The man who was supposedly the supervisor never went to the lab, didn't even have a card key to enter it and lacked technology knowhow to oversee equipment purchases or testing.

The lab's three to four employees spent almost $1.2 million on computer hardware and software that was mostly not useful for official functions but appealed to their fancy. They bought the "latest tech toys for their personal use" a whistleblower said. An official of the SEC Office of Information Technology referred to the lab as "a toy box" in testimony. Employees took the equipment home and used it for personal purposes. So the GAO suggestion on how to improve inspections led to SEC personnel putting stock exchange information at risk and wasting taxpayer money.

These were the findings of an investigation that covered several years through October 2011, the post-Madoff period when the SEC was supposedly undergoing far-reaching reforms. Paradoxically, those very reforms provided opportunities for further corruption.

To put into practice the reform recommendations of the Boston Consulting Group, the chief operating officer of the SEC insisted on hiring another consultant — though his colleagues argued the agency itself could implement the reforms. He steered most of the work to the one consultant where his friends were partners and principals. This preference allowed that consultant to make over $1 million a month.

Weber, in his lawsuit, suggested an interesting explanation along the lines of scratch-my-back-and-I-will-find-a-way-to-scratch-yours-later. The SEC chief operating officer was a former managing vice president of Capital One Financial. Weber was investigating the possibility that this man may have favored the consultant as payback for regulatory favors he received earlier when he was at Capital One. But the chief operating officer put Weber on leave, possibly to impede the inconvenient investigation into the matter of hiring the consultant.

The lagged payback is suggestive of a pattern. Regulators may favor a party who later on, after circumstances have changed and the connection is no longer obvious, pushes a plum their way. What from the outside looks innocuous may be a long-due payback to a regulatory ally.

Diverse as these scandals are, they have in common the extreme hubris of the officials concerned. They were told to reform, they were chastened, they were under scrutiny — it did not matter. They felt free to visit porn and gaming sites, dispense with computer security, buy themselves the computer stuff they fancied, get their allies lucrative consulting gigs and engage in assorted misconduct.

The misbehaving bureaucrats show little concern that they will be called to account. Again, we have to assume they are rational. Their lack of fear is rationally grounded – government bureaucrats are rarely called to account. The mindset that they are unlikely to suffer serious consequences for their actions is based on experience. Even porn surfers could not be fired, despite a roaring scandal and demands for reform from members of Congress.

This culture is rooted in the reality of the regulatory state, which endows bureaucracies with a high degree of independence. Organizational reshuffles that take place under the name of reform do not change the fundamental situation. Members of the bureaucracy even use the reforms to further their own purposes at the expense of taxpayers.

Outrageous as the Madoff and Stanford failures and later scandals were, the agency did not suffer real reverses. On the contrary, it gained new authority and resources. It was given immense new powers by the Dodd-Frank Act, which should be called a Lobbyist Job Creation Act, so many opportunities did it provide for political rent extraction and need for protection against others' rent seeking. Jobs for regulatory insiders boomed, to the benefit of former SEC staffers.

As a result, financial bureaucrats have even less to fear. If forced out of the government, they have plenty of places to go, to help industry people protect against or take advantage of the rules they helped create. Why would they worry about what people think of their behavior? Given the current structure of the regulatory system, neither the public nor Congress can really get to them.

Galbraith's bad kings are no more but in their place are free-wheeling corrupt surrogates. People have a poor impression of government not because they are unduly influenced by the history of oppression by ancient rulers but because of what they see close to home, when they look at Washington today. While Congress usually gets the blame for this, we should not forget the fourth arm of government that runs regulation land.

So the promised administrative utopia turned out to be a dystopia of bureaucracies gone amuck. What can be done?

CHAPTER ELEVEN: To Keep Regulation Honest

Looked at closely, financial regulation bears a striking similarity to a Ponzi scheme that promises highly attractive returns. The scheme may make some profit but its main effect is to transfer wealth. Similarly, financial regulation has not protected investors as promised these 80 years. But it does transfer wealth—foremost to regulatory insiders and their allies.

Another similarity is noteworthy. A Ponzi scheme is a vortex that pulls in people and money. Even Newton could not resist the lure and was drawn back into the South Sea scam. Regulation, also, builds on itself—the more it fails, the more rules pile up. Failure is attributed either to a lack of regulation or shortage of proper staff and money. This results in more powers and more resources for regulators after every major debacle, including the most recent financial crisis.

A third common ground is that such operations look exceptionally successful and may continue to look fine for a long time. Berger, Madoff and Stanford took different paths, but all three were known as exceptional money managers. Failure is invisible until it crops up seemingly with no warning. But in fact financial disasters do not happen quickly; they are in the making below the surface.

The SEC was celebrated as the outstanding agency, a triumph of the regulatory state. It is not possible to pinpoint exactly when it degenerated into the current feral bureaucracy where self-seeking functionaries ignore gigantic swindles and engage in all manner of malfeasance. But it could not have suddenly happened; the organizational culture that makes for this behavior must have started in the earlier bureaucracy with its supposedly exceptional record.

That brings us to the question of what to do. To think up reforms in the abstract is all too easy. Experience shows how hard it is to make a reform work as intended. Far more likely that the desired change will not be achieved, that the unintended consequences will create new problems, that the net effect will be nil or negative. To have a real chance of altering this pattern, we need to overcome the myths.

The Quack Medicine

Myth number one is the perennial cure offered for all regulatory ills — better staff. This notion is so persistent because it is part of the larger vision of elite surrogates taking care of public interest. In fact, Landis' claim that good men can make bad laws work is a fallacy. That approach has turned out to be a surefire way to create bureaucracies that are dysfunctional as far as public goals are concerned but highly effective in protecting their own and other special interests.

The real causality is the other way around — dysfunctional rules and organizational culture make people behave badly. Appointing strong individuals is at best a temporary nostrum. At worst, such individuals further corrupt the organization by taking arbitrary actions to achieve their own ends.

Tullock defines an efficient organization as one where self-regarding opportunists will do the right thing for the common benefit. Someone interested only in his own career will try to bring about the accepted goals of the organization because that is the way to advance. Conversely, in a bad setting an idealist is under pressure to behave like an opportunist or get sidelined.

Private companies operating in a competitive market have a built-in efficiency feature — if customers are not satisfied, the business goes down. Market discipline does not work perfectly to force companies to function well, but sooner or later it weeds out the dysfunctional ones. By contrast, regulatory agencies are legally endowed with monopoly power in controlling certain aspects of an industry and do not go bankrupt.

As we saw, the old-fashioned ideal of controlling public bureaucracies by keeping them strictly subject to Congressional directives was set aside in the early 20th century. Agencies are deliberately organized so as to be immune to political pressure. They face no real discipline. There is no longer an oversight mechanism, leaving aside how effective it was in the past. In any event supervising today's Byzantine regulatory apparatus is not practical. Rules are so numerous and complex that neither politicians nor the electorate can possibly keep track of them.

This two-fold Schumpeterian lack of oversight problem, combined with the Buchanan motive problem, has no obvious solution. How to build a public bureaucracy that functions well on its own power was the holy grail of Commons' career and the reason for his later unhappiness with regulatory agencies. Try as he did, he failed to find a way to design an organization where the members did what they are supposed to do. Nobody succeeded at this.

No matter how carefully put together, regulatory bureaucracies are dominated by rational self-seekers who have no reason to be stewards of the public interest. The nub of the matter, as Whitman and Rizzo (2007) point out, is that public decision makers create costs and benefits for numerous people – including future generations – but face only the costs and benefits that affect themselves.

Even so, the "right people" solution is still trotted out whenever regulatory failures surface. This despite the fact that several decades ago Stephen Breyer debunked it in no uncertain terms. Proposals to improve agencies by getting better personnel "seem only to scratch the surface of the regulatory problem," he wrote.[342]

Presumably governments do not on purpose appoint wrong people; incompetent and corrupt administrators are not part of an official plan. Dysfunctional bureaucracies are a side effect of policies that are typically defended as promoting the public interest. They gain power because politicians present regulation as a solution to social or economic ills. The regulatory state necessarily empowers regulatory bureaucracies and they naturally use that power to further their own ends.

Breyer acknowledged that reforms aiming to counter corruption are inherently limited. Take conflict of interest rules that attempt to ward off corruption from revolving-door relationships. The required delay before a former SEC lawyer can represent customers to the Commission has no real impact — rational SEC employees will factor in this delay and plan accordingly. The lifetime federal ban against representing parties the regulator has been involved with sounds more effective, but all it means is that the ex-regulator can't appear before the commission for such parties — he or she can still advise them.

Landis argued against any such limit on the ground that this would make it more difficult to attract qualified staff. Breyer says effective rules against the revolving door imply a major change in the nature of government employment. By restricting agency personnel's ability to move to the private sector, effective rules would create a population permanently committed to civil service careers. This would move the United States closer to European countries run by high-prestige bureaucracies where people spend their entire professional lives.

Whether such a system is desirable was unclear to Breyer, who did not believe that better salaries, status or publicity for regulators will solve the problems of regulation. The salary of a commission chairman is equal to a cabinet undersecretary's and commissioners of major agencies such as the SEC enjoy considerable status and prestige — though the latter has dimmed due to scandals since Breyer wrote about regulatory reform in the 1980s.

Reading Mises' comments on the old German system, one is apt to say that it is not desirable to have more powerful agencies constituted of career bureaucrats. True, public choice arguments emphasize the capture of regulators by the businesses they regulate and forbidding regulators to take jobs with those businesses may reduce such capture. But that is not the only issue.

Bureaucrats form so formidable an interest themselves – apart from those they regulate – that their burgeoning presence reduces the public's say in government, whatever the other weaknesses in collective decision making. Mises saw the emergence in European states of a large class of men dependent on the government for their careers as a "serious menace to the maintenance of constitutional institutions."

The cases we looked at demonstrated the power of the bureaucracy's own interest, through which all decisions are refracted. Whether there is capture by the regulated on a particular issue and the form it takes depends on what the bureaucrats decide is best for themselves. The notion that better staffing can resolve so deep-seated a governmental dysfunction would almost be funny were it not a massive sham that enables Ponzi regulation.

Those Who Believe in Good Government

To recap, it should be clear that if financial regulation is to be broadly beneficial, it cannot rely on the good intentions, altruism or expertise of government bureaucrats. Neither can the public or elected officials effectively supervise the regulatory state. The real question is how financial regulation can minimize Buchanan, Hayek and Schumpeter problems. The short, obvious answer is to economize on benevolence, knowledge and oversight.

If there is to be a net social benefit from regulation, it has to not require anyone's goodwill. One way to escape the fake benevolence trap is to rely on competition. The policing of fraud could be systematically outsourced to outside lawyers and financial analysts. Qualified lawyers and analysts could openly bid for a service contract to do a specified number of examinations of financial firms, with the lowest bidder automatically awarded the contract.

If it turns out that there was fraud going on and the private investigators missed it, their compensation could be clawed back and their right to bid for such jobs denied. This would make it the examiners' self interest to identify problems. But any outsourcing is just another source of patronage for a bureaucracy. Judging from experience, privatization will almost certainly add to corruption.

That said, routine open bidding for certain tasks is certainly doable. The selection of receivers and trustees for estates is an obvious area where competition among qualified lawyers would advance the public good. Why not have open bidding by qualified applicants rather than handing estates to the friends of lawyers and regulators? Lawyers often compete to get hired for private lawsuits; they would similarly compete for receiver jobs. Yet the SEC does not use open bidding to designate receivers or trustees.

The required tasks can be specified — sell whatever assets are left, make a plan for retuning money to investors and execute the plan once it is approved by a court. The qualified bidder who will perform these tasks for the lowest compensation gets the job.

Possibly the work could include clawing back payments of ersatz profits, but there is no reason for a receiver to engage in open-ended litigation. If investors wish, they can hire lawyers to sue other parties on their behalf, likely for contingency payments for successful litigation.

Like other reform proposals, the suggestion to use competitive bidding poses a paradox. Such reforms have been proposed before for government agencies and sound like the obvious thing to do. And yet these seemingly sensible ideas are not applied. Breyer, outlining measures against conflicts of interest, asked why "these suggestions have not been welcomed by all those who believe in good government."

At the time Breyer was an appeals judge. Named to the Supreme Court in 1994 by President Carter, he became known for a pragmatic approach in line with the legal realist heritage of the left-leaning liberal side of the court. However, though his intellectual and political orientation can be traced to the New Deal, Breyer developed a somewhat more qualified perspective compared to the arch-regulator Landis.

By the late 20th century notorious regulatory failures had emerged, the result of the ambitious interventionism that produced a great multitude of regulations, many of them so arcane and obscure as to be understood only by the specialists paid to make and administer them. His awareness of the failures shows in Breyer's somewhat more cautious approach.

Reform ideas such as outsourcing via competitive bids or more stringent conflict of interest rules may be rejected as bound to be ineffective. Perhaps some of the recommendations are not real solutions or are impractical. But another explanation has the virtue of simplicity. In his analysis Breyer assumes away the Buchanan problem — he ignores the interests of policy makers and regulators. That the latter do not adopt certain reforms suggests that their interest is not served by the proposed changes.

There is another way to economize on the benevolence and knowledge of public actors and the need for oversight to make them behave. But this, too, is an old idea.

Limits

James Madison eloquently explained the reason laws should be limited in length and complexity. "It will be of little avail to the people that the laws are made by men of their own choice," he wrote in Federalist Paper no. 62. "if the laws be so voluminous that they cannot be read, or so incoherent that they cannot be understood ..." If voters can't read or understand laws, they have no control over legislation.

Short and readily comprehensible laws impose boundaries on what a government can do. The principle that elected governments work best within boundaries had roots in Britain — it was Burke who said an all-powerful parliament must impose limits on itself in order to function properly. Through the centuries, others expressed similar ideas.

Schumpeter thought democracy works well enough as long as there are no serious issues, when the "problems of public policy are so simple and so stable that an overwhelming majority can be expected to understand them and to agree about them."[343] That the range of political decision making should not be extended too far was a condition for successful electoral rule.

A more recent version of the argument comes from Ilya Somin, who points out that the more the government does, the greater the variety of policies and programs, the more there is beyond electoral knowledge and oversight.[344] Conversely, the less government there is for citizens to know and the fewer the questions to be decided, the easier oversight will be. As Somin puts it, "Democratic control of government may increase when there is less government to control."[345]

When the scale and, especially, the scope of government expands – as it has over the past century – not only ordinary citizens but political elites can't understand what the government is doing. Even professional social scientists have only a superficial knowledge of the activities of government agencies in areas outside their expertise. No one can absorb more than a tiny fraction of the burgeoning body of information, so that we are all ignorant of most policymaking, however well-meaning our efforts to learn.

Breyer was among those who advised policy makers to strive for simplicity. His guideline for regulation is to concentrate on major dangers with great risks, not minor problems. "Regulators of great intelligence, with genuine goodwill, working extremely hard, are nonetheless unlikely to deal effectively with borderline cases," he wrote in 1982.[346]

These are just a few of the injunctions over the years to limit the number and complexity of laws and rules. Despite coming from both sides of the political spectrum, the counsels to keep it simple had no visible impact. Thus a recent proponent of the idea, the new paternalist Cass Sunstein, another Harvard law professor, claims to have successfully simplified certain rules while he was regulation czar in the first Obama presidency.[347] But in fact that administration imposed an immense number of new rules on finance and healthcare, many of unprecedented complexity, with the Dodd-Frank Act and Affordable Care law for medical insurance.

If the key to successful policy making in a democracy is to keep policies few and simple so that at least some of the electorate and its representatives can grasp the basic issues, the United States must have breached the threshold a long time ago. The problems of the SEC are part of this larger trend.

Financial regulation is beyond the awareness of the public unless something dramatic happens, like a big crisis or fraud scandal. Even then, the system is so massive and intricate that you have to study it as a career to have any real chance of learning how it functions. It is proof against oversight not only by voters and elected politicians but also wide swatches of the policy establishment, leaving the country at the mercy of cabals of unknown bureaucrats working behind closed doors.

To reduce the dependence obviously requires shrinking regulation to fewer and simpler rules. Keep regulators' field of action small and simple enough to be observable by many. This will allow less recourse to the supposed "benevolence" of surrogates.

As Breyer observed about other reform ideas, the fact that putative believers in good government have not applied the simplicity principle for a century suggests the forces pushing in the opposite direction are powerful. Perhaps proponents of regulation seek something other than good government. Nevertheless, I will sketch a proposal for simplicity in financial regulation.

What Is the Aim?

As we saw, financial regulators' remit expanded over time. Initially the object was to make sure corporations provided accurate information to shareholders. By 1940 the SEC was to regulate finance "in the public interest or for the protection of investors" a broader program with two possibly conflicting parts — investors and the public may not have the same interest. By 2013 the SEC described its objectives as "to protect investors, maintain fair, orderly and efficient markets, and facilitate capital formation." Of that manifold mission, only the first part, to protect investors, has a reasonably clear-cut interpretation. In large part it must mean to tamp down on fake claims by corporate sponsors and money managers.

The relative clarity is demonstrated by the fact that we know the goal was not met and the SEC left investors to fend for themselves in the face of phony information, or worse, misled them through its own actions or inactions. The other parts of the mission are so nebulous that I can't tell whether regulators pursue those goals or just include them in the mission statement in order to give the appearance of meeting demands from Congress in the aftermath of crisis.

The SEC confused the issue of fraud by expanding the definition to include insider trading, which does not involve deception and hence is not really fraud. Into the 1960s it was not even a clear-cut crime but became one through an interpretation of the 1934 Act by an SEC chairman.[348] Boudreaux (2009) and Manne (1966) argue that insider trading is in fact useful for conveying accurate information to markets. It helps prices adjust quicker to underlying corporate realities, keeping them honest. So at least some versions should not be illegal at all.

That is persuasive to my mind. But in recent years the SEC focused on insider trading cases and extended the meaning of the term so that it is no longer limited to corporate executives but seemingly applied to anyone who happens upon some information. This was probably to showcase regulators' efforts after their many failures and scandals. But whether prosecuting insider trading – especially so broadly – benefits or harms the investing public is an open question.

In the relatively straightforward matter of protecting investors by deterring false claims, the interest of agency staff runs counter to what the public expects of it. Amid the Madoff and Stanford affairs, certain SEC lawyers expressed the opinion that stamping out fraud should not be their job — they prefer that to be the responsibility of the FBI and the police. This attitude goes back to Landis, who disliked having to enforce rules.

One can see why bureaucrats would rather not to be held responsible for failing to stop schemes. They prefer to make rules without being bothered about the tricky part, getting people to obey those rules. If freed from enforcement duty, they could endlessly spin rules without having to worry about what's happening in reality. Failures would not be their problem.

But regulators face a political dilemma. It is hard to explain to politicians, let alone the public, what the SEC does if it has no responsibility for tamping down on financial fraud. The agency was created to prevent securities issuers from bamboozling shareholders. True, the bureaucracy would face less public relations risk if its responsibility was limited to making rules, leaving enforcement to others. But then it would have a harder time justifying its powers, budget and even existence.

In fact agency higher ups use the fraud card whenever they want certain policies, because this is the most politically effective ruse they possess. They used it in 2003, when they proposed a requirement for hedge fund managers to register with the SEC.

Initially the reason given for the new rule was to monitor any risk to the financial system. That rationale proved insufficient. For one thing, manager registration does not help with systemic risk, which can be more effectively monitored by observing the flow of transactions going through brokerages and banks. That means cooperating with other regulatory entities, in particular the Federal Reserve and the Commodity Futures Trading Commission. As is widely recognized, bureaucrats are disinclined to share their turf with other bureaucrats.

Therefore the official defense of the hedge fund registration rule did not emphasize systemic risk and instead focused on the prevention of fraud, citing a growing number of hedge fund cases, Manhattan Capital among them. Two SEC commissioners objected and voted against the rule. One of them, Paul Atkins, pointed out that the examples of fraud cited to defend the rule did not in fact point to registration as a solution — most of the managers nabbed for fraud were either · already registered or managed funds that were too small to warrant registration under the new rule.[349]

Some were engaged in garden-variety fraud that did not involve a real hedge fund but just used the label — they could easily avoid registering and use some other story to con people. Mandatory registration would make no difference. Atkins questioned the notion that regulators can ferret out malfeasance via regular examinations. It was not even possible to identify bad practices at investment advisers with straightforward strategies. Yet proponents of registration claimed that it would help identify illegal practices sooner.[350]

Any con artist worth his salt is capable of keeping up the game while filing an SEC registration form, maintaining records and fielding routine examinations as required. Berger concocted the fraud thanks to a registered broker, the SEC forced Madoff to register and Stanford's scheme took place largely via a registered broker-dealer and investment advisory business. The examiners and forms could not stop the schemes. In the Madoff and Stanford cases, even persistent complaints did not lead to the apprehension of the fraudsters.

The SEC does not need registration to pursue fraud. It has the authority to intervene when there is any suspicion, whether or not the suspect is registered. What registration does is to mislead investors into thinking a manager is relatively safe. Making registration mandatory merely reassures a larger mass of people, giving them a false sense of security. How it benefits the public is unclear at best.

Yet registration is advocated as if it were a solution against fraud. After the SEC rule was overturned by an appeals court in 2006, the 2010 Dodd-Frank law reinstituted registration for most hedge fund managers. This is yet another useless complexity.

No new law is required for the SEC to pursue the one goal almost everyone agree on. The agency should be responsible only for deterring the dissemination of false information by funds or companies. That is doable and, if done right, would benefit investors. Fake information leads to not just losses but also the misuse of resources and misdirection of investment. Preventing it would also enhance the efficiency of markets, though the immediate aim is to stop deception.

What is required is an effective system for checking information and taking action when inconsistencies show up. Since there is too much information for everything to be checked, the staff should do random checks. Randomly picked firms' reports can be inspected for inconsistencies and random names questioned in person.

356

Randomness is essential to discourage deception. When fund managers or companies are selected by other, substantive criteria, then those whose chances of being chosen are slim will not be deterred from fudging their message if they have a mind to do so. True randomness means that anyone's information can be examined at any time.

Special considerations by the staff – such as whether a certain manager is influential or a firm might be a future employer – would have no effect as long as the targets are picked randomly. In addition, to remove personal considerations from an inspection or enforcement action, it makes sense to rotate staff so that no single person makes the key decisions. Otherwise, enforcement staff could still go easy on a target they have reason to favor and, conversely, impose needless hardship on people for political or personal reasons.

The best way to help investors make better decisions is to open to them a database of examinations done and the findings with respect to each company or fund manager. That way an investor can see the issues raised by examiners even if the SEC takes no other action. Whereas the present system is particularly misleading — investors were impressed that Madoff and Stanford were closely watched by regulators and apparently had only minor problems in repeated investigations.

Certain proclivities are persistent. While regulators are often not enthusiastic about tackling a wily crook, especially one with connections, once a scheme ends they insist on taking over the estate. When it comes to overseeing an estate worth many millions or even billions of dollars, no official argues that some other agency should be responsible — no throwing that particular hot potato to someone else. In international turf disputes regarding an estate, they invariably favor their own, as in the Stanford case.

This may be because that's how they see the legal question. Or it may be the politically correct response. But it is difficult to avoid the suspicion regulators desire the patronage opportunity represented by turning a large estate over to a group of lawyers. It appears that the sequel to fraud is what financial regulators truly preside over, extracting from financial regulation what is best for themselves. At that stage there is no issue of stopping the scheme or catching the perpetrator, and as for the investors, they're lucky if they last the many years it will take to get back what remains of their assets.

The solution is obvious — hold an open auction for qualified lawyers, pick the lowest bidder to provide a standard package of services to the estate. In view of the fact that all these years the SEC has not instituted this simple principle for honest procurement, I doubt that it can be instituted. Higher echelons of the bureaucracy apparently do not want to change their ways.

Gresham Law of Organization

If the benevolence of regulators is one big myth, their presumed competence to alleviate any market ill is another. A realistic assessment of experience shows that the Hayek problem is ever present. Any attempt to make sense of the regulatory state has to ask, what are its agents capable of doing? Really?

Organizations, when they work, are powerful tools for achieving results. One thinker who took a hopeful view of bureaucratic functioning was Herbert Simon, who early in his career worked for an association of municipal agencies and studied their problems. Putting together what he learnt from reading Commons with what he saw in municipalities, he argued that organizations can expand human rationality.

Later Simon initiated a large-scale project at Carnegie Mellon to study behavior in organizations — mostly private companies, but the same framework can be applied to government organizations. So it came about that Commons indirectly inspired the behavioral theory of the firm in the mid-20th-century.

Simon and his colleagues Richard Cyert and James March analyzed the functioning of organizations from the point of scarce cognitive resources. How do members of an organization behave, given that mental facility is limited? A key behavioral insight is that people try to avoid uncertainty. Making decisions under uncertainty is difficult, so we try to evade such decisions.

Cyert, March and Simon came up with a "Gresham's Law" of organization. The original Gresham's Law says bad money drives out good money. Gresham's Law of organization says routine will drive out non-routine. Routines involve little or no uncertainty and economize on knowledge and cognitive processing — at the micro level of an organization as well as the broad institutional context. Once you have a routine, following it requires little thought, like decisions from a known menu. For individual members of an organization, routines are easy and efficient.

Activities in an organization vary in their goals and deadlines. The simpler and clearer the goal, the easier it is to attach rewards for success in achieving it or penalties for failure. Research showed that members of an organization allocate their time to activities that are subject to explicit time pressure, have simple goals and come with rewards or punishments.

Such activities are highly programmed. The risk of making a mistake is small because you follow established routine. The timing and what specifically is to be achieved are also clearly determined. By contrast, novel activities or plans have less clarity in goals, timing and how to proceed. Members of an organization gravitate to activities that are programmed while non-routine functions are put aside. Specialized teams have to be charged with non-programmed missions such as long-term strategy and innovation, if these are to be undertaken at all.

Among the guidelines Simon, Cyert and March suggested are the following. These are meant to help an organization effectively utilize the information processing and analytical abilities of its members.

- Use simple rules.
- Avoid decision-making procedures that require prediction of uncertain events.
- Change rules only when there is a strong and obvious reason to do so.
- Do not change them all at once. Change them sequentially, preferably one at a time, getting feedback on the consequences of a change before making the next one.

Simplicity comes across as the holy grail of both organizations and regulation, ever desirable yet ever elusive. Elaborate requirements clearly strain the knowledge and rational decision making facility of both regulators and the regulated. This damages the ability of any government organization to achieve its given goals.

Ambitious goals can take attention away from the core function of the organization. Thus the SEC, enmeshed in attempts to root out vaguely defined insider trading and nebulous systemic risk, is more likely to ignore real fraud. The more it is supposed to do, the less it is likely to accomplish for investors. The solution is to institute better routines to catch real fraud.

People who make their way up a bureaucratic ladder become experts at side-stepping non-routine challenges as much as possible. Having to go out of the regular pattern is both difficult and dangerous; someone who does this frequently will be regarded as unsafe and is unlikely to be promoted in a hierarchical organization. Hence those who become higher-level bureaucrats avoid non-routines both by experience and inclination — otherwise they would not make it to the top echelons.

Gresham's Law of organization implies that bureaucrats will attend to the most routine parts of regulation and go through highly programmed motions. For instance, they will make sure forms are filled and filed on time. This in itself is not very helpful — Madoff and the Stanford company filled their SEC registration forms but that did nothing for investors. Of course, the forms are supposed to act as a control over managers, but that goal is not really served.

Professional con men understand the conventional bureaucratic mindset. Stanford asked for piles of compliance paperwork to protect his scheme. For investors, this is the worst of all worlds. On the surface, regulatory requirements are met. The con game is concealed behind the appearance of pro forma regulatory compliance.

In the Madoff and Stanford investigations supervisors who were long-time regulators decided not to pursue the matter. That further pursuit was beyond the known parameters and beset by obvious career risk, for one thing because Madoff had contacts with top regulators and Stanford was protected by a network of politicians and high-end lawyers. Taking on the risk was clearly unappealing to the supervisors, even though mid-level examiners found evidence that they believed justified further scrutiny of Madoff and Stanford.

These were unusual situations that bureaucrats try to avoid. Such calculations are internal to a bureaucracy and typically not known to the politicians who set the goals, let alone to the public who pays for the system and is the ultimate bearer of the costs imposed by regulation. Because the Madoff and Stanford cases caught so much attention, the agency was forced to make some disclosure of what happened. In the usual run of affairs such decisions would be made with nobody outside the bureaucracy being any wiser.

In these examples routine got in the way of useful regulatory action, but it is possible to use organizational routine to good purpose. What is needed is a set of routines that achieve the desired end — to invert Landis' saying, good rules will force bad bureaucrats to do something useful.

Were the SEC's mission effectively slimmed down to maintaining the accuracy of financial information, it can rely on simple checking and follow-up rules applied to randomly selected targets. Rules can define danger signs and mandate questioning a money manager if, say, three danger signs are present. Such routines reduce the need to make decisions or predictions.

Certainly expertise can play a useful role, but only under certain conditions. Cognitive scientists find that people learn to make better judgments or predictions if:[351]
- There are stable regularities in the subject they observe.
- They observe those regularities for a prolonged time.
- They get clear feedbacks as to the accuracy of their judgments.

Translated to a regulatory setting, this suggests staffing the SEC with accountants (rather than lawyers) who will check randomly selected records. By repeatedly observing the same type of data, they can become specialists in detecting the inconsistencies that are the sign of misinformation.

Narrowing the goal and specifying the routines to be used would reduce the discretion of the staff, thereby going against the trend that started with the New Deal. The point is to institute rules, rather than the preferences of bureaucrats, as the principle of regulation. Then the SEC could become a genuine deterrent to fraud.

To specify a doable, slimmed-down mission requires not tacking on whatever desirable notion may be suggested by the latest headlines. This is always a huge political temptation, by way of showing something is being done about some problem or another. Another temptation is to expand what is meant by the original goal. To keep the mission simple, the word fraud should not be used for everything under the sun. Fraud is properly defined as deception and the peddling of false information. Insider trading does not meet the definition because insiders use correct information to trade. (Whether such trading should be a crime is a separate question.)

Non-routine functions such as strategic plans are sometimes farmed out to consultants. The risk involved in hiring outside service providers is demonstrated by the problem of trustees for estates and the consultant investigation I described above. If agency staff have discretion in picking the providers, favoritism will inevitably taint the choices. In theory it is possible to avoid this by soliciting bids from interested and qualified consultants and automatically picking the lowest bidder. But in practice hiring consultants creates potential for corruption.

Moreover, the benefit is illusory. Consultants are not likely to suggest actions that displease those who hire and pay for them. If perchance a consultant's recommendations run counter to the preferences of the bureaucracy that is supposed to implement the report, it goes without saying that the bureaucrats will resist. Given the uncertain benefit and certain cost, it is hard to make a case that consultants are useful for reforming regulatory agencies.

Ending the Ponzi Regulation Cycle

The regulatory governance system we live in is a result of arguments and beliefs that go back 80 years or more. Back in the time these ideas were espoused with great enthusiasm as the cure for age-old ills. Now that the results are in, that enthusiasm has dimmed a notch, though the vision of a regulatory state that solves a vast array of economic and social problems retains its hold on many.

This follows a pattern observed in other areas by the philosopher Isaiah Berlin: "The history of thought and culture is …a changing pattern of great liberating ideas which inevitably turn into suffocating straitjackets, and so stimulate their own destruction …."[352] To early 20th century reformers, classical legal precepts were suffocating, even though the protection provided by the rule of law had been liberating in the preceding era. By the 21st century, however, earlier financial reformers' promises to protect the weak, resolve conflicts and help people make rational choices had proved to be a chimera.

The bureaucracies built to bring about those promises are beset by seemingly unsolvable knowledge, interest and oversight problems. I've discussed these under separate rubrics identified by the names Hayek, Buchanan and Schumpeter, the foremost thinkers who forced the recognition of the issues. But of course in reality the problems interact — bureaucrats lack knowledge of what people want and pursue their own interest, hence the lack of oversight by voters and elected politicians means that the regulatory system serves regulators rather than the other way around as intended.

I've pointed to several features of financial regulation that bring to mind a Ponzi scheme. The main one is that it makes false claims. What fraud victims get in return for the large sums paid to SEC-designated trustees is emblematic of the broader issue. The benefit the public supposedly receives for the resources consumed by financial regulation is not real. Whereas the payments that go to lawyers, lobbyists and regulators, the waste of time and energy that could be productively used — those costs are genuine.

While the claims to remedy ills are bogus, certainly in the financial area, the regulatory state imposes an all-too-real straitjacket on society. It has become a vast waste of resources and a tool for organized small groups – foremost among them government bureaucrats and their cronies – to exploit the rest of the population. Instead of making society more efficient and egalitarian as promised, it is a source of inefficiency and inequity.

Worse, failures bring more of the same. Regulators do not stop or even encourage shenanigans during good times. This makes for a spiraling trajectory. Financial regulation fails to correct the problem it was supposed to address; in response, more regulation and bureaucracy is created; then comes another failure and yet more rules and bureaucracy. Cumulative expansion follows cumulative failure. The more regulators fail, the more they gain.

While the growth of the regulatory state and the bureaucratic powers to run it are intentional – advocated by lawyers, policy analysts, pundits; legislated by Congress – its consequences are to a large extent unintended. One side effect is the increasingly convoluted character of the system. Nobody openly favors layer upon layer of arcane rules, yet such has been the trend for the past century. Regulations, like tax laws, become ever more rococo even as generation after generation of would-be reformers keep calling for simplicity and transparency.

Increasingly ornate regulatory programs rely on greater skills and, more critically, good intentions on the part of the bureaucrats. As the fraud debacles show, skills and public mindedness are in extremely short supply. To assume these qualities will be forthcoming when experience indicates otherwise is no different from a fraudster assuming that he will eventually make good despite the fact that so far he has lost money.

The emergence of out-of-control bureaucracies is an unavoidable consequence of regulatory expansion. Nobody has found a practical way to design better public organizations where the staff is motivated to do the right thing without the discipline imposed by a competitive market. Yet the same dysfunctional bureaucracy that failed earlier is expected to come up with an ever growing number of rules on ever more complex issues. Continued failure is preordained, but that has not stopped the spiraling regulatory state.

This trajectory, so clearly counter to public interest, makes one suspect the motives behind the lofty claims made for financial regulation. If Congress and the White House truly want honest regulation, they have to do something other than what they've done so far. If they don't, they're going on with Ponzi regulation. Realistically achievable goals should not require the impossible, namely benevolent and knowledgeable surrogates who need no oversight.

While one can point to many problems, the root cause of bureaucratic dysfunction is the old vision and its influence on policy. It is time to put aside early 20th century conceptions of a regulatory system staffed with public-minded experts yielding wide discretionary powers. Regulators should not be left free to do what they choose. Instead, they need to be given a specific, narrow mission – such as find and eradicate false financial information – that can be achieved through doable routines.

We should not expect more, and certainly not assume that regulators are selfless proxies for society or capable of knowing how to enhance mass well being. Comforting though that gauzy illusion may be in an uncertain world, it obscures reality and encourages government agents to be irresponsible and corrupt.

NOTES

[275] Boskin 2013 and 2012.

[276] Hayek 1978, 3, n3. See Caldwell 2004 for a well rounded study of Hayek's wide-reaching intellectual contributions.

[277] Vanberg 1989 does a fascinating comparison of Carl Manger with Commons.

[278] The discussion here is limited to only one aspect of Hayek's thought. However, it is related to other strands. Caldwell 2004 gives a sense of the connections in Hayek's work.

[279] Hayek 1978, p. 34.

[280] Hayek 1978, 7

[281] For a somewhat different analysis of Hayek's writings on institutional evolution, see Birner 2009 and Birner & van Zijp 1994.

[282] See James Otteson 2010, who calls this "the great mind fallacy".

[283] Hayek 1944 p. 1

[284] Hayek 1978, p. 72

[285] Scott Scheall asked this question while presenting Scheall 2013.

[286] Galbraith 1958.

[287] An early reply to this claim came from Frédéric Bastiat, who wrote about legal plunder – also known as taxes - under both imperial and democratic governments. The subject of taxation is beyond the scope of this book, but see Leef 2012 and Murray 2011 for counters to the general benevolence claim for interventionism.

[288] Sugden 2011 points out the similarity.

[289] Thaler and Sunstein 2008 is probably the best known soft paternalist text; they prefer to call their agenda "libertarian paternalism"—also see Sunstein and Thaler 2003.

[290] The second volume of *Democracy in America*, with this warning at the end, gives a darker view of the country than the first volume.

[291] Tocqueville 1840, George Lawrence translation, 1969 printing, p. 694.

[292] "Gentle" democratic despotism as foreseen by Tocqueville sounds somewhat similar to "participatory fascism" as defined by Robert Higgs and Charlotte Twight. See n.312 below.

[293] Thaler and Sunstein 2008 and Sunstein & Thaler 2003.

[294] Rosenberg 1994, pp. 47, 61

[295] For various aspects of entrepreneurship, see Harper 2003, Endres & Woods 2010, Rajagopalan and Wagner 2013, Endres & Harper 2013.

[296] Schumpeter 1950, p. 258.

[297] Downs (1957) highlighted the insignificance of any one vote, with the implication that voters have no reason to learn more about politics.

[298] Somin 1998 and 2004.

[299] Caplan 2001 and 2007.

[300] For a commentary on Caplan's thesis, see Bass 2007.

[301] 1950, p. 261

[302] Carpini and Keeter 1996

[303] Somin 1998

[304] Friedman 1998, p. 397.

[305] For the new theory of regulation, see the seminal 1971 paper by George Stigler.

[306] Peltzman 1989.

[307] Buchanan and Congleton 1998, p. 19

[308] Buchanan, Tullock and Tollison. 1980.

[309] Olson 1965, p. 72

[310] See Yandle for the role of trust in the financial system.

[311] Coase initially used transaction costs to explain why firms exist. This work also led to the realization that private parties can't price in external costs and benefits because of transaction costs, reshaping environmental policy to create property rights such as emissions permits that reduce transaction costs.

[312] Higgs has argued that the U.S. system has become participatory fascism—a term coined by Charlotte Twight. See Higgs 2012.

[313] North 1990, p. 63.

[314] Jarrell 1981.

[315] Winston 2006.

[316] This and the next section draw on Sowell 1995 and Sowell 2007.

[317] Not that these thinkers are alike in every respect. See Salerno 1993 for a key difference in the works of Mises and Hayek.

[318] "Reflections on the Revolution in France" 1790, in Burke 1999.

[319] Friedman 1998, p. 405.

[320] Schumpeter 1950 p 294

[321] Schumpeter 1950 p 299

[322] Mises 1944, p. v.

[323] On the cyclicality of enforcement and regulation, see Aviram 2008, Ribstein 2003 and 2006, Shughart and Robert Tollison 1985.

[324] Different authors point to different reasons for the cyclicality of regulation-making and enforcement. These explanations are in general not mutually exclusive.

[325] Schumpeter 1950 p 294

[326] Mises 1944, p. 47.

[327] Tullock, 1965, p. 69.

[328] Wilson 1989.

[329] Tullock 1993, p.52

[330] Breyer 1982, p. 351.

[331] This incident, described in Ch. 3 above, was analyzed by Seligman 1985.

[332] Luparello 2009.

[333] An online search for George Washington's farewell address returns 280,000 hits while one for Eisenhower 's shows 113,000, but the comparison is not fair because references to Washington had a head start of 150 years.

[334] Posner 2008 and Epstein, Landes and Posner 2013. Krecké 2014 discusses the Posner model.

[335] One has to read about the numerous frightful impositions on children by these two judges to understand the enormity of their behavior—see Ecenbarger 2012.

[336] Cowen 2000.

[337] New York State Commission on Judicial Conduct, 2005.

[338] By Mary Randolph; 9th edition came out in 2012. Amazon sells a number of similar titles.

[339] Information in this matter comes from US Securities and Exchange Commission Office of the Inspector General, 2011b, Sept. 16.

[340] Jaffe 2011.

[341] Holzer 2011.

[342] Breyer 1982, p. 345.

[343] Schumpeter 1950, p. 267

[344] Somin 2004.

[345] Somin 1998 p. 435.

[346] Breyer 1982, p. 185.

[347] Sunstein 2013a is on this subject.

[348] See above, Chapter Three.

[349] Atkins 2006 and 2004.

[350] A court of appeals overturned the SEC registration rule in 2006 but a similar rule was included in the 2010 Dodd-Frank Act, defended along the lines described in the text.

[351] Kahneman 2011 discusses these conditions in chapter 22.

[352] Berlin 1998, p. 76.

BIBLIOGRAPHY

Abrams, Fred. 2010. "Peter Madoff & His Competing Claimants," *Asset Search Blog*, July 17.

Abramovitz, Moses. 1989. *Thinking about Growth*. Cambridge University Press.

Ackerman, Andrew. 2012. "SEC Loses Bid to Get SIPC to Pay Stanford Ponzi Claims," *Wall Street Journal*, July 3.

Ackerman, Andrew. 2011. "SEC Suit Pursues Payouts by SIPC," *Wall Street Journal*, Dec. 13.

Akerlof, George. 1970. "The Market for Lemons: Quality Uncertainty and the Market Mechanism," *Quarterly Journal of Economics*, August.

Associated Press. 2006. "U.S. Says It Found Problems In Enron Bankruptcy Billing," *New York Times*, March 28.

Arvedlund, Erin. 2009. *Too Good To Be True: The Rise and Fall of Bernie Madoff*. Portfolio.

Arvedlund, Erin. 2001."Don't ask, don't tell: Bernie Madoff Is so secretive, he even asks his investors to keep mum," *Barron's*, May 7.

Atkins, Paul S. 2006. "Protecting Investors through Hedge Fund Advisor Registration: Long on Costs, Short on Returns," *Annual Review of Banking & Financial Law*, v. 25.

Atkins, Paul S. 2004. Statement by SEC Commissioner at Open Meeting Considering Proposed Registration under the Advisers Act of Certain Hedge Fund Advisers, July 14.

Aviram, Amitai. 2011. "Forces Shaping the Evolution of Private Legal Systems," in *Law, Economics and Evolutionary Theory*, P. Zumbansen and G. Calliess (eds.), Elgar.

Aviram, Amitai. 2008. "Counter-Cyclical Enforcement of Corporate Law," *Yale Journal on Regulation*, Winter.

Aviram, Amitai. 2007. "Bias Arbitrage," *Washington and Lee Law Review*, Summer.

Ayotte, Kenneth and David A Skeel Jr. 2006. "An Efficiency-Based Explanation for Current Corporate Reorganization Practice," *The University of Chicago Law Review*, Winter.

Badinter, Robert and Stephen Breyer (eds.) 2004. *Judges in Contemporary Democracy; An International Conversation*. New York University Press.

Bailey, Elizabeth. 2002. "Narcissism, Entitlement and the Sour Smell of Excess," *Financial Times*, June 15/June 16.

Banner, Stuart. 1997. "What Causes New Securities Regulation? 300 Years of Evidence," *Washington University Law Quarterly*, v. 79.

Barberis, Nicholas & Richard Thaler. 2003. "A survey of behavioral finance," in *Handbook of the Economics of Finance*, Constantinides, M. Harris & R. M. Stulz (eds.), v. 1, Elsevier.

Barber, William. 1990. "Government as a Laboratory for Economic Learning in the Years of the Democratic Roosevelt," in *The State and Economic Knowledge. The American and English Experiences*, Mary Furner and Barry Supple (eds.), Woodrow Wilson Center Series, Cambridge University Press.

Barron, David; Elizabeth West and Michael Hannan. 1998. "Deregulation and Competition in the Financial Industry," *Industrial and Corporate Change*, March.

Bass, Gary. 2007. "Clueless: An Economist Argues that Voters are Biased, Irrational, Manipulable and Plain Ignorant. Is Democracy Dangerous?" *New York Times Magazine*, May 27.

Bazerman, Max H. and Ann E. Tenbrunsel. 2011. *Blind Spots: Why We Fail to Do What's Right and What to Do About It*, Princeton University Press.

Becker, Gary. 1985. "Public Policies, Pressure Groups, and Deadweight Costs," *Journal of Public Economics*, v. 28.

Becker, Gary. 1968. "Crime and Punishment: An economic Approach," *Journal of Political Economy*, March-April.

Benson, Bruce L. and David W. Rasmussen 1996. "Predatory Public Finance and the Origins of the War on Drugs, 1984–1989," *Independent Review*, Fall.

Berg, Scott. 2013. *Wilson*. Putnam.

Berger, Michael. 1996-1999. *Wall Street Notes*, various issues.

Berger, Michael.1995-1996. "Market Watch," *Barron's*, various issues.

Berle, Adolf and others. 1934. *America's Recovery Program*. Books for Libraries Press, 1970 reprint.

Berle, Adolf and Gardiner Means. 1932. *The Modern Corporation and Private Property*. Harcourt Brace. 1967 edition.

Berlin, Isaiah. 1997. "Two Concepts of Liberty," in *The Proper Study of Mankind: An Anthology of Essays*, Farrar, Straus and Giroux. (Article first published in 1958).

Bicchieri, Cristina. 2006. *The grammar of society: The nature and dynamics of social norms*. Cambridge University Press.

Biddle, Jeff. 1990. "The Role of Negotiational Psychology in J.R. Common's Proposed Reconstruction of Political Economy," *Review of Political Economy*, v.2.

Biggs, Barton. 2008. *Hedgehogging*. Wiley.

Bikhchandani, S., D. Hirshleifer and I. Welch. 1998. Learning from the Behavior of Others: Conformity, Fads and Informational Cascades. *Journal of Economic Perspectives*, v. 12.

Birger, Jon and Chris Isidore. 1998. "Stocks of Banks, Brokers to Face Further Turmoil," *Crain's New York Business*, September 28.

Birnbaum, Jeffrey H. 2005. "The Road to Riches Is Called K Street: Lobbying Firms Hire More, Pay More, Charge More to Influence Government," *Washington Post*, June 22.

Birner, Jack. 2009. "From Group Selection to Ecological Niches. Popper's Rethinking of Evolution in the Light of Hayek's Theory of Culture," in S. Parusnikova and R.S. Cohen, *Rethinking Popper*, Springer.

Birner, Jack and R. van Zijp. 1994. *Hayek, Coordination and Evolution: His Legacy in Philosophy, Politics, Economics and the History of Ideas.* Routledge.

Blackburn, Simon. 2006. "Home Truths about the Real Value of Truth," *Financial Times,* July 29/30.

Boettke, Peter J.; Zachary Caceres and Adam Martin. 2012 "Error is Obvious, Coordination is the Puzzle," *Hayek and Behavioral Economics,* Roger Frantz and Robert Leeson (eds.) Palgrave-MacMillan, Forthcoming.

Boettke, Peter J. 2010. "What Happened to 'Efficient Markets'?" *Independent Review*, Winter.

Boettke, Peter J., Christopher J. Coyne, Peter T. Leeson 2007. "Saving government failure theory from itself: recasting political economy from an Austrian perspective," *Constitutional Political Economy*, v. 18.

Boettke, Peter J. and Peter T. Leeson. 2003. "Hayek, Arrow and the Problems of Democratic Decision-Making," *Journal of Public Finance and Public Choice*, , v. 20.

Boskin, Michael. 2013. "Taming Leviathan," Project Syndicate, January 27.

Boskin, Michael. 2012. "The Anatomy of Government Failure," *Wall Street Journal*, October 25.

Boudreaux, Donald. 2009. "Learning to Love Insider Trading," *Wall Street Journal*, October 24.

Boulding, Kenneth. 1957. "A New Look at Institutionalism," *American Economic Review Papers and Proceedings of the 68th Annual Meeting of the American Economics Association.* v. 47.

Bradley, Michael and Michael Rosenzweig. 1992. "The Untenable Case for Chapter 11," *Yale Law Journal,* v. 101.

Bray, Chad. 2012. "Feeder Funds Lose in Ruling," *Wall Street Journal*, Jan. 6.

Bray, Chad. 2011. "SEC's Top Lawyer Sued in Madoff 'Clawback' Case," *Wall Street Journal*, Feb. 23.

Brennan, Geoffrey and James Buchanan. 1985. *The reason of rules: Constitutional Political Economy*. Cambridge University Press.

Breyer, Stephen. 1982. *Regulation and Its Reform*. Harvard University Press.

Brush, Silla and Jim Snyder. 2009. "Stanford Maintained Big Washington Presence," *The Hill*, Feb. 17.

Buchanan, James and Roger Congleton. 1998. *Politics by Principle, Not Interest*. Cambridge University Press.

Buchanan, James. 1991. *Economics and Ethics of Constitutional Order*. Ann Arbor: University of Michigan Press.

Buchanan, James; G. Tullock; and R.D. Tollison. 1980. *Toward a Theory of Rent-Seeking Society*. Texas A&M University Press.

Buchanan, James. 1975. *The Limits of Liberty: Between Anarchy & Leviathan*. University of Chicago Press.

Buchanan, James and Gordon Tullock. 1962. *The Calculus of Consent*. Ann Arbor: University of Michigan Press.

Buchwald, Jed and Mordecai Feingold. 2012. *Newton and the Origin of Civilization*. Princeton University Press.

Burke, Edmund. 1999. *Portable Edmund Burke* Ed. Isaac Kramnick, New York: Penguin.

Butos, William and Thomas McQuade. 2006. "Government and Science: A Dangerous Liaison?" *Independent Review*, Fall.

Calkins, Laurel Brubaker and Andrew Harris. 2011. "Stanford Judge Says Receiver May Need to End Search for 'Pot of Gold'" *Bloomberg News*.

Caldwell, Bruce. 2010. *Studies on the Abuse and Decline of Reason: Texts and Documents*. University of Chicago Press.

Caldwell, Bruce. 2004. *Hayek's Challenge: An Intellectual Biography of F.A. Hayek*. University of Chicago Press.

Caplan, Bryan. 2007. *The Myth of the Rational Voter. Why Democracies Choose Bad Policies*. Princeton University Press.

Caplan, Bryan. 2001. "Rational Irrationality and the Microfoundations of Political Failure," *Public Choice*, v. 107.

Caribbean360.com. 2011. "Investors question Antigua Stanford liquidators," August 18, accessed at http://www.caribbean360.com

Carpini, Michael X. Delli and Scott Keeter. 1996. *What Americans Know about Politics and Why It Matters*. Yale University Press.

Chanos, James. 2003. Prepared Statement for the US Securities and Exchange Roundtable on Hedge funds, May 15.

Chellel, Kit. 2011. "Stanford Bank Liquidators Dispute Predecessor's $18 Million Fee,"
Bloomberg News, October 12.

Choi, Young Back. 1993. *Paradigms and Conventions: Uncertainty, Decision Making, and Entrepreneurship*. University of Michigan Press.

Chorvat, Terrence and Kevin McCabe. 2005. "Neuroeconomics and Rationality," George Mason University Law and Economics Working Papers Series.

City of New York Office of the Comptroller. 2005. Audit Report on the Estate Management Practices of the Kings County Public Administrator. June 29.

Coase, Ronald. 1992. "The Institutional Structure of Production," *American Economic Review*, September.

Coase, Ronald. 1960. "The Problem of Social Cost," *Journal of Law and Economics*, October.

Coase, Ronald. 1937. "The Nature of the Firm," *Economica*, November.

Coates, Dennis; J.C. Heckelman; B. Wilson. 2010. "The Political Economy of Investment: Sclerotic Effects from Interest Groups," *European Journal of Political Economy*, v.26.

Coats, A. W. 1983. "John R. Commons as a Historian of Economics: The Quest for the Antecedents of Collective Action," *Research in the History of Economic Thought and Methodology*, v. 1.

Coffee, John C. Jr. 2006. *Gatekeepers: The Professions and Corporate Governance*, Oxford University Press.

Cohen, Laurie , Aaron Lucchetti, and Marcus Baram. 2005. "Even as his World Imploded, Mr. Vilar Pledged Millions," *Wall Street Journal,* June 10.

Commons, John R. 1950. *The Economics of Collective Action*. Manuscript edited by Kenneth Parsons. MacMillan Co.

Commons, John R. 1934a. *Institutional Economics. Its Place in Political Economy*. MacMillan Co.

Commons, John R. 1934b. *Myself*. MacMillan Co.

Commons, John R. 1931. "Institutional Economics" *American Economic Review*, v. 21.

Commons, John R. 1924. *Legal Foundations of Capitalism*. MacMillan & Co.

Connett, David and Stephen Foley. 2009. "The Stanford Files: FBI's first probe was 20 years ago," *The Independent*, February. 22.

Couch, Jim F. and William F. Shughart. 1998. *The Political Economy of the New Deal*, Edward Elgar.

Cowen, Tyler. 2005. "Self-Deception as the Root of Political Failure," *Public Choice*, September.

Cowen, Tyler and Eric Crampton (eds.). 2004. *Market Failure or Success: The New Debate*, Edward Elgar Publishing.

Cowen, Tyler. 2000. *What price fame?* Harvard University Press.

Craig, Susanne. 2004. "Bear Stearns Continues Its Contrarian Ways," *Wall Street Journal*, November.

Crandall, Robert W. 1993. "Regulation and the 'Rights' Revolution: Can (Should) We Rescue the New Deal?" *Critical Review*, Spring-Summer.

Crews, C. Wayne. 2013. *Ten Thousand Commandments. An Annual Snapshot of the Federal Regulatory State, 20th edition*. Competitive Enterprise Institute.

Croft, Jane. 2011. "Stanford liquidators to access $20m of assets," *Financial Times*, August 4.

Croft, Jane. 2010. "US receiver loses case over Stanford's assets," *Financial Times, February 25.

Csikszentmihalyi, Mihaly. 1993. *The Evolving Self. A Psychology for the Third Millennium,* HarperCollins.

Cyert, Richard. and James March. 1963. *The Behavioral Theory of the Firm,* Prentice Hall.

Dalmady, Alex. "Duck Tales — Stanford International Bank," *VenEconomy Monthly,* January 2009.

De Bedts, Ralph. 1964. *The New Deal's SEC. The Formative Years,* New York and London: Columbia University Press.

DeLong, Brad and Konstantin Magin, 2005. "The Last Bubble Was Brief, But It Was Still Irrational," *Financial Times,* April 19.

Donaldson, W. 2003. Testimony Concerning Investor Protection Implications of Hedge Funds Before the Senate Committee on Banking, Housing and Urban Affairs, April 10.

Downs, Anthony. 1957. *An Economic Theory of Democracy.* New York: Harper.

Dunbar, Nicholas. 2000. *Inventing Money: The Story of Long-Term Capital Management and the Legends Behind It.* Wiley

Eichenwald, Kurt and Daniel Wakin. 2005. "The Double Ups and Downs of a Philanthropist," *New York Times,* May 30.

Economist. 2012. "Over-Regulated America. The Home of Laissez-Faire Is Being Suffocated by Excessive and Badly Written Regulation," Feb 18.

Encinar, M.I. and Muñoz, Felix Fernando. 2006. "On novelty and economics: Schumpeter's paradox," *Journal of Evolutionary Economics,* 16:3.

Endres, Anthony, and David Harper. 2013. "Wresting Meaning from the Market': A Reassessment of Ludwig Lachman's Entrepreneur," *Journal of Institutional Economics,* September.

Endres, Anthony and C. R. Woods. 2010. "Schumpeter's Conduct Model of the Dynamic Entrepreneur: Scope and Distinctiveness," *Journal of Evolutionary Economics,* 20.

Epstein, Richard A. 2013. "The Takings Clause and Partial Interests in Land: On Sharp Boundaries and Continuous Distributions," *Brooklyn Law Review*, 78:2.

Epstein, Richard A. 2011a. "The Dangerous Experiment of the Durbin Amendment," *Regulation*, v. 34, Spring.

Epstein, Richard A. 2011b. "The Constitutional Paradox of the Durbin Amendment: How Monopolies Are Offered Constitutional Protection Denied to Competitive Firms," *Florida Law Review*, v. 63, pp. 1307

Epstein, Richard A. 2006. *How Progressives Rewrote the Constitution*. Cato Institute.

Epstein, Richard A. 2002. "Implications for Legal Reform," in *Regulation through Litigation*, W. Kip Viscusi, ed., Brookings Institution Press.

Epstein, Richard A. 1998. *Principles for a Free Society. Reconciling Individual Liberty with the Common Good.* Perseus Books.

Epstein, Richard A. 1990. "The Independence of Judges: The Uses and Limitations of Public Choice Theory," *Brigham Young University Law Review*.

Epstein, Richard A. 1988a. "The Mistakes of 1937," *George Mason Law Review*, 11, winter.

Epstein, Richard A. 1988b. "Rent Control and the Theory of Efficient Regulation," *Brooklyn Law Review*.

Epstein, Lee, William M. Landes and Richard A Posner. 2013. *The Behavior of Federal Judges: A Theoretical and Empirical Study of Rational Choice.* Harvard University Press.

Ernst, Daniel. 2009. "Lawyers, Bureaucratic Autonomy, and Securities Regulation During the New Deal," Georgetown University Law Center Faculty Working Papers, posted on http://scholarship.law.georgetown.edu/fwps papers/115

Ecenbarger, William. 2012. *Kids for Cash. Two Judges, Thousands of Children, and a $2.8 million Kickback Scheme.* The New Press.

Ferguson, John. 1970. *Socrates: A Sourcebook.* Macmillan.

Feuer, Alan. 2005. "Venit, Vidit, Vicit. Then He Was Charged with Fraud," *The New York Times,* May 15.

Folsom, Burton Jr. 2008. *New Deal or Raw Deal? How FDR's Economic Legacy Has Damaged America.* Simon & Schuster.

Frankel, Tamar. 2012. *The Ponzi Scheme Puzzle: A History and Analysis of Con Artists and Victims,* New York: Oxford University Press.

Fraser, Steve and Gary Gerstle (eds.) 1989. *The Rise and Fall of the New Deal Order 1930-1980.* Princeton University Press.

Friedman, Jeffrey. 1998. "Public Ignorance and Democratic Theory," *Critical Review,* Fall.

Friedman, Milton and Rose. 1998. *Two Lucky People,* University of Chicago Press.

Friedman, Milton. 1962. *Capitalism and Freedom,* University of Chicago Press.

Fusfeld, Daniel R. 1954. *The Economic Thought of Franklin D. Roosevelt and the Origins of the New Deal.* Columbia University Press.

Galbraith, John Kenneth. 1971. *The New Industrial State.* Second ed. New American Library.

Galbraith, John Kenneth. 1958. *The Affluent Society.* Second Ed. Houghton & Mifflin Co.

Galbraith, John Kenneth. 1952. *American Capitalism: The Concepts Of Countervailing Power.* Reprint by Kessinger Publishing, 2010.

Gapper, John. 2005. "The Danger of Rewriting Chapter 11" *Financial Times,* October 13.

Gilbert, Daniel. 2005. *Stumbling on Happiness.* Vintage Books.

Goode, Erica. 2003. "Stalin to Saddam: So Much for the Madman Theory," *New York Times,* May 4.

Goodwin, Doris Kearns. 2013. *The Bully Pulpit: Theodore Roosevelt, William Howard Taft and the Golden Age of Journalism.* Simon & Schuster.

Grant, James. 2008. *Mr. Market Miscalculates: The Bubble Years and Beyond.* Axios Press.

Hamilton, Alexander, James Madison and John Jay. 1961. *The Federalist Papers.* New American Library. Originally published 1787-88.

Harper, David & Anthony Endres. 2012. "The anatomy of emergence, with a focus upon capital formation," *Journal of Economic Behavior & Organization*, 82.

Harper, David. 2003. *Foundations of Entrepreneurship and Economic Development.* Routledge.

Harris, Andrew and Laurel Brubaker Calkins. 2011. "Stanford's US, Antiguan Receivers Vie in Court for Control of His Assets," *Bloomberg News*, Dec. 21.

Harter, Lafayette G. Jr. 1965. "John R. Commons — Social Reformer and Institutional Economist," *American Journal of Economics and Sociology*, January.

Harter, Lafayette G. Jr. 1962. *John R. Commons. His Assault on Laissez Faire.* Oregon State University Press.

Hayek, Friedrich A. 1979. *The Counter-Revolution of Science: Studies on the Abuses of Reason.* Liberty Press.

Hayek, Friedrich A. 1978. *New Studies in Philosophy, Politics, Economics and the History of Ideas.* University of Chicago Press.

Hayek, Friedrich A. 1976. *Law, Legislation and Liberty: v. 2, The Mirage of Social Justice.* University of Chicago Press.

Hayek, Friedrich A. 1973. *Law, Legislation and Liberty: v. 1, Rules and Order.* University of ChicagoPress.

Hayek, Friedrich A. 1945. "The Use of Knowledge in Society," *American Economic Review*, v. 35.

Hayek, Friedrich A. 1944. *The Road to Serfdom.* University of Chicago Press.

Hayes, Edward. 2009a. "Madoff Inquiry Focusing on Emails," *US Financial Services News*, June 16.

Hayes, Edward. 2009b. "SEC Faces Wrath of Whistleblower," *US Financial Services News*, February 13.

Helland, Eric and Alexander Tabarrok. 2006. *Judge and Jury: American Tort Law on Trial*, Independent Institute.

Helland, Eric, Jonathan Klick and Alexander Tabarrok. 2005. "Data Watch: Tort-Uring the Data," *Journal of Economic Perspectives*, 19.

Helland, Eric and Alexander Tabarrok. 2003. "Contingency Fees, Settlement Delay and Low-Quality Litigation: Empirical Evidence from Two Datasets," *Journal of Law, Economics and Organization*, v. 19.

Henriques, Diana. 2011. *The Wizard of Lies. Bernie Madoff and the Death of Trust.* Times Books

Higgs, Robert. 2012. "Once More, with Feeling: Our System Is Not Socialism, but Participatory Fascism," The Independent Institute Blog, October 30.

Higgs, Robert. 2011. "Economic Analysis and the Great Society," *The Freeman*, May 26

Higgs, Robert. 2011. "Ideological and Political Underpinnings of the Great Society," *The Freeman*, March 15.

Higgs, Robert. 2004. *Against Leviathan. Government Power and a Free Society.* The Independent Institute.

Higgs, Robert. 1987. *Crisis and Leviathan. Critical Episodes in the Growth of American Government.* Oxford University Press.

High, Jack. 1993. "Self-Interest and Responsive Regulation," *Critical Review*, Spring-Summer.

Hirschfield, Marc and George Klidonas. 2011. "Avoidance Actions in Ponzi Scheme Bankruptcy Cases," Published by the American Bar Association Business Bankruptcy Committee for the Association's business bankruptcy April meeting. Accessed at http://www.bakerlaw.com/articles/american-bar-association-avoidance-actions-in-ponzi-scheme-bankruptcy-cases-4-1-2011/

Hodgson, Geoffrey M. 2004. *The Evolution of Institutional Economics.* Routledge.

Hodgson, Geoffrey M. 1993. *Economics and Evolution: Bringing Life Back into Economics*, University of Michigan Press.

Hodgson, Geoffrey M. 1988. *Economics and Institutions: A Manifesto for a Modern Institutional Economics*, University of Pennsylvania Press.

Hofstadter, Richard. 1962. *Anti-Intellectualism in American Life*. Vintage Books, a division of Random House.

Holzer, Jessica. 2013. "Accord Reached over SEC Firing," *Wall Street Journal online*, June 9.

Holzer, Jessica, and Andrew Ackerman. 2012. "Report Faults Former SEC Inspector General," *Wall Street Journal online*, October 5.

Holzer, Jessica . 2011b. "Ex-SEC Lawyer's Madoff Ties Face Scrutiny. Watchdog to Urge Justice Department Review of Whether Conflict-of-Interest Laws Were Broken," *Wall Street Journal online*, September 17.

Holzer, Jessica. 2011a. "SEC Leasing Flap Intensifies," *Wall Street Journal*, July 7.

Horwitz, Steven. 1994. "Systemic Rationality and the Effects of Financial Regulation: Rejoinder to Kindleberger," *Critical Review*, Fall.

Horwitz, Morton J. 1992. *The Transformation of American Law 1870-1960. The Crisis of Legal Orthodoxy*. Oxford University Press.

Ikeda, Sanford. 1997. *Dynamics of the Mixed Economy*. Routledge.

Ishmael, Stacy-Marie. 2009. "Sir Allen's Antigua, or the curious case of Stanford International Bank," *Financial Times* Alphaville blog, Feb. 17.

Jaffe, Matthew. 2011. "SEC Still Struggling to Stop Its Porn Problem," *ABCNews.com*, June 1.

Jarrell, Gregg A. 1981. "The Economic Effects of Federal Regulation of the Market for New Security Issues." *Journal of Law and Economics*, December.

Jones, Ashby. 2009. "With Dueling Letters, A Squabble Over Madoff Funds Begins," April 8, *Wall Street Journal* Law Blog.

Kahneman, Daniel. 2011. *Thinking, Fast and Slow.* Farrar, Straus Giroux.

Karkkainen, Bradley. 2004. "'New Governance' in Legal Thought and in the World: Some Splitting as an Antidote to Overzealous Lumping," *Minnesota Legal Review,* v. 89.

Kary, Tiffany. 2008. "Bear Stearns Wins Trial Over Hedge Fund's Collapse," *Bloomberg News,* June 27.

Kates, Steven. 2010. "Influencing Keynes: The Intellectual Origins of the General Theory," *History of Economic Ideas,* v.28, n.3, pp.33-64.

Katznelson, Ira. 2013. *Fear Itself: The New Deal and the Origins of Our Time.* Liveright.

Keller, James. 2009. "Is Deregulation to Blame?" *Claremont Review of Books,* Fall.

Kindleberger, Charles P. 1994. "Theory vs. History: Reply to Horwitz," *Critical Review,* Fall.

Kindleberger, Charles P. 1978. *Manias, Panics and Crashes. A History of Financial Crises.* Basic Books.

Kirtzman, Andrew. 2010. *Betrayal: The Life and Lies of Bernie Madoff.* Harper Perennial.

Kirzner, Israel M. 1999. "Creativity and/or Alertness: A Reconsideration of the Schumpeterian Entrepreneur," *Review of Austrian Economics,* v. 11.

Kirzner, Israel M. *1997. How Markets Work: Disequilibrium, Entrepreneurship and Discovery.* Coronet.

Klein, Daniel B. 1997. "Trust for Hire: Voluntary Remedies for Quality and Safety," *Reputation: Studies in the Voluntary Elicitation of Good Conduct,* University of Michigan Press.

Klick, J. and G. Mitchell. 2006. Government Regulation of Irrationality: Moral and Cognitive Hazards, *Minnesota Law Review,* 90.

Koch, Charles H. Jr. 1996. "James Landis: The Administrative Process," *Administrative Law Review*, Summer.

Koellinger, Philipp, Maria Minniti and Christian Schade. 2007. "I Think I Can, I Think I Can...: A Study of Entrepreneurial Behavior." *Journal of Economic Psychology*. 28.

Koppl, Roger. 2002. *Big Players and the Economic Theory of Expectations*. Palgrave Macmillan.

Krecké, Elisabeth. 2014. "The Figure of the Judge in Law and Economics," *Norms and Values in Law and Economics*, Nicolas Mercuro (ed.), Routledge. Forthcoming.

Kroszner, Randall S. 1998. Rethinking Bank Regulation: A Review of the Historical Evidence," *Journal of Applied Corporate Finance*, v.11.

Kurdas, Chidem. 2012b. "Madoff Trustee Partners' Bonanza," *HedgeFundSmarts.com*, November 8.

Kurdas, Chidem. 2012a. *Political Sticky Wicket: The Untouchable Ponzi Scheme of Allen Stanford*. Amazon e-book and paperback, September 15.

Kurdas, Chidem. 2011b. "Ex-SEC Counsel $140,000 Madoff Benefit," *HedgeFundSmarts.com*, September 20.

Kurdas, Chidem. 2011a. "Madoff Joke: Whistleblower Travails," *HedgeFundSmarts.com*, February 2.

Kurdas, Chidem. 2009b. "Regulation Will Stop Future Madoffs? It Just Ain't So!" *The Freeman*, May.

Kurdas, Chidem. 2009a. "Does Regulation Prevent Fraud? The Case of Manhattan Hedge Fund," *Independent Review*, Winter.

Kurdas, Chidem. 2006b. "FBI Focuses on Hedge Funds," HedgeWorld.com, October 26.

Kurdas, Chidem. 2006a. "Greenspan: Bubbles are Unstoppable, Hedge Funds Prevent Mistakes," HedgeWorld *Inside Edge,* September 22.

Kuznets, Simon. 1952. "Long-Term Changes in the National Income of the United States of America since 1870,' *Income and Wealth of the United States*, Bowes and Bowes.

Landis, James M. 1938. *The Administrative Process*. Yale University Press.

Lattman, Peter. 2013. "Suit Offers a Peek at the Practice of Inflating a Legal Bill," *New York Times*, March 25.

Lattman, Peter. 2007."Bankruptcy Court Ruling Roils Hedge-Fund Servicers," *Wall Street Journal* law blog, February 16.

Lee, Gary, G. Larry Engel and Kenneth Krys. 2007. "Cross-Border Recovery Strategies for Insolvent Hedge Funds," a report distributed by law firm Morrison & Foerster, June.

Leef, George C. 2012. "Stealing You Blind: How Government Fat Cats Are Getting Rich Off of You," *The Freeman*, October.

Levenson, Thomas. 2009. "Commentary: Even a genius can get suckered," *CNN.com*, July 29.

Lichtman, Allan J. 1987. "Tommy the Cork; the secret world of Washington's first modern lobbyist - Thomas G. Corcoran," *Washington Monthly*, February.

Loasby, Brian. 1999. *Knowledge, Institutions and Evolution in Economics*. Routledge.

LoPucki, Lynn M. 2006. *Courting Failure: How Competition for Big Cases is Corrupting the Bankruptcy Courts*. The University of Michigan Press.

Lowenstein, R. 2000. *When Genius Failed: The Rise and Fall of Long-Term Capital Management*. Random House.

Luparello, Stephen. 2009. Testimony on the Financial Industry Regulatory Authority before the Subcommittee on Capital Markets, Insurance and Government Sponsored Enterprises, of the Committee on Financial Services, U.S. House of Representatives February 4.

MacKay, Charles. 1932 edition. *Extraordinary Popular Delusions and the Madness of Crowds*. L.C. Page & Co., original publication 1841.

Madrick, Jeff. 2009. "They Didn't Regulate Enough and Still Don't," *The New York Review of Books*, Nov. 5.

Maiello Michael and Daniel Kruger. 2001. "Bear Trap" *Forbes Magazine* online edition, June 11.

Manne, Henry. 1966. *Insider Trading and the Stock Market*. Free Press.

March, James and Herbert Simon. 1958. *Organizations*, Wiley.

MarHedge. 2002. "Judge Kills Bear's $1.9b Berger Bill," Marhedge.com, April 19.

Markopolos, Harry et al. 2011. *No One Would Listen*. WILEY.

McCraw, Thomas K. 1984. *Prophets of Regulation*. Belknap Press of Harvard University Press.

McElhatton, Jim. "Both Parties Scheme for Ponzi cash," *The Washington Times*, July 26, 2011.

McGrane, Victoria. 2009. "Lobbyists on Pace for Record Year," *Politico*, December 22.

MacKay, Malcolm. 2013. *Impeccable Connections: The Rise and Fall of Richard Whitney*. Brick Tower Press.

Marcus, David. 2013. "The Reason Dewey & LeBoeuf Failed," *The Deal Pipeline*, October 14.

McKean, David. 2004. *Tommy the Cork: Washington's Ultimate Insider from Roosevelt to Reagan*. Vermont: Steerforth Press.

Meek, Andy. 2009. "After the Fall: The Messy Cleanup of Stanford Financial," *Memphis Daily News*, Sep 28.

Meiners, Roger E. and Bruce Yandle (eds.). 1989. *Regulation and the Reagan Era Politics, Bureaucracy and the Public Interest*. Independent Institute.

Menand, Louis. 2013. "How the Deal Went Down. Saving Democracy in the Depression," *New Yorker*, March 4.

Milakovich, Michael, and Kurt Weis. 1975. "Politics and Measures of Success in the War on Crime," *Crime and Delinquency*, January.

Miller, Ross. 2002. *Experimental Economics. How We Can Build Better Financial Markets*. John Wiley & Sons.

Mitchell, William and Randy Simmons. 1994. *Beyond Politics: Markets, Welfare and the Failure of Bureaucracy*. Westview Press.

Mises, Ludwig von. *Human action: A Treatise on Economics*. Yale University Press.

Mises, Ludwig von. 1944. *Bureaucracy*. New Haven: Yale University Press.

Mitchell, Wesley C. 1937. *The Backward Art of Spending Money and Other Essays*, McGraw-Hill.

Mokyr, Joel. 1992. "Technological Inertia in Economic History," *The Journal of Economic History*, June.

Muñoz, Felix Fernando, Encinar, M.I., & Cañibano, C. 2011. "On the role of intentionality in evolutionary economic change," *Structural Change and Economic Dynamics, 22*

Murray, Iain. 2011. *Stealing You Blind: How Government Fat Cats Are Getting Rich Off of You*. Competitive Enterprise Institute.

Nasaw, David. 2012. *The Patriarch. The Remarkable Life and Turbulent Times of Joseph P. Kennedy*, Penguin Press.

Newman, Andy. 2003. "Judges Say Democratic Official Issued List of Favored Lawyers," *New York Times*, December 16.

Norman, Jesse. 2013. *Edmund Burke: Philosopher, Politician, Prophet*. Basic Books.

North, Douglass, John J. Wallis and Barry R. Weingast. 2009. *Violence and Social Orders. A Conceptual Framework for Interpreting Recorded Human History*. Cambridge University Press.

North, Douglass. 1993. "What Do We Mean by Rationality?" *Public Choice, 77*.

North, Douglass. 1990. *Institutions, Institutional Change and Economic Performance*. Cambridge University Press.

North, Douglass. 1966. *The Economic Growth of the United States 1790-1860*. W.W. Norton & Co.

Oakeshott, Michael. 1991. *Rationalism in Politics*. Liberty Fund.

Ocrant, Michael. 2001. "Madoff Tops Charts; Skeptics Ask How," *MAR/Hedge*, May.

O'Driscoll, Gerald. 2011. "Money, Prices and Bubbles," presented at the Colloquium on Market Institutions and Economic Processes at New York University, March 21.

O'Driscoll, Gerald and Lee Hoskins. 2006. "The Case for Market-Based Regulation," *Cato Journal*, Fall.

O'Driscoll, Gerald, Mario Rizzo and W.R. Garrison. 1996. *The Economics of Time and Ignorance*. Routledge.

Olson, Walter. 2011. *Schools for Misrule: Legal Academia and an Over-Lawyered America*, Encounter Books.

Olson, Mancur. 1982. *The Rise and Decline of Nations*. Yale University Press.

Olson, Mancur. 1965. *The Logic of Collective Action: Public Goods and the Theory of Groups*. Harvard University Press.

Ostrom, Elinor. 2005. *Understanding Institutional Diversity*, Princeton University Press.

Ostrom, Elinor and Sue Crawford. 1995. "A Grammar of Institutions," *American Political Science Review*, September.

Ostrom, Elinor. 1990. *Political Economy of Institutions and Decisions*, Cambridge University Press.

Otteson, James. 2010. "Adam Smith and the Great Mind Fallacy," *Social Philosophy and Policy Foundation*.

Paganelli, Maria Pia.2012."David Hume on Public Credit," *History of Economic Ideas* xx

Paganelli, Maria Pia. 2011. "Is a Beautiful System Dying? A Possible Smithian Take on the Financial Crisis and its Aftermath" *The Adam Smith Review*, 6

Peltzman, Sam. 1989. "The Economic Theory of Regulation after a Decade of Deregulation," *Brooklyn Papers in Economic Activity. Microeconomics*.

Posner, Richard A. 2008. *How Judges Think*. Harvard University Press.

Posner, Richard A. 2003. *Law, Pragmatism and Democracy*. Harvard University Press.

Posner, Richard A. 2001. *Frontiers of Legal Theory*. Harvard University Press.

Posner, Richard A. 1995. *Overcoming Law*, Harvard University Press.

Posner, Richard A. 1993. "Nobel Laureate: Ronald Coase and Methodology." *Journal of Economic Perspectives,* Fall.

Rajagopalan, Shruti and Richard Wagner. 2013 "Legal Entrepreneurship within Alternative Systems of Political Economy," *American Journal of Entrepreneurship,* 6(1).

Rakoff, Jed. 2014. "The Financial Crisis: Why Have No High-Level Executives Been Prosecuted?" *New York Review of Books*, January 9.

Ramstad, Yngve. 2001. "John R. Commons's Reasonable Value and the Problem of Just Price," *Journal of Economic Issues*, v. 35.

Ratcliffe, R. G. 2009. "Ben Barnes Reclaims Spot in Spotlight with Stanford," *Houston Chronicle,* March 10.

Reed, Christopher. 1999. "The Damn'd South Sea," *Harvard Magazine*, May.

Regan, William and Allison Wuertz. 2013. "Second Circuit Affirms Dismissal of Madoff Trustee's Common Law Claim," *National Law Review*, July 1.

Ribstein, Larry E. 2006. "Fraud on a Noisy Market," *Lewis & Clark Law Review*, Spring.

Ribstein, Larry E. 2003. "Bubble Laws," *Houston Law Review*, v.40.

Ritchie, Donald A. 1980. *James M. Landis. Dean of the Regulators*. Harvard University Press.

Rizzo, Mario. 2013. "The Problem of Rationality: Austrian Economics between Classical Behaviorism and Behavioral Economics," Forthcoming, *Oxford Companion to Austrian Economics*.

Rizzo, Mario. 2011. "The Rule of Discretion versus the Rule of Law: Soros Gets Nailed," *ThinkMarkets.wordpress.com*, October 14.

Rizzo, Mario and Glen Whitman. 2009. "The Knowledge Problem of New Paternalism," *Brigham Young University Law Review*, n. 4.

Rizzo, Mario. 2009. "Little Brother Is Watching You: New Paternalism on the Slippery Slopes," *Arizona Law Review*.

Rizzo, Mario. 2005. "The Problem of Moral Dirigisme: A New Argument against Moralistic Legislation," *NYU Journal of Law & Liberty*, v.1.

Rizzo, Mario. 1999. "Which Kind of Legal Order? Logical Coherence and Praxeological Coherence" *Journal des Economistes et des Etudes Humaines*.

Roberts, Dan. 2005. "How to Stay Afloat — US Businesses Embark on a less Sheltered Voyage Through the Courts," *Financial Times*, October 21, p.11.

Romano, Roberta. 2005. "The Sarbanes-Oxley Act and the Making of Quack Corporate Governance," *Yale Law Journal*, May.

Romer, Paul M. 2010. "What Parts of Globalization Matter for Catch-Up Growth?" *American Economic Review* and NBER Working Paper No. 15755.

Rosenberg, Nathan 1994. *Exploring the Black Box: Technology, Economics and History*. Cambridge University Press.

Rosiak, Luke. 2010. "Texas Politico Rapidly Rises to No. 1 Overall Donor, Now No. 1 bundler," Sunlight Foundation Reporting Group, January 6.

Roth, Zachary. 2010. "A Washington Tale: As Feds Closed In, Stanford Boosted Efforts To Buy Influence," *TPMMuckraker*, January 5.

Rothfeld, Michael. 2011. "Madoff Trustee, Fairfield Liquidators Join Forces," *Wall Street Journal* online, May 10.

Rutherford, Malcolm. 2006. "Wisconsin Institutionalism: John R Commons and His Students," *Labor History*, May.

Salerno, Joseph. 1993. "Mises and Hayek Dehomogenized," *Review of Austrian Economics*, v.6. n. 2.

Sandler, Linda. 2012. "New York Accused Madoff Trustee of Intimidation," *Bloomberg News,* Sept. 4.

Sandler , Linda and David Voreacos. 2011. "Lautenberg Foundation Appeals Ruling in Bid to Continue Suit of Madoff Kin," *Bloomberg News*, March 29.

Sandomir, Richard and Ken Belson. 2011. "Madoff Decision Is Significant Setback to Owners of Mets," *New York Times*, August 17.

Sawer, Patrick. 2008. "Cricket Tycoon Sir Allen Stanford Caught up in Spying Row," *The Telegraph*, Nov. 9.

Scheall, Scott. 2013. "Economics and Ignorance," presented to the Colloquium on Market Institutions and Economic Processes at New York University, October 7.

Schumpeter, Joseph A. 1991. *The Economics and Sociology of Capitalism*. Richard Swedberg, ed. Princeton University Press.

Schumpeter, Joseph A. 1954. *History of Economic Analysis*. Oxford University Press.

Schumpeter, Joseph A. 1950. *Capitalism, Socialism and Democracy*. New York: Harper & Row.

Schwarz, Jordan A. 1987. *Liberal: Adolf A. Berle and the Vision of an American Era*.
Free Press of Macmillan.

Seligman, Joel. 1985. *The SEC and the Future of Finance*. Praeger.

Seligman, Joel. 1982. *The Transformation of Wall Street: A History of the Securities and Exchange Commission and Modern Corporate Finance*. Houghton Mifflin.

Sherrer, Hans. 2006. "The Inhumanity of Government Bureaucracies," in *The Challenge of Liberty. Classical Liberalism Today*, Robert Higgs and Carl Close (eds.), Independent Institute.

Shlaes, Amity. 2008. *The Forgotten Man: A New History of the Great Depression* Harper Perennial.

Simon, Herbert. 1991. *Models of My Life*. Basic Books.

Simon, Herbert. 1982. *Models of Bounded Rationality*. Cambridge, Mass.: MIT Press.

Simon, Herbert. 1978. "Rationality as Process and Product of Thought," *American Economic Review, Proceedings*, 68.

Simon, Herbert. 1957. *Models of Man*. New York: Wiley.

Simon, Herbert. 1947. *Administrative Behavior*. New York: MacMillan.

Singh, Rachael. 2010. "Vantis enters administration," *Accountancy Age*, June 30.

Shiller, Robert. 2000. *Irrational Exuberance*. Broadway Books.

Shogren, Alex. 2000c. "Court Appointed Receiver to Distribute Remaining Assets – Bear Stearns Issues Another Statement," HedgeFund.net, January 20.

Shogren, Alex. 2000b. "Receiver Appointed – But Are the Investors Who Withdrew in 1999 Out of the Woods?" HedgeFund.net, January 20.

Shogren, Alex. 2000a. "If It Seems too Good to be True..." HedgeFund.Net January 15.

Shughart, William F. 2013. "James Buchanan and Gordon Tullock A Half-Century On," in Dwight R. Lee (ed.), *Public Choice, Past and Present: The Legacy of James Buchanan and Gordon Tullock*, Studies in Public Choice, Randall Holcombe (series ed.), Springer.

Shughart, William F. 2004. "Bending before the Storm: The U.S. Supreme Court in Economic Crisis, 1935–1937," *The Independent Review*, Summer.

Shughart, William F. and Robert Tollison.1998. "Interest Groups and the Courts," *George Mason Law Review*, summer.

Shughart, William F. 1988. "A Public Choice Perspective of the Banking Act of 1933," *Cato Journal*, 7, Winter.

Shughart, William F., Robert Tollison and Brian L. Goff. 1986. "Bureaucratic Structure and Congressional Control," *Southern Economic Journal*, 52, April.

Shughart, William F., Ryan Amacher, Richard Higgins and Robert Tollison. 1985. "The Behavior of Regulatory Activity over the Business Cycle: An Empirical Test," *Economic Inquiry*, January.

Shughart, William F. and Robert Tollison. 1985. "The Cyclical Character of Regulatory Activity," *Public Choice*, 45.

Smallberg, Michael. 2012. "SEC Official Cited for Whistleblower Retaliation Announces Departure," *Project on Government Oversight Blog*, August 12.

Smith, Adam. 1976. *An Inquiry into the Nature and Causes of the Wealth of Nations*. Edited by R. H. Campbell and A. S. Skinner, Oxford Clarendon Press.

Solomon, Deborah. 2009. "Questions for Arthur Levitt: Money Manager," *New York Times* online, January 25.

Somin, Ilya. 2004. "When Ignorance Isn't Bliss: How Political Ignorance Threatens Democracy," *Policy Analysis* series from the Cato Institute, September 22.

Somin, Ilya. 1998. "Voter Ignorance and the Democratic Ideal," *Critical Review*, Fall.

Soros, George. 2003. *The Alchemy of Finance*. Wiley.

Sowell, Thomas. 2007. *A Conflict of Visions. Ideological Origins of Political Struggles*. Revised edition. Basic Books.

Sowell, Thomas. 1995. *The Vision of the Anointed. Self-Congratulation as a Basis for Social Policy.* Basic Books.

State of New York Commission on Judicial Conduct. 2005. Determination in the Matter of the Proceeding Pursuant to Section 44, Subdivision 4, of the Judiciary Law in Relation to Michael H. Feinberg, Surrogate, Kings County. February 10.

Sternsher, Bernard. 1964. *Rexford Tugwell and the New Deal.* Rutgers University Press.

Stigler. George J. 1971. "The Theory of Economic Regulation," *Bell Journal of Economics and Management Science,* Spring.

Stigler. George J. 1964. "Public Regulation of the Securities Markets," *Journal of Business,* April.

Stiglitz, Joseph. 2013. *The Price of Inequality: How Today's Divided Society Endangers Our Future.* W. W. Norton & Co.

Stiglitz, Joseph. 2010. *Freefall: Free Markets and the Sinking of the Global Economy.*
W. W. Norton & Co.

Stoffel, Brian. 2012. "You're Wrong about Madoff, and that Ignorance Will Hurt You," *The Motley Fool,* April 27.

Stone, Isidor F. 1989. *The Trial of Socrates.* Doubleday.

Story, Louise and Gretchen Morgenson. 2011. "SEC Chairwoman Under Fire over Ethics Issues," *New York Times,* March 9.

Sugden, Robert. 2011. "The Behavioral Economist and the Social Planner: To Whom Should Behavioral Welfare Economics Be Addressed?" *Papers on Economics and Evolution,* Max Planck Institute of Economics, December 20.

Sunstein, Cass. 2013a. *Simpler: The Future of Government.* Simon & Schuster.

Sunstein, Cass. 2013b. "It's For Your Own Good!" *New York Review of Books,* March 7.

Sunstein, Cass. and Richard Thaler. 2003. "Libertarian paternalism," *American Economic Review, Papers and Proceedings* 93.

Sunstein, Cass. 1994. "On Costs, Benefits, and Regulatory Success: Reply to Crandall," *Critical Review,* Fall.

Swedberg, Richard. 1991. *Schumpeter: A Biography*. Princeton University Press.

Sweeney, John. 2009. "Stanford Drug Informer Role Claim," *BBC News*, May 9.

Schweizer, Peter. 2013. *Extortion: How Politicians Extract Your Money, Buy Votes, and Line Their Own Pockets*. Houghton Mifflin Harcourt Trade.

Tabarrok, Alexander, and Eric Helland. 1999. "Court Politics: The Political Economy of Tort Awards," *Journal of Law and Economics*, April.

Tabarrok, Alexander. 1998. "The Separation of Commercial and Investment Banking: Morgans vs. Rockefellers," *The Quarterly Journal of Austrian Economics* 1.

Tabarrok, Alexander and Tyler Cowen. 1992. "The Public Choice Theory of John C. Calhoun," *Journal of Institutional and Theoretical Economics*, v. 148.

Taleb, Nassim Nicholas. 2007. *The Black Swan. The Impact of the Highly Improbable*. New York: Random House.

Taleb, Nassim Nicholas. 2001. *Fooled by Randomness. The Hidden Role of Chance in the Markets and in Life*. Texere.

Taylor, John and Kenneth Scott, editors. 2012. *Bankruptcy Not Bailout: A Special Chapter 14*. Hoover Institution Press.

Taylor, John. 2009a. *Getting Off Track: How Government Actions and Interventions Caused, Prolonged, and Worsened the Financial Crisis*. Hoover Institution Press.

Taylor, John. 2009b. "The Financial Crisis and the Policy Responses: An Empirical Analysis of What Went Wrong," National Bureau of Economic Research papers, January.

Thaler, Richard and Cass Sunstein. 2008. *Nudge: Improving Decisions About Health, Wealth, and Happiness*. Yale University Press.

Tichenor, Daniel and Richard Harris. 2002-2003. "Organized Interests and American Political Development" *Political Science Quarterly*, v. 177.

Tichi, Cecilia. 2009. *Civic Passions: Seven Who Launched Progressive America*, University of North Carolina Press.

Tocqueville, Alexis de. 1969. *Democracy in America*. Translation by George Lawrence. two volumes, originally published 1835 and 1840. HarperCollins.

Tollison, Robert D.1991. "Regulation and Interest Groups," in J. High (ed.), *Regulation: Theory and History*, University of Michigan Press.

Tollison, Robert D. 1983. "Difficulties Facing Regulatory Reform: Comment," in W.C. Stubblebine and T.D. Willett (eds.), *Reaganomics: A Midterm Report*, ICS Press.

Toronto Globe and Mail. 2002. "For Wall Street Firms It's No Longer a Family Affair," Theglobeandmail.com, May 29.

Tran, Q Vinh. 2006. *Evaluating Hedge Fund Performance*. Wiley.

Tugwell, Rexford G. 1992. *The Diary of Rexford G. Tugwell: The New Deal, 1932-1935*. M. V. Namorato, ed. Greenwood Press.

Tugwell, Rexford G. 1982. *To the Lesser Heights of Morningside: A Memoir*. University of Pennsylvania Press.

Tullock, Gordon. 1993. *Rent Seeking*. Edward Elgar.

Tullock, Gordon. 1971. *The Logic of the Law*. Basic Books.

Tullock, Gordon. 1965. *The Politics of Bureaucracy*. Public Affairs Press.

Tversky, Amos and Daniel Kahneman. 1974. "Judgment Under Uncertainty: Heuristics and Biases," *Science*, v. 185.

United Kingdom High Court of Justice, Chancery Division. 1999. Diem Consultants Inc., Claimant, and Manhattan Capital Management Inc., Defendant, Claim no. 99-04334, issue date October 13.

US District Court at the Northern District of Texas, Dallas Division. 2009 on. Stanford Financial Group Receivership, case # 3-09-CV-0298-N, various documents.

US Bankruptcy Court for the Southern District of New York. 2008 on. Securities Investor Protection Corp. liquidation, Bernard L. Madoff, debtor, case # 08-1789, various documents.

US Bankruptcy Court for the Southern District of New York. 2000 on. Manhattan Investment Fund Ltd. et al, debtors, cases # 00-10922 and 00-10921, various documents.

US Bankruptcy Court for the Southern District of New York. 2001 on. Manhattan Investment Fund Ltd., Helen Gredd v. Bear, Stearns Securities Corp., case # 01-2606, various documents.

US Congress House Judiciary Subcommittee on Courts, Commercial and Administrative Law Hearing. 2011. "Chapter 11 Bankruptcy Venue Reform Act of 2011," September 8.

US District Court for the Southern District of New York. 2009 on. Irving Picard v. JP Morgan Chase and related entities, case # 11-cv-00913, various documents.

US District Court for the Southern District of New York. 2009 on. Irving Picard vs. HSBC Bank plc and related entities, case # case # 11-cv-00 763, various documents.

US District Court for the Southern District of New York. 2000 on. USA v. Berger, case # 00-cr-877-1, various documents.

US District Court for the Southern District of New York. 2000-2003. Cromer Finance Ltd. and Prival N.V. vs. Michael Berger et al., case # 00-cv-2284 (DLC), various documents.

US District Court for the Southern District of New York. 2002. Helen Gredd, v. Bear Stearns Securities Corp. Case # 01 Civ. 4379, various documents.

US District Court for the District of Columbia. 2012. David P. Weber vs. US Securities and Exchange Commission and Mary L. Schapiro. Complaint, November 15, case # 1:12-cv-01850-RWR.

US District Court for the District of Columbia. 2012. US Securities and Exchange Commission v. Securities Investor Protection Corporation, Opinion and Order, July 3.

US District Court for the Southern District of Texas. 2009 on. Securities and Exchange Commission v. Stanford International Bank and related entities and persons, Case #3:09-cv-0298-N, various documents, last accessed dated June 1, 2012.

US District Court for the Southern District of Texas. 2009 on. United States v. James M. Davis. "Plea Agreement" Case # H-09-335, August 27.

US Government Accountability Office 2012b. *Securities Investor Protection Corp. Customer Outcomes in the Madoff Liquidation Proceeding.* September.

US Government Accountability Office. 2012a. Report to Congressional Requesters. *Securities Investor Protection Corporation: Interim Report on the Madoff Liquidation Proceeding,* March.

US House of Representatives Subcommittee on Oversight and Investigations of the Committee on Financial Services. 2011. Hearing on "The Stanford Ponzi Scheme," May 13.

US Senate Committee on Banking, Housing and Urban Affairs. 2010. Hearing on "Oversight of the SEC Inspector General's Report on the 'Investigation of the SEC's Response to Concerns Regarding Robert Allen Stanford's Alleged Ponzi Scheme' and Improving SEC Performance," September 22.

US Securities and Exchange Commission Administrative Proceedings. 2012. Various documents, last accessed August 31.

US Securities and Exchange Commission press release. 2009. "David M. Becker Named SEC General Counsel and Senior Policy Director," February 6.

US Securities and Exchange Commission Office of the Inspector General. 2012b. Memorandum by Jon Rymer, interim inspector general, November 30.

US Securities and Exchange Commission Office of the Inspector General. 2012a. *Investigation into Misuse of Resources and Violations of Information Technology Security Policies within the division of Trading and Markets.* August 30.

US Securities and Exchange Commission Office of the Inspector General. 2011b. *Investigation of Conflict of Interest Arising from Former General Counsel's Participation in Madoff-Related Matters.* September 16.

US Securities and Exchange Commission Office of Inspector General. 2011a. *SEC's Oversight of the Securities Investor Protection Corporation's Activities.* March 30.

US Securities and Exchange Commission Office of the Inspector General. 2010. *Investigation of the SEC's Response to Concerns Regarding Robert Allen Stanford's Alleged Ponzi Scheme.* March 31.

US Securities and Exchange Commission Office of the Inspector General. 2009b. *Investigation of Failure of the SEC to Uncover Bernard Madoff's Ponzi Scheme.* Public version, August 31.

US Securities and Exchange Commission Office of the Inspector General. 2009a. *Investigation of Fort Worth Regional Office's Conduct of the Stanford Investigation.* June 19.

US Securities and Exchange Commission. 2004. Registration under the Advisers' Act of Certain Hedge Fund Advisers; Proposed Rule, *Federal Register,* Dec. 10, 69.

US Securities and Exchange Commission. 2002. *In the Matter of Financial Asset Management Inc.,* Releases no. 8052, 45224, 2007 and 1485; Administrative procedure.

US Securities and Exchange Commission. 2000. *SEC Charges Hedge Fund and Its Adviser with Fraud,* January 18.

Vanberg, Victor. 2006. Human Intentionality and Design in Cultural Evolution," *Evolution and Design of Institutions,* C. Schubert & G. Wangenheim (eds.) Routledge.

Vanberg, Victor. 1989. "Carl Menger's Evolutionary and J. R. Commons' Collective Action Approach to Institutions: A Comparison," *Review of Political Economy,* v. 1.

Vaughn, Karen. 1999. "Hayek's Implicit Economics: Rules and the Problem of Order," *Review of Austrian Economics*, v.11.

Walker, Jack. 1991. *Mobilizing Interest Groups in America: Patrons, Professions and Social Movements.* University of Michigan Press.

Waters, Richard and Juliana Ratner. 2002. "Wall Street's Faithful Bull," *Financial Times*, August 17/18.

Whalen, Charles J. 2008. "John R. Commons and John Maynard Keynes on Economic History and Policy: the 1920s and Today," *Journal of Economic Issues*, March.

Whalen, Charles J. 1989. "John R. Commons's Institutional Economics: A Re-Examination," *Journal of Economic Issues*, June.

Whitehouse, Kaja. 2013. "$2B for Madoff victims is going nowhere fast,"
New York Post, September 16.

Whitman, Douglas Glen and Mario Rizzo. 2007. "Paternalistic Slopes," *New York University Journal of Law & Liberty*, 2.

Wilchins, Dan. 2006. "Refco Judge Rejects Trustee, Abadi Eyes Unit," *Reuters*, January 10.

Williamson, Oliver E. 1996. *The Mechanisms of Governance*, Oxford University Press.

Williamson, Oliver E. 1985. *The Economic Institutions of Capitalism*, Free Press.

Wilson, James Q. 1998. "Idealizing Politics," *Critical Review*, Fall.

Wilson, James Q. 1991. *Bureaucracy: What Government Agencies Do and Why They Do It.* Basic Books.

Wilson, James Q. and Richard J. Herrnstein. 1985. *Crime and Human Nature.* Simon and Schuster.

Wilson, James Q.(ed.) 1982. *The Politics of Regulation,* New York: Basic Books.

Wilson, James Q. and George L. Kelling. 1982. "Broken Windows. The police and neighborhood safety" *The Atlantic*, March.

Winston, Clifford; Robert W. Crandall and Vikram Maheshri. 2011. *First Thing We Do, Let's Deregulate All the Lawyers*. Brookings Institution Press.

Winston, Clifford. 2006. *Government Failure vs. Market Failure. Microeconomics Policy Research and Government Performance*. Washington, DC: AEI-Brookings Joint Center for Regulatory Studies.

Witt, Ulrich. 2003. *The Evolving Economy*. Edward Elgar.

Wolf, Charles Jr. 1993. *Markets or Governments: Choosing Between Imperfect Alternatives*. MIT Press.

Wyatt, Edward. 2011. "SEC Head Admits Misstep in a Madoff Ethics Issue," *New York Times*, March 11.

Yandle, Bruce. 2010. "Lost Trust. The Real Cause of the Financial Meltdown," *Independent Review*, Winter.

Zywicki, Todd. J. and Edward Peter Stringham. 2011 "Common law and economic efficiency," *Production of Legal Rules, Encyclopedia of Law and Economics* v. 7, Francesco Parisi (ed.), Edward Edgar.

Zywicki, Todd. J. 2006. Is Forum Shopping Corrupting America's Bankruptcy Courts?" *Georgetown Law Journal*, 94.

INDEX

www.ingramcontent.com/pod-product-compliance
Lightning Source LLC
Chambersburg PA
CBHW060316200326
41519CB00011BA/1743